Transnational Currents in a Shrinking World

Transnational Currents in a Shrinking World

1870–1945

Emily S. Rosenberg

The Belknap Press of Harvard University Press
CAMBRIDGE, MASSACHUSETTS
LONDON, ENGLAND

For Norman

Originally published as Chapter 5 of *A World Connecting: 1870–1945*, ed. Emily
S. Rosenberg (Cambridge, MA: Belknap Press of Harvard University Press, 2012),
a joint publication of Harvard University Press and C. H. Beck Verlag.
German language edition © 2012 by C. H. Beck Verlag.

Maps by Isabelle Lewis
Book design by Dean Bornstein

Library of Congress Cataloging-in-Publication Data

Rosenberg, Emily S., 1944–
    Transnational currents in a shrinking world: 1870–1945 / Emily S. Rosenberg.
        pages   cm
    Includes bibliographical references and index.
    ISBN 978-0-674-28133-2 (alk. paper)
    1. Transnationalism. 2. Internationalism. 3. Social networks. I. Title.
    JZ1320.R67   2014
    305.8009'041—dc23   2013031962

Contents

Introduction

"The extension and use of railroads, steamships, telegraphs, break down nationalities and bring people geographically remote into close connection. . . . They make the world one." So wrote David Livingstone, the famed British missionary-explorer whose accounts of Africa became widely influential in the West.[1] By the late nineteenth century, this commonplace sentiment echoed throughout the world, expressed in some form or other both by those who celebrated the shrinking world and by those who feared it.

The observation that the late nineteenth-century revolutions in transportation, communication, finance, and commerce were transforming loyalties and sensibilities, limiting or even eliminating spatial distance, animated the creation of an ever-widening array of international and transnational networks during the era from the mid-nineteenth to the mid-twentieth century. C. A. Bayly has aptly called the steps toward what is now often termed globalization the "Great Acceleration." In many older historical writings it was assumed that Europeans shaped the onset of the "modern" age during this era and then, for better or worse, exported its characteristics to other regions through emerging structures of empire, trade, and cultural hegemony. Bayly, however, conceives of the world during this era "as a complex of overlapping networks of global reach, while at the same time acknowledging the vast differentials of power which inhered in them." Europeans were often able to "bend to their will existing global networks," he writes. Yet "it was the parasitic and 'networked' nature of Western domination and power which gave it such strength, binding together, and tapping into, a vast range of viable networks and aspirations."[2]

This book joins the work of many recent scholars in emphasizing networks. Although Euro-Americans played a significant role in the creation and spread of modernity in this era, the many social and cultural networks that increasingly crisscrossed the globe helped to coproduce and accelerate the transformations. It recognizes that state-building projects, imperial dynamics, demographic movements, and economic interrelationships leave significant global interconnections unexamined, and that today's dense and varied social networks and cultural entanglements have important forerunners. A wide range of new international agreements and institutions expanded the realms of intergovernmental connections. In addition, many non-state networks existed more or less independently from governments (or sometimes operated loosely through them). These networks connected people through aspiration, expertise, and affiliation of various kinds. This book, in short, is concerned with how transnational social and cultural currents circulated across and beyond national states and drew the world together in new ways.[3]

To begin, it will be helpful to imagine the usual territorial map of the world with pastel-colored countries and empires grouped into continents separated by blue seas. It is within the invisible assumptions of such a map that most history has been written. The conventions of professional history writing, after all, emerged in the late nineteenth century in association with the accelerated processes of state building, empire building, and mapmaking. Textbooks, for example, often use maps to illustrate the rise and fall of territorial control. Contrasting colors display the before-and-after borders of controlled or claimed realms. Examples would be the common use of before-and-after maps of World War I, the partition of Africa, the expansion of Japan in the 1930s and early 1940s, the shrinkage and then enlargement of the Soviet empire after the Bolshevik Revolution, and so forth. Such maps exemplify how history is generally taught and learned with reference to geographically bounded national states, and they exemplify the extent to which history centers on questions related to why and how those shifting borders moved. Of course, such maps are enormously helpful in visualizing the world, and one would not seek their eradication. Geographical information provides a solid basis for visualizing world history. But such maps also silently construct realms of inquiry that mostly relate to the decisions and actions of those expanding and contracting, appearing and disappearing, yellow, pink, and green entities named states.

Other kinds of maps can be, and have been, devised. If the world is mapped according to population, for example, the "sizes" of countries or regions look far different from when they are plotted according to geographic territory. Consider, further, how the world changes shape when remapped according to data on per capita income, urbanization, energy consumption, numbers of people living less than fifty miles from their place of birth, or any other of dozens of indicators. Even though less common, these kinds of maps may track historical information that seems just as important for understanding the world's past as are those more familiar maps delineating territorial borders.

This book tries to construct, through words, yet another kind of map that is even more intricate. Perhaps possible to conjure only in the flexible dimensions of the imagination, this map directs attention not to a particular territorial place or to the information that might be contained therein but to the dynamic connections, both visible and invisible, between and among places. Such networks and connecting flows, in all their variation, cannot literally be charted onto geographical space, but they nonetheless constitute a mental map that may recast the terrain of history writing. Livingstone and so many of his contemporaries around the world claimed to be witnessing a revolution in geographic space and the allegiances it commanded. Historians need to conjure new maps in order to capture and then raise questions about the amazing acceleration of interconnectivity that was shrinking distance and complicating identities.

The chapters that follow suggest some of the interwoven pathways that might make up a mental map of social and cultural transnational history. No world or global history can be comprehensive, and this one does not attempt to cover every transnational network in every area of the world through this long and complicated era. Because the idea of transnational history remains a concept under construction, however, I have tried to map what might be some major categories and interpretive themes for these networks. I have then illustrated these with examples from throughout the world, sometimes making reference to the more conventional realms of national states ("Japan," "Argentina," "the United States," "Germany," and so on) while still attempting to hold at bay the assumptions of nation-state primacy conveyed through their naming. The focus is not primarily on separate geographies but on those flows that spanned geographical boundaries. The concern of this book is the fluid realm of the "trans-."

To illuminate transnational networks, the central metaphor of *currents* provides appropriate imagery for this age of electricity. The globalizing currents examined here emerge unevenly and in complex fashion. The metaphor of currents moves away from a spoke-and-wheel, center-and-periphery framework to suggest crisscrossing flows of power and an interactive, though usually asymmetrical, reciprocal dynamic.

The idea of "currents" suggests a number of associated words that serve to illuminate the global interactions analyzed here. Currents, for example, can run through circuits. They may pulse in one direction or be interactive; they may flow from point to point or charge a more generalized field. They come together in nodes, which are points of collection and retransmission. They may be conveyed along lines that may be singular or of blended and woven character. They have both a visible and an invisible quality. Currents move, connect, and draw together but are also subject to disruption, overload, and shock.

Currents can be smooth, even pleasing, but always carry the danger of interruption. In short, the vocabulary of currents suggests linked contingency and variability, process and transformation rather than static structure. All of these connotations prove useful in schematizing the world as it came into being during this era of accelerating interconnections.

It seems helpful to elaborate further on some of the ways that this metaphor will do its interpretive work in the chapters that follow.

1. Currents, of course, move through networks. Networks among states and interconnections among peoples often transcended boundaries and drew different nationalities and cultures together. Some of these networks were highly utilitarian and served an array of specific functions. Many new organizations, for example, sought to facilitate global connections through the international standardization of norms and through institutionalizing regulatory and legal regimes. Other networks were more visionary, linked to ideas and affiliations that their adherents held in common and wanted to project transnationally. Older world histories that centered primarily on states and empires often lost sight of the variety of visions that animated individuals who operated and held strong allegiances across political boundaries.

Global networks often transcended geographical boundaries, but they nonetheless participated in other kinds of boundary drawing. In fact, the more that some types of boundaries were challenged and erased, the more new networks might shore up others in new ways. The simultaneous erasure and creation of difference and distinction, of course, were interrelated. The language and categories of disease, gender, race, cultural affinities, religion, and science, for example, often transcended geographical boundaries at the same time as they created new grammars and registers of difference. Cultural currents could foster inclusion, exclusion, and rearrangement of human relationships; their effects could be sometimes transitory and sometimes more lasting.

2. Although global networks were not coterminous with bounded states or imperial systems or regional affiliations, neither were they free of them. Transnational currents complicate the interpretive terrain of world history along both a spatial and a chronological axis. First, the globalizing networks in this era assumed shape within the context of Western Europe's nation building, empire building, and growing economic and cultural hegemony. Nations and empires were spaces, themselves assembled through networks of various kinds, that attempted to regularize and delineate the movement of people, goods, and ideas. Secondly, in the West most conceptions of what was "global" and "international" implied an inevitable and presumably progressive universalizing of certain Western ideas and experiences. The extension and imposition of Western universalism played an important role in constituting many global networks. Thus *transnational networks developed not necessarily in opposition to the hardening boundaries of nationalism or of empire, or as a stage of progress beyond them, but sometimes as counterparts to state and empire building. At the same time, networks also beckoned beyond territoriality toward a newer world in which fast-moving technologies of representation, with multiple and shifting codes of meaning, challenged the fixity of space and identity.*

3. An examination of global currents helps direct attention to particular people who shaped the emergent networks and affiliations and who served as conduits for exchanges connecting several planes of analysis. A focus on people and their connections can help make visible how the realms of the transnational, the national, and the local intersected in ways both dangerous (for whom?) and liberating (for whom?). *Using the metaphor of currents with nodes of connectivity facilitates an analytical process that scales back and forth, seeing large and seeing small while concentrating on the interactivity and often unevenness among local, regional, and global levels.*[4]

4. Historians writing within a postcolonial sensibility have tried to break loose from the earlier era's rigid conceptions of territorial bound-

aries and from its teleological assumptions of geographic, racial, and class destiny. Many have sought to build a new appreciation for the networked interactivity that characterized what Mary Louise Pratt has called "contact zones." Contact zones are "social spaces where cultures meet, clash, and grapple with each other, often in contexts of highly asymmetrical relations of power, such as colonialism, slavery, or their aftermaths." Pratt sees a shrinking world's clash of cultures not simply as a story of loss, imperialism, and oppression, but also as one about mutual borrowings, diverse if unequal forms of power, trickster reversals, possible harmonies, and substantial confusion. Anthropologist Anna Tsing suggests that, in transnational space, the global and the local meet in unpredictable encounters, which she calls moments of "friction."⁵ *Within the friction of contact zones, which multiplied within the connective currents that networked the globe in this period, there was creativity as well as oppression, coproduction as well as imposition of "imperial knowledge." Currents brought diverse kinds of transformations.*

5. Thus, this book endorses anthropologist Arjun Appadurai's insistence that the presumed universalism of modernism nested together with diverse oppositions. *Claims of universalism and particularism bred each other; the global and the local interacted to produce uniformity as well as diversity. The world became increasingly characterized by what I will call "differentiated commonalities"—that is, commonalities that nevertheless manifested themselves differently depending on the unpredictable frictions arising from geographical, temporal, and sociocultural locations.*⁶

6. Currents also appropriately connote the age of electricity. The global spread of electricity was a feat of science, engineering, and finance that embedded almost mystical qualities within this age of rationality. It aptly exemplified *the unity between two often-dichotomized aspects of "modern" life—reason supported by exacting taxonomies and accounting practices, and emotion charged through fluid spectacularity.*

By dramatically shrinking time and space, electricity's progeny—illumination, telephony, movies, and much more—all seemed one part science and one part miracle.

Concepts of "modernity" are the subjects of an enormous scholarship, of course, and this book develops a particular view. It projects "the modern" as emerging from two, seemingly contradictory, impulses. Promises of "order and progress" expressed one impulse. It emphasized rationality, science, engineering, corporate organization, and classification. It exalted the application of expertise and often worked to stabilize hierarchies of gender and race and geographical space. A second impulse arose within various new forms of entertainment and the changing media of mass communications. Characterized by spectacle, image, flow, surprise, and disjuncture, it appealed to a kind of emotional knowledge that was often self-styled as "popular." Science/spectacle, expertise/entertainment, order/disorder are, of course, only schematic opposites. It was within the combinations and clashes of these false poles that emerged the messy diversities and contradictions that have characterized modern life.[7]

7. The metaphor of currents whose dynamics are driven by polarities presents an even broader interpretation of modernity. Currents carry power, experience charge, and often activate their energy through polarities. Similarly, the emerging modernism of this increasingly networked era was one in which seemingly binary poles emerged as coproductive counterparts: *homogenization and differentiation, the global and the local, trans- or internationalism and nationalism, reason and spectacle. All of these sets are composed not of opposites but of nested complements that operated in creative tension with each other.*

There are dangers in any interpretive or metaphorical schema, and two of these need to be considered at the outset. Electricity brings with it a language and presumption of "enlightenment," of bringing "light" to and illuminating, "dark" continents and peoples. The metaphor itself can frame the discursive constructions of the age of electricity, hiding as much as it reveals. Authors, and readers, however, cannot escape the entrapments of language and discourse; they can only strive for the kind of critical reflection that will mitigate the hazards. In addition, the idea of mapping networks and currents may leave invisible the many people in the world who remained relatively untouched by them or who became more *dis*connected. Swaths of the earth, particularly in the interiors of Africa and Asia, may have been partially or largely "off-grid" in the transnational connectivity of the age, perhaps remaining in localized networks or perhaps intentionally self-shielded from outsider threats. Still, any idea that continental interiors held timeless people living the unchanged ways of their ancestors has proved to be an Orientalist cliché. Transnational currents could have secondary and tertiary ripple effects, touching even very remote people in uneven and unpredictable ways. In some cases the borders and restrictions that colonial rule imposed, of course, also worked to restrict networks: Colonial powers in Africa, for example, often destroyed prior long-distance trading and cultural networks. Extractive production brought some areas into greater contact with global networks of economic and social exchange while it made others more isolated. The forging of some networks thus could mean the disarticulation of others.[8] The frame of transnational currents, in short, cannot hope to capture either a connotation-free or a total story of all the localities in the world. Indeed, no schema could succeed in achieving linguistic neutrality and an accounting of all lives on the planet.

Despite potential hazards, I seek to use selective examples to show the possibilities inherent in focusing history around the dynamic, if uneven, flows of transnational currents. Focusing on five areas—international agreements and institutions, social networks and attachments, nodes of exhibition and collection, epistemic affiliations based on expertise, and the spectacular flows of mass media and consumerism—this book provides a tentative map for some of the transnational global connectivities that preceded the popularization of the word *globalization* in the 1960s and 1970s. These currents are diverse in character and in operation; they comprise neither a coherent global project nor a new stage of history that is beyond the national or imperial state. Although there is by now an enormous amount of research on transnational networks, their representations in this book are necessarily partial and contain overlapping chronologies. Chronological time is important: the kind of networks that once mostly abetted the rise of European dominance developed circuitry that helped undermine European power as the twentieth century wore on. Still, chronological time, like geographical space, is less important in this book than the thematic elaborations. The five themes that follow suggest that "complex interconnectivity," a term that John Tomlinson has given to the era since 1970, is no less a descriptor for the period 1870 to 1945.[9]

CHAPTER ONE

Currents of Internationalism

In the early twentieth century, the British writer Norman Angell electrified the imaginations and hopes of people who called themselves
"internationalists." A small man scarcely five feet tall who had officially
dropped his given last name "Lane" to become known by his penulti-
mate name "Angell," Norman had moved to America at the age of seventeen and headed west. In his six years in America, he worked briefly
as a tutor on a southern plantation, a cowboy, a homesteader near the
"fearful, weary, merciless desert" around Bakersfield, California, and a
journalist.[1] From 1905 he began serving as the Paris editor for the
Daily Mail and, after returning to England in 1912, he took up politics. Angell's short book *The Great Illusion* (1910) made him famous.
Angell was a complicated man—sickly, moody, shy—but his ideas resonated internationally, and he proved to be a compelling speaker. *The
Great Illusion* was translated into twenty-five languages, sold over
two million copies, and briefly spurred a movement called "Norman
Angellism."

The thesis of *The Great Illusion* (from which the famous antiwar
film *The Grand Illusion* would later derive its mocking title) held that
military clashes had become obsolete because the integration of finance
and commerce in European countries made war counterproductive.
Conquest, he argued, added nothing to the wealth of a nation or its
citizens. Reworking the popular Darwinian beliefs of his day, Angell
wrote that war "involves the survival of the less fit. . . . Warlike nations
do not inherit the earth" but "represent the decaying human element"
of "primitive instincts and old prejudices." In many nations of the

world "Norman Angellism" had its converts. In the United States in 1913 no less a figure that the president of Stanford University, David Starr Jordan, proclaimed that war was "impossible." "The bankers will not find the money for such a fight, the industries will not maintain it, the statesmen cannot."[2]

Angellism was only one manifestation of a widespread conviction that the revolution in communications, travel, and trade would shrink the world and create greater harmony. In China, the reformist ideas of Sun Yat-sen, Kang Youwei, and Liang Qichao, for example, had taken shape from these men's late nineteenth-century travels around the world. Kang cited the telegraph, the Universal Postal Union (UPU), and international law as evidence of a trajectory from which states might one day organize themselves into a world parliament. Liang, who between 1902 and 1907 published an influential biweekly journal called the *New Citizen,* expressed the hope that emerging international news services might promote a cosmopolitanism that would eliminate national and factional hostilities.[3]

The world of the late nineteenth and early twentieth centuries did indeed see the development of newly established "international institutions," defined by some scholars today as "persistent and connected sets of rules, often affiliated with organizations, that operate across international boundaries. Institutions range from conventions to regimes to formal organizations."[4]

A seeming paradox lay at the heart of these newly institutionalized international networks. The rhetoric of internationalism often suggested that its advocates transcended "narrow" nationalism and embraced a progressive universalism that would, incrementally, come to replace national states. People who considered themselves internationalists frequently lashed out against what they regarded as excessive or militant nationalism. Yet, as the very word *international* suggests, the "national" constituted the building block of the "international" realm, and most internationalists pursued projects that created cooperative forums and regulatory regimes among bounded states—states that were consolidated along a European model.

The boundary-strengthening moves of states and of empires thus emerged not as preconditions for or in opposition to internationalism but often as its necessary accompaniments. Indeed, most of the international regulatory peacekeeping regimes that took shape in the nineteenth and twentieth centuries attracted support precisely because so many people believed they might serve, or even universalize, the interests of their national states.

A close look at the emergence of international networks dissolves any possible paradox involved in linking the emergence of "internationalism" together with the attempts to harden the delineation of national and imperial borders. In this period the most successful international institutions sprang primarily from a Euro-American impulse that sought to refashion the world into an assemblage of "advanced" states that could project and protect their imperial realms while using cooperative institutions to spread a universalistic Western ethos. Internationalism most often came dressed as a Western project, but as we will see, its visions also contained many variations that inspired movements in diverse directions, including nationalisms linked to anticolonialism.

This chapter positions World War I as a major watershed for internationalism. In the late nineteenth century, the promise and problems of accelerating technological change drew delegates from states together to regularize practices, particularly those related to global communication and transportation. The shrinking globe also spurred ideas that international law might broaden its scope from addressing specific practices (such as navigation) to shaping larger regimes of arbitration and peacekeeping. Before the Great War, a wide variety of associations blossomed under the sunny optimism that international political institutions might keep pace with the globalization occurring in the economic and technological realms. International networks were generally elite affairs, and many Euro-American leaders assumed that nationalistic warfare had become a relic of a less enlightened past and that imperialism and internationalism would eventually uplift the globe into an era of shared "civilization" and progress.

World War I dealt a blow to such dreams. Specific internationalist projects continued, and many of the international regulatory regimes developed over the period remained as vital mechanisms that promoted the connectivities of the age. The war's destruction, however, shattered prewar optimism, and interwar internationalism seemed propelled more by fear than by hope. Could international rivalries and militarism be contained? As a greater diversity of people and ideas entered the international arena, disagreements widened rather than narrowed, and the label *internationalism* became fraught with ever more contradiction and multiplicity of meaning. As first one and then another world war wreaked incomprehensible devastations, fewer and fewer people could assume that movement toward a common definition of "civilization" provided the inevitable telos of history.

Ordering Space and Time

In the second half of the nineteenth century, the telegraph became the most visible symbol of a shrinking and interlocking world. Facilitating communication across distances through telegraphy, a task driven by strategic and business interests, became one of the earliest arenas for the creation and coordination of international norms and practices. Underwater telegraph cables successfully spanned the English Channel in 1851 and only fifteen years later, amazingly, traversed the Atlantic Ocean. Connecting first Europe and North America, telegraphy spread into the Middle East, Asia, and Latin America during the 1870s. Britain's extension of telegraph lines from London to India in 1870, to southern Africa in the 1880s, and between Australia and Canada in the early 1900s illustrates the importance of telegraphy to imperial systems. World War I proved the telegraph's significance for national war strategies, including intelligence gathering.[5]

The International Telegraph Union, founded in Paris in 1865 and subsequently retitled the International Telecommunication Union (ITU), sought to standardize and regulate international telecommunications. International telegraph lines had adapted a version of Morse code, a system of short and long clicks that Samuel B. Morse pioneered in the United States in the 1840s for his Western Union company. The ITU made this practice its global standard. The new organization also, in time, came to allocate radio spectrum and devise procedures for international telephone calls. Europe developed an international telephone system in the 1920s, but reliable transoceanic telephone and a functioning global network did not emerge until well after World War II. In Europe, states owned telegraph and telephone services, and the United States, where ownership by private business generally prevailed, remained reluctant to join the ITU as a formal partner until after World War II. Still, the United States nonetheless sent observers and participated in various standard-setting conferences. Both states and enterprises embraced these emerging international norms that, by helping curb monopolistic or overly nationalistic practices, facilitated commercial and social connections across the entire system. The preeminent historical account of the ITU claims that, as the first genuine international organization, the ITU became the model for subsequent international bodies, including the League of Nations.[6] The ways in which telegraphy mixed national and imperial aspirations with international regulation are illustrative of emerging international regimes.

Closely related in structure and function to the ITU, the Universal Postal Union (UPU), founded initially as the General Postal Union in 1874, regularized the carrying and delivery of international mail. Nationalized, government-run postal services had emerged along with the

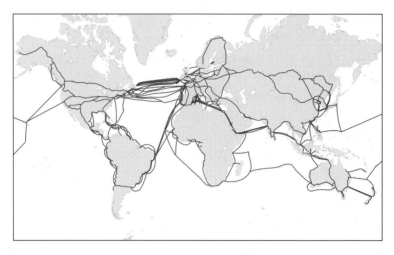

International network of major telegraph and cable lines, 1924.

nation-building efforts of modern states. The United States, for example, had consolidated its services into a single postal district and had, in 1863, introduced free home delivery of mail in its largest cities. Hoping to expand the possibility of correspondence worldwide, US officials then called for an international postal congress. Similarly in England, Rowland Hill's midcentury reforms had introduced inexpensive, pre-paid, and uniform rates. Building on such beginnings, Heinrich von Stephan, the German postal minister who had standardized postal exchange in Bismarck's Germany, led an effort to form an ongoing international organization. In 1874, European nations, the United States, Russia, Turkey, and Egypt entered an agreement to cooperate in creating a shared postal space, and within two years Japan, Brazil, Persia, and many European colonies joined. The Union soon included every country in the world.

The Union sponsored ingenious efficiencies. Before the UPU, each country had to negotiate a separate treaty with every other; after the UPU's establishment, one treaty would link a country to the Union.

Then all correspondents in the participating nations could post to each other by paying a flat, relatively inexpensive rate that did not depend on distance or on diplomatic status. Stamps of member nations were accepted for the whole international route, making additional stamps from countries along the route of transit unnecessary. Each country retained the monies it collected for international postage. As with the ITU, the UPU compellingly illustrated how national objectives dovetailed with the creation of international rule-setting and enforcement mechanisms.[7]

The rapid spread of a coherent global postal system under the UPU spurred the growth of literacy and of letter writing. It helped generate a revolution in written communication and print media. Postal reform coincided, for example, with the rise of postcards, which Austria introduced in 1869 and Germany embraced during the Franco-Prussian War of 1870–1871 to facilitate military communications. The Americans introduced a "penny postcard" in the 1870s, helping democratize letter writing by encouraging inexpensive, briefer, and more casual communication.[8] Soon advertisers discovered that efficient postal services and postcards could create bonds with customers. Mass letter writing took on a new commercial function. Book and magazine publishing also became global industries that continued targeting their elite purchasers but also developed new products to appeal to new middle- and working-class buyers. By 1914 the major industrial nations in Europe, the United States, and Japan all had mandated schooling for children up to age fourteen, and all had reached roughly 90 percent literacy fifteen years after that. International regulatory regimes often benefited the largest companies within the countries with greatest literacy rates because those firms could most easily profit from a globalizing market.

The burgeoning industry of publishing, benefiting from streamlined postal systems and rising literacy rates, also turned to international rule setting to safeguard authors' rights and bolster markets. The Berne

Convention of 1886 began to unify procedures related to literary property, and a Publishers' International Congress, formed at the end of the century, tried to secure the interests of the huge international publishing houses in Germany, France, Britain, and America.

It would be hard to overstate the importance of the revolution in print media in this era. Fueled by growing literacy, revolutions in technologies of production, and regulatory agreements, it linked people and spread ideas even as it entrenched inequalities between those who were part of the world of print and those who were not.

As international rules for electronic and written communications became standardized and more businesses and individuals broadened their contacts, the regularization of time seemed urgent. Cycles of sun and moon had governed the preindustrial world, but a predictability that transcended distance was critical to an interconnected and industrial world. In the mid-nineteenth century, as Britain and then Germany moved toward regularized time zones within their national spaces, the rules about time in the United States and most other countries remained chaotic and governed by local authorities. In 1870 Philadelphia's noon came twenty minutes after Pittsburgh's. An American train traveler from Washington to San Francisco would have to reset his or her timepiece over two hundred times in order to be current with each locality through which the train passed. Ships could not clearly communicate their positions at sea because of multiple national meridian systems; Greenwich, Paris, Berlin, Bern, Uppsala, St. Petersburg, Rome, and others each promoted its particular status as an anchor for a different prime meridian.

The new speed of railroads, shipping, and telegraphs necessitated the coordination of global space and time. Without a standard time, how could business appointments be kept; how could travelers meet; how could trains and ships stay safe? With their special need for rationalized scheduling, railroads often led the way. In the United States in 1883 railroads standardized their time zones to accord to Britain's

Greenwich-based system, and most towns embraced this reform that some opponents derisively called "Vanderbilt time."

The International Meridian Conference, held a year later in Washington, DC, brought together twenty-five nations, which represented most countries in the Americas and in Europe in addition to Turkey, Japan, and Hawai'i. Although France had been committed to its Paris prime meridian (and did not accept the new system until 1911), Britain prevailed in the diplomatic wrangling. The conference accepted the Observatory of Greenwich as the initial meridian for longitude. Establishing longitudes west and east from Greenwich until they met at an "international date line" in the Pacific Ocean, the conference's technicians of time also urged the universal adoption of a standardized twenty-four-hour day. Although most of rural China, India, and elsewhere continued to use sundials and to observe a plethora of local times, over the next several decades most nations gradually adopted a system of twenty-four time zones—a system that the Meridian Conference of 1884 had discussed but not mandated.[9]

As much of the world was standardizing time, new inventions and practices readjusted how time might be valued, understood, and experienced. The telephone collapsed distance into simultaneity. Stop-action photography froze time in a moment. The electric light pushed back the hours of darkness. Railroad sleeping cars (pioneered by Pullman in the United States and Wagons-Lits in Europe) sped passengers with great comfort across much longer distances, including the fabled Orient Express route that opened from Paris to Istanbul in 1889. Automobiles spurred construction of more and better roads. The electric clock, invented in 1916, introduced a fluid motion to the second hand. Motion pictures played with time by slowing, accelerating, and punctuating it. Artistic and literary modernism broke with established traditions to toy with new sensibilities of time and space; Salvador Dalí's *The Persistence of Memory* (1931) famously bent and distorted watches that symbolized time's passage. Frederick Taylor chopped up time and motion to accelerate the work processes of industrial labor, while typewriters sped up the pace of office work. The international networks that synchronized the world and its people thus altered economic, cultural, and emotional realms, stimulating new visions of globality that sparked both hope for universalist understandings and dread of machinelike conformity.[10]

The rationalization of time gave encouragement to other standardization movements. Efforts emerged to coordinate railroad track gauges and scales. The Treaty of the Meter, signed by many industrial countries in 1875, created an International Bureau of Weights and Measures to monitor the spreading metric system. (Britain and the United States remained outside of the metric zone.) The International Electrotechnical Commission (IEC), formed in 1906 as one of the earliest nongovernmental standardizing bodies, codified electrical standards and symbols. Its 1938 International Electrotechnical Vocabulary contained over two thousand terms in English, French, German, Italian, Spanish, and Esperanto. Engineers, the new professionals who seemed to be the heroes of the era, led many of these movements toward the coordination of national, regional, and international systems. Supporting such efforts, the International Statistical Institute (ISI), founded at The Hague in 1885 as a semigovernmental organization, linked the statistical offices of various governments. The statistics gathering of the League of Nations assumed some of the ISI's tasks in the interwar era, when the trade among ninety countries began to be monitored in statistical terms. Statistical calculations emerged to track international comparisons in balance of payments, unemployment, price levels, and national income.

The expanding matrix of statistics, especially after World War I, elaborated a new branch of knowledge in which the very conception of an "economy" was national in its orientation but transnational in its scope. The Weimar Republic and the Third Reich led the way in using economic statistics as a way of engineering national power. Yet the emergence of economic analysis became itself a transnational endeavor, as professionalizing "economists" borrowed and adapted ways of examining the "economy" as a sphere separated from "politics" and "society."[11]

International standardization, dominated by European governments and the United States, cascaded from one arena of life into others.[12] Enthusiasm for the principles of uniformity and efficiency, of course, mingled with foreboding and with nostalgia for local practices. International networks emerged in tandem with localized, sometimes anti-imperial, resistance to their spread, and they also took shape within competing claims on universality among clashing national standards. Still, the importance of the standardization movements of the era can hardly be overstated. They provided the infrastructure for the spread of all kinds of transnational currents in a shrinking world.

International Networks for Sports

In a movement parallel to the ordering of communication and time, the International Olympic Committee (IOC) sought to facilitate and standardize competition in sports. French nobleman Baron Pierre de Coubertin, an early champion of the Olympic Games, convened the initial IOC in 1894, and Athens hosted the first modern games in 1896, attracting three hundred athletes from thirteen countries. The next two games became appendages of world fairs, one held in Paris in 1900 and one in St. Louis in 1904. Coubertin and the IOC then tried to establish a regularized tradition by holding games in Athens in 1906 and in London in 1908.

Coubertin promoted the Olympic Games as a way of fostering an international community around sporting events. The games, he argued, would bolster manliness, transcend national differences, and foster respect for others. With the theme of "peaceful internationalism," he aimed to inspire young men to build strength of body and character. Such idealistic notions of transcending the state through state-sponsored

A postcard depicting the Panathinaiko Stadium in Athens, site of the first modern Olympic Games in 1896. As international mail improved, picture postcards became a popular way of communicating without having to write long, descriptive letters. (© Rykoff Collection/Corbis)

competitions were consistent with the pre–World War I internationalist spirit, but critics emerged even from the beginning. Some charged that the games were insignificant, while others suggested that competitions might stir, rather than dampen, nationalism. Indeed, the games in Stockholm in 1912 foreshadowed the tensions that were mounting toward war. Moreover, sporting events tended to be the province of elite and male participants, linked as they were to presumed qualities of leadership. Controversy grew over the issue of female participation. The push to bring women into the Olympics accelerated in view of the growing popularity of the Women's World Games, held in 1922 and every four subsequent years until the late 1930s.[13]

The popularity of international sporting competitions in the early twentieth century sparked the creation of a body to oversee the worldwide game of football (soccer). The Fédération Internationale de Football Association (FIFA), founded in Paris in 1904, held an unsuccessful international competition in 1906 but established recognition for itself after a competition held in conjunction with the London Olympics of 1908. FIFA's membership expanded beyond Europe before World War I, as South Africa, Argentine, Chile, Canada, and the United States made application.

The world wars illustrated how both nationalism and internationalism became woven into the fabric of sporting events. The disruption in travel, the military enlistment of athletes, and the national hatreds generated by World War I hurt international sport. The Olympic movement and FIFA both foundered. The Olympic Games scheduled for Berlin in 1916 were not held, and the immediate postwar Olympic and FIFA matches attracted fewer nations and even less public interest than their prewar counterparts. The mid-1920s and early 1930s, however, brought some recovery. FIFA introduced the World Cup competitions in 1930, and the IOC successfully staged Olympic Games in Paris in 1924, in Amsterdam in 1928 (where female athletes finally participated in five track-and-field events), and in Los Angeles in 1932 (made famous by the amazing all-around athlete Mildred "Babe" Didrikson).[14] At the infamous Berlin Olympics of 1936, however, Adolf Hitler tried to showcase the Aryan race and German power. His ethno-nationalistic displays, very visibly challenged when the African-American Jesse Owens won four gold medals, tarnished the rhetoric of internationalism that surrounded the games.[15] The global military struggles of the World War II era postponed any revival of a supposedly harmonious "Olympic spirit." Although many scholars of the Olympics present international and national impulses as being contradictory, they clearly were also complementary. One had first to be national in order to compete in international games.

Sports projected the hegemonies found in other internationalist arrangements. Both the Olympics and football (soccer) claimed to symbolize a global community united in sport, but the organizing bodies reflected not only national loyalties but also imperial and gender allegiances. Universalized values and rules, in sports as in other domains, emanated from the powerful states and citizens who could view international rules and gatherings as being consistent with their own views. As football spread to European colonies in Africa, the Caribbean, and Asia, and as baseball spread to zones of American influence, each colonial power portrayed the expansion of its favorite sport as the elixir that promoted civilization and manliness. Officials, missionaries, and educational initiatives in both informal and formal colonies became associated with the spread of national sporting preferences. Gender and racial distinctions were both reinforced and challenged within the expansion of international sports.

Legal Internationalism and Arbitration

The proliferation of international institutional structures dating from the late nineteenth century seemed to confirm the possibility that nations could develop supranational regulatory regimes. It was only a short leap from devising specific functional collaborations such as the ITU and the IPU to imagining that states themselves might form leagues or federations for even more ambitious purposes, especially legal arbitration or multilateral peacekeeping.

Some theorists proclaimed that the global networks of trade and communications would make sovereign states obsolete. In the 1860s, lawyers from various European countries began to assert a "scientific" view of law, suggesting that universal legal principles should gradually be codified and spread.[16] Universities established chairs in international law, and professional gatherings of lawyers discussed how to standardize legal systems.

Creating law for the world was bound up in the sense of civilizing mission, so strong in the West, and fit with the evolutionary, progressive view of history that was becoming hegemonic. The idea of an emerging legal order both spread a sense of one-world universalism and also became a way of dividing "civilized" nations from the "backward" areas that seemed in need of transformation. Within this discourse of transformative universalism, the turn of the century witnessed many attempts to develop a body of international law and to create venues for its enforcement and for the arbitration of disputes.[17]

Most scholars agree that the emergence of the concept of international law generally developed from the law of the sea. Hugo Grotius's interest in developing international law, for example, had stemmed from his reflections on freedom of the seas. As the largest arena of space between and among national states, the seas raised complicated issues of jurisdiction, and the 1913 International Convention on Safety of Life at Sea (formulated in the wake of the *Titanic* disaster) provided an important step toward a multilateral process of lawmaking and law enforcement. This and other international legal agreements, which attempted to ensure free flow of maritime transport and to protect innocent passage through territorial waters, aimed to convert the world's waterways from arenas of conflict to safe commercial highways.

Many late nineteenth-century European politicians and jurists pursued the dream that international arbitration could replace war as a means of settling disputes. An active group of legal internationalists, operating through several influential associations, had been building a context for legal arbitration over the course of the late nineteenth century. The so-called *Alabama* Treaty of 1873 between Britain and the United States, for example, dealt with claims arising from the British-made Confederate cruiser that had sunk seventy Union ships during the American Civil War. Setting a precedent for the competence of arbitral tribunals, the treaty defined the rights and duties of neutrals and provided momentum behind the inclusion of arbitration clauses in other multilateral treaties, such as the Congo Act of 1885 and the Anti-Slavery Act of 1890.[18] In 1889 the Inter-Parliamentary Union (IPU), formed by peace activists William Randal Cremer and Frédéric

Passy, joined together countries with parliaments (twenty-four by 1913) to advance methods of international arbitration.

The Hague Peace Conferences of 1899 and 1907 represented the high point of prewar internationalist attempts to substitute law and arbitration for war and force. International politicians, intellectuals, and jurists had picked up on an idea promoted by Tsar Nicholas II of Russia to hold a major international conference to standardize precepts of international law and procedures for arbitration. The idea of convening such conferences at The Hague electrified many of those who were advocating diverse forms of peace activism and international lawmaking. Henri Dunant, the founder of the Red Cross, played a significant role in persuading world powers to accept the tsar's proposal. Austrian baroness Bertha von Suttner, a prolific journalist and author of a widely translated 1889 bestseller *Die Waffen Nieder! (Lay Down Your Arms!)*, helped galvanize the burgeoning international peace movement behind the idea. She had earlier helped convince Alfred Nobel, the inventor of dynamite, to dedicate money in his will to establishing a prize for a person who would work "most effectively for the fraternization of mankind, the diminution of armies, and the promotion of Peace Congresses."[19] The eccentric British journalist William Thomas Stead founded a new weekly in London called *War against War* to further his International Peace Crusade and to promote the gathering at The Hague. The Universal Peace Congress, composed of a growing number of men and women activists who met yearly to advance the cause of arms limitation, also backed the idea.

The conferences at The Hague did not simply endorse lofty goals about peace; they attempted to devise practical measures to build a structure of international law. The internationalism represented at The Hague, although limited in scope, transcended Europe and the United States to include China, Japan, Siam, Turkey, Persia, and Mexico (in the 1907 conference, seventeen other delegations from the American continent also joined the New World contingent). Delegates pursued three specific aims: to promote the peaceful settlement of disputes, to restrict the "excessive" cruelty of warfare (for example, restrictions on "dumdum" bullets and projectiles that would harm civilians), and to limit arms races and the burdens they placed on national treasuries.

The idea of arbitration as a way not of ending but of preventing conflict may have been the most important concept to come out of meetings at The Hague, although specific problems of jurisdiction remained. Participating nations signed a convention for the Pacific Settlement of International Disputes. They created the Permanent Court of Arbitration, or World Court, which operated before the outbreak of World War I and was reconstituted after the war as the International Court of Justice (1922–1945), associated with the League of Nations. Agreements also codified laws of war, including rules for the opening of hostilities, the rights of neutral nations and persons, the status of merchant ships, and the conduct of naval and land warfare.[20]

Judged in the context of the stirring speeches, the expectations set by the participating luminaries, and the lavish ceremonies, banquets, and press coverage, the outcomes of The Hague conferences have often been trivialized. The conferences were, after all, followed closely by outbreak of the Great War. But they did clearly tap into important characteristics of the age—the interest in establishing international standards and the vision that legal regimes could gradually transcend national borders and come to govern the behavior of states just as they governed individuals within successful states. The conferences comprised expressions both of the fear that national competition might lead to devastating warfare and of the hope that global communications and other networks might facilitate a new international order with mechanisms to keep the peace.[21]

Before the outbreak of the Great War, coinciding with the optimism that helped promote The Hague conferences, the idea that major wars had become obsolete circulated among "internationalists" around the world. New England anti-imperialist Raymond Landon Bridgman, for example, published "The First Book of World Law" in 1911. Bridgman proclaimed that "for more than a generation true world law has been growing," and he provided a compendium of agreements relating to everything from communications to sanitation to world government. He wrote that "within a comparatively short time the organization of all mankind into a political unit has advanced rapidly" and that an unwritten World Constitution of widely accepted tenets already formed the basis for an emerging World Organization.[22] In many parts of the world, as has been noted, people read Norman Angell's *The Great Illusion* and hailed him as a prophet. The "guns of August" that touched off World War I, of course, proved that nationalism easily trumped the internationalists' dreams of convergence and peace. Efforts to build international institutions, however, persisted through the war and after.

A League of Nations

The staggering casualties that the Great War inflicted on a generation of European men (almost ten million soldiers dead; perhaps twice that many wounded) seemed to confirm the folly of military contests. Although it seems clear, in retrospect, that the devastations of the Great War fostered the growth of communist and fascist authoritarianism and planted the seeds of World War II, the war initially appeared to strengthen the hands of those who advocated new international mechanisms for the peaceful settlement of disputes. The idea of a League of Nations embodied the early twentieth-century internationalist faith that liberal capitalist democracies, benign imperial administrations, and international bodies might all promote a system that would civilize the rest of the world and spread universalized norms.[23]

US president Woodrow Wilson became the most prominent voice for building a postwar peace through a kind of world federalism based upon international legal standards. His vision that collective security arrangements and "self-determination" of peoples would curb aggressive nationalism and ethnic grievances became globally influential. Wilsonian faiths, however, were fraught with contradiction. Wilson's country would never join the League of Nations, though that body is forever associated with his name, and his conception of self-determination turned out to be excruciatingly limited.

As president, Wilson had developed his ideas about internationalism as he steered his foreign policy through a series of crises with Mexico and confronted the outbreak of war in Europe in 1914. Only leagues of cooperating, democratic nations, he came to believe, could discipline the rapacious forces let loose by revolutions and wars. For the Western Hemisphere, he had proposed a Pan American Pact that would organize collective action among nations to solve wrongdoing within the hemisphere (wrongdoing to which Wilson, of course, assumed the United States would never be party, although many Latin Americans felt otherwise). The pact itself went nowhere, but after the European war began in 1914, Wilson drew closer to advisers who were generally influenced by Angell, Jordan, and others who advocated international arrangements, arms reduction, and a repudiation of nationalism as the path to peace. Once in the war, Wilson proposed his Fourteen Points (1918), a plan for a postwar reconstruction of the international system along lines that he believed would eliminate the root causes of war.

Around the world, reformers and internationalists of various stripes saw in Wilson, and perhaps in the United States, a reason to believe that a new order actually could come from the sorrows of war. Two of the president's Points would have especially profound influence. One was "self-determination," a vague concept that Wilson advanced as an antidote to the instabilities raised by ethnic tensions in the old Austro-Hungarian Empire but one that colonial subjects around the world quickly embraced as a rallying cry for their own national aspirations. The second was "collective security," a concept to be embodied in a League of Nations. Conceiving of the new world-to-be in terms of individual, self-determining states that would come together in a pro-tofederation, Wilson's vision embodied the aspirations that had buoyed so many of the internationalist currents before the war.[24]

In some ways Wilson was an unlikely midwife to the vision that became styled as a "new diplomacy" based upon open covenants, "peace without victory," self-determination, and collective security among democratic nations. An aloof intellectual who had been president of Princeton University, Wilson had dispatched troops into Mexico, installed US military rule in Haiti, tightened US military control in the Dominican Republic, and implanted a US administration into Nicaragua. America's first southern president since before the Civil War, he had brought racial segregation to his nation's capital and had appointed many southern Democratic segregationists as top diplomats around the world.

Yet Wilson also had deep ties to international circles that advocated for labor rights, feminism, anti-imperialism, and even socialism. His blueprint for a conflict-free world of self-determining democracies and laws resonated within the agendas of many reformers throughout the world, including anticolonial leaders in China, India, Egypt, Korea, and elsewhere. Many internationalists at home and abroad, even if they decried Wilson's various compromises and rigidities, had been inspired by his belief in the concept of a league of self-determining states. Although Wilson met opposition at the 1919 Peace Conference at Versailles and then from his own Senate, which ultimately refused to ratify the Treaty of Versailles because of the article creating the League, his League of Nations exemplified many of the hopes—and contradictions—of the era's internationalists.[25]

By 1918, as old autocratic empires (Russian, Austro-Hungarian, German, and Ottoman) fell apart and a dozen new republics were proclaimed, liberal internationalists such as President Wilson hoped that postwar cooperation among emerging democratic states might vindicate the horrible costs of war. Wilson's idea that war could be an in-

NOT ROOM FOR BOTH

The Covenant of the League of Nations struggling to unseat the Constitution of the United States. This political cartoon, published in the *San Francisco Chronicle,* supported President Woodrow Wilson's Republican opponents, who charged that the League of Nations would curtail the nation's sovereign powers. The US Senate refused to ratify the Treaty of Versailles because the treaty established the League. (© Bettmann/Corbis) strument for bringing stability and international understanding, however, was always delusion. From 1914 into the early 1920s, much of the world witnessed epic-scale devastation: deaths from the world war, casualties associated with the Russian, Mexican, and Chinese revolutions, ravages from influenza and other epidemic diseases, and displacements of populations associated with wartime's rising nationalism. In Europe, the self-styled seat of civilization, perhaps over fifteen million people perished from these combined causes, and this death toll affected societies and cultures in profound ways, becoming both a symbol of instability and a further cause of it.

New dictatorships, nourished by demographic dislocations and new ideologies, quickly challenged any idea of an emerging liberal republican norm. The Bolshevik revolutionary regime, which came to power in Russia in 1917, provided inspiration and support for a transnational communist movement advocating more power for working classes. It also promoted a doctrine of self-determination that, unlike Wilson's, was merged directly with anti-imperialism, thereby appealing globally to nationalists seeking independence from colonial powers. Liberal republicans in many countries, faced with postwar economic instability and threats to their power from communist movements, often moved rightward. Partly in response to the growing strength of communist parties and the weaknesses of liberal parliaments, various forms of nationalist dictatorships and fascist regimes came to Italy, Spain, and Portugal in the 1920s and to Germany and Japan in the 1930s. Corporative states with varied degrees of authoritarianism also emerged in Mexico, Brazil, Argentina, and elsewhere. The League's structure of internationalism could hardly contain such political and economic polarization—much less the virulent nationalisms within which the many consolidating dictatorships thrived. The structures of the League were ill-suited to cope with what Eric Hobsbawm called the "age of extremes" and the clashing imperial aspirations that ultranationalism nourished.

Still, the League was a significant conduit for transnational connections in the interwar period. Headquartered in Geneva, it had thirty-two original member states, and thirteen additional states were invited to join. With a structure vaguely reminiscent of the IPU and inspired by plans from The Hague Peace Conferences, the League was the first international organization devoted to a broad agenda that included arbitration of disputes, the prevention of war, and the international coordination of social and economic programs. It drew together the transnational connections that had been emerging among groups of professionals since the nineteenth century and brought them under a single international umbrella. The secretariat of the League in the early 1930s employed over seven hundred staff members from all over the world, although those from Europe were by far in the majority. The dense network of people working in League-sponsored economic, social, and cultural organizations in the interwar era probably constituted the League's most lasting impact. One scholar writes that the representations of the League at the time of its creation "conjured images of a globe crisscrossed by streams of electrical energy."[26]

Internationalist legal thinkers saw the League as the kernel that might grow into a global legal system. The Permanent Court of International Justice heard disputes between states from 1920 to 1940, and various League institutions worked on codifying international law, especially in the areas of communications, transportation, and arms control. The League also promoted restricting opium traffic (resulting in the Geneva Convention of 1931), protecting women from trafficking and children from exploitation, opposing the continuation of slavery, facilitating intellectual and cultural exchange, and resettling refugees.

The League's Economic and Financial Organization (EFO) extended the practice of standardization by collecting economic statistics on national economies and on the international economy as a whole. It widened its purview beyond data collection when leading nations and bankers urged active intervention to help stabilize postwar economies in crisis. Drawing upon the expertise of leading economists in Europe, the EFO began to advocate particular policies related to tariffs, trade, monetary systems, production, and poverty. It hosted the World Economic Conferences in 1927 and 1933. Although the EFO clearly failed to prevent the world from slipping into depression during the 1930s, its statistical yearbooks and networks of economists provided a basis for the creation of international economic agencies after World War II.

The League of Nations Health Organization (LNHO), formed in 1923 in response to postwar epidemics, also coordinated national policies to promote international norms. With one-third of its scientific work subsidized by the Rockefeller Foundation, the LNHO linked together public health experts from nations and regions throughout the world to collect data and to standardize statistical and epidemiological practices, such as cataloging blood types. It encouraged the establishment of public health programs globally and reported regularly on health conditions throughout the world. League-promoted sanitation programs helped lower death rates.[27]

The International Labour Organization (ILO), established in the Treaty of Versailles partly in an effort to forestall the appeal of communism in the wake of the Bolshevik Revolution, became one of the League's most activist bodies. The ILO built on a long but fairly ineffective tradition of international conferences convened by labor activists. In the 1870s leading labor reformers had begun to hold international gatherings, and an International Association for Labour Legislation (IALL) met in Paris in 1900 to informally coordinate national rules and expose countries with labor abuses. The resolutions of such international forums, however, had little impact on national legislation. The ILO, having more formalized institutional backing, accelerated efforts to advance rights for workers and labor unions. Its first annual conference in October 1919 adopted six conventions dealing with workplace safety, work hours, and protection for women and children who worked in industry. Gradually, many countries ratified the ILO's conventions, although the deepening depression of the 1930s slowed the pace of ratification. In 1926 the ILO established a supervisory system that monitored how states were applying its standards.[28]

Within the ILO, however, various approaches clashed along lines of nationality and ideology. The ILO recognized trade unions and employers as partners with national states—a tripartite form that merged "public" and "private" sectors in ways that invited disagreements. Moreover, even among pro-labor groups, the ILO was frequently beset with competing views on the style of labor activism—ranging from conservative unionists such as American Samuel Gompers to a spectrum of ·less accommodationist leaders. Generally the organization supported a liberal capitalist system operating through cooperating national states, however, and opposed an alternative transnational labor movement that was being promoted through the Soviet Union's Third International.

The League's relationship to colonialism was similarly uncertain, as the League both undermined and buttressed the justifications for colonialism. The war victors stripped the defeated powers, Germany and the Ottoman Empire, of their colonies and converted these holdings into mandates. This action in effect repudiated the colonialism exercised by defeated nations and provided a structure for a presumably more enlightened tutelage. Mandates were to be administered by designated "advanced" nations until ready for self-government, and the mandate administrator had to pledge to protect the "native" and minority populations and to "develop" the territory. The mandate system, however, sanctioned and rejustified foreign administration, and the League did little to interfere with the empires of the war's victors. Colonial peoples who had hoped that Wilson's calls for postwar self-determination would challenge colonial rule were bitterly disappointed. For them, the League inscribed colonialism into a Euro-centered internationalism rather than offering a more inclusive blueprint. Nationalist movements, which were growing in colonialized areas, embraced and continued to organize around the language of self-determination even as they rejected the postwar settlement that restored and relegitimized the colonial order. A new anticolonialist internationalism took shape.[29]

After the Great War and paralleling the League's efforts at standardization, countries created additional structures to establish common rules. Most of these disciplinary authorities did not threaten the sovereignty of national states but simply enhanced states' abilities to facilitate the global reach of citizens and businesses. The overriding interest of all states seemed to be in providing speed, security, and safety in international commerce and communication. The International Broadcasting Union of 1925 (later absorbed into the ITU) handled issues of newly emergent broadcast radio. The International Commission for Air Navigation and International Air Traffic Association, created in 1919, developed technical and safety standards for aircraft, although commercial aviation remained quite limited before World War II. International shipping conferences promoted agreements on maritime safety. The Hague Codification Conference of 1930 tried to settle a broad range of issues relating to how nationality and citizenship status should be determined.

Despite, or really because of, the Great War, the efforts at arms limitation also experienced some rebirth. The Washington Treaty of 1922, despite its flaws and omissions, attempted to limit certain categories of naval armaments and to curb a renewal of the pre–World War I arms race. The 1925 Geneva Protocol to the Hague Convention, a response to public outcry over the wartime use of mustard gas and fears that even more deadly agents would be developed, prohibited "the use in war of asphyxiating, poisonous or other gases, and of bacteriological methods of warfare." Sixty-one nations ultimately signed the Kellogg-Briand Pact of 1928, which outlawed war, but the multilateral agreement provided no mechanism for enforcement or determining fault. Peace movements that denounced nationalism surged in many countries during the early 1930s, even as ultranationalist fascist governments reshaped politics in Italy, Germany, and Japan and armed for war.

In 1935 the Nobel Peace Prize went to Norman Angell, the well-known peace pamphleteer of a quarter century earlier. In his acceptance speech Angell articulated the arguments that still animated those who placed their hopes for peace in international law and a League of Nations. War, he said, "is made, not usually by evil men knowing themselves to be wrong, but is the outcome of policies pursued by good men usually passionately convinced that they are right."[30] Only the application of law and the mediations of a body such as the League of Nations, he concluded, could curb the passions and the overzealous patriotism that led to violence. The optimism of Angell's earlier writings, however, only faintly echoed. Networks of internationalists no longer exuded confidence that they formed a vanguard in a natural progression by which new economic and cultural interconnections would morph into international rules and bodies that could keep the peace.

The disruptions and revolutions arising from World War I had fostered ideologies of communist and then fascist authoritarianism, and the Great Depression, which fell most heavily on parliamentary democracies and liberal capitalist regimes, strengthened the self-confidence of these dictatorships. In the early 1930s Joseph Stalin consolidated his power in the Soviet Union, fostered a famine in Ukraine that would kill perhaps three million people, and laid the foundations for institutions that, in 1937 and 1938, would carry out a Great Terror of targeted murder directed at dissenters, peasants, and members of national minorities. The year Angell accepted his prize, Italian armies invaded Ethiopia. Hitler was promoting his program to remake and "purify" Germany, and in the next few years he laid plans for an expanding German Reich in which Jews and Eastern Europeans would be "cleansed" away to make room for German settlers and "civilization."

As Nazi ideology became more extreme and dedicated to warfare, these proposals hardened into the systematic implementation of a "final solution" to the "Jewish problem" through mass slaughter. By the time of Hitler's defeat in May 1945, approximately six million Jews—or two-thirds of the prewar population of European Jews—and been killed; millions of other "undesirables"—Roma, homosexuals, disabled persons, Poles and other Eastern Europeans—had also met their deaths; and documents suggest that the mass killing of non-Germans in the lands that Hitler wished to resettle to the east had just begun. Japanese leaders, also linking "civilization" with their own plans to build a settler colony, sent hundreds of thousands of farmers and technicians to develop Manchuria while their army and the notorious Unit 731, which conducted horrific human experimentation, consolidated control over inhabitants. Japan's military leaders moved into China and promised to keep extending their reach into Southeast Asia.[31]

As Angell and many of his internationalist contemporaries watched the governments of Japan and then Germany leave the League of Nations, launch their expansionist programs, and touch off new wars in Asia and Europe, they increasingly embraced the need for collective military action against fascism. They continued to advocate for an even stronger international body that could build alliances among democracies, but they could no longer sustain the idea that the new connecting currents of the twentieth century would render war-making a "Great Illusion." Well-functioning global economic markets and effective parliamentary forms had deteriorated in tandem. The currents of transnational connections that some internationalists had once hoped would spread cooperative institutions instead swept most of the world into the vortex of a second world war. In a linked world, alliances, affiliations, ethnic and class hatreds, and research on modern war-making techniques quickly fed the global conflagration. The internationalism of the late nineteenth century turned defensive and fearful in the mid-twentieth century's increasingly interconnected, yet increasingly militarized, world.[32]

The world's second war in the twentieth century, like the first one, both curtailed and also spread global interconnections. The Great Depression and the rising tide of autarchic nationalism and regional blocs had chipped away at the institutions of the global economy, but the war also underscored, for many, the need to rebuild a functioning world system. British prime minister Winston Churchill and US president Franklin D. Roosevelt met aboard a warship in Newfoundland in August 1941 and issued a statement called the Atlantic Charter, which tried to sketch out internationalist aims for the postwar period. Endorsing lower trade barriers, global economic and social cooperation, freedom of seas, disarmament, and a fair peace, the Charter expressed standard internationalist positions. Within a few months, all of the "United Nations" of the wartime alliance accepted the Charter's principles. As the war dragged on, the importance of building transnational ties of all kinds became ever more compelling to all belligerents: access to raw materials throughout the globe proved strategically critical, as did being able to maintain global transportation and communications systems. In addition, the huge wartime mobilizations of people—for both war work and war fighting—sent millions away from their homes and introduced them to new countries and cultures. Internationalists of the interwar era—and there were by then many versions of what, specifically, internationalism should champion—still might hope for some kind of postwar reconstruction of a functional world order.

The United Nations Organization and the Bretton Woods economic agreements, created as World War II ended, emerged from both the hopes and the fears that had come to animate internationalism over the previous century. They also embodied the contradictions of earlier international agreements, bodies, and rule-setting regimes. Like the League, these institutions advanced an internationalism that often masked agendas for national and imperial advantage. The San Francisco Conference that forged the new United Nations in 1945, for example, hailed Jan Smuts for having been present at the creation of the League. Smuts spoke eloquently about the need for a new institution that would preserve justice and the "fundamental rights of man." But Smuts epitomized the imperial and racial ideology of British colonialism, and he was there to preserve its values from what he regarded as the misguided humanitarianism that might cast his own country of South Africa in a bad light. Smuts, writes Mark Mazower, was a member of the generation "who sought to prolong the life of an empire of white rule through international cooperation." Similarly, international meetings at Bretton Woods in 1944 to reconstruct the global financial system signaled the limitations, more than the promise, of new postwar cooperative institutions. Stalin refused to attend; Britain and the United States clashed; lesser countries and colonies had little voice; and the newly created financial bodies initially proved so ineffective that the British financial system veered into near collapse in the year after the war ended.[33]

~

In the late nineteenth century, the revolutions in communications and transportation brought by the industrial age promoted a flowering of efforts to imagine the world as a single field. At the same time, the growth of new fortunes, extracted from growing global economic networks, financed a host of international initiatives and structures designed to bring national leaders together to spread regularity of practices and common ideas about law. In the pre–World War I era, marked by the ascendancy of Western nations and dominated by transnationally networked elites, many projects on behalf of international cooperation and perpetual peace reflected an ebullient optimism about the future.

To those involved in them, the variety of international bodies that emerged from the late nineteenth century seemed to be constructing universalized values and practices that could, over time, bring nations and the people they governed into cooperative and standardized arrangements. The destruction of the twentieth-century wars and the brutalities of imperial regimes, however, showed the limitations and naïveté of such visions of universality.

The world history of convergences and "progress," which turn-of-the-century internationalists had hoped to witness and enact in the twentieth century, had turned dark by 1945. By the end of World War II, the past half century seemed the story of ruin, war, depression, lost generations, and misbegotten colonial adventures. Some important infrastructure of the cooperative rule-setting regimes remained—regulations on telegraphs, mail, time, and measurement, for example, along with efforts to draw together laws and statistics—but most seemed narrowly technical matters rather than steps into some postnational or convergent future. The infant United Nations began to take up work done by the League, but the emergence of anticolonialism and a budding Cold War brought myriad challenges to the visions of earlier internationalists.

Significant voices, of course, had scoffed throughout the period at any idea that internationalism might promise a new universalistic age. Throughout the era, the rivalries sharpened by nationalism, frightening new weaponry, and hatreds bred in colonialism had provided clear-eyed warnings. Mark Twain wrote bitter essays against the self-deceptions and silences of imperialists. Joseph Conrad probed the darkness at the heart of colonial relationships. Growing anticolonial networks, their hopes spurred and then spurned by Wilsonian internationalists who talked of self-determination, coalesced to challenge Western frameworks of convergence and to amplify the voices of those who felt disenfranchised and marginalized within emerging international bodies.

International conventions and rule-making institutions thus forged important global networks, but these often favored people already endowed with economic and political power. The contradictions of "internationalism" became manifest in the bloodletting of World War I, the rise of communist and fascist authoritarianism, the brutalities of and resistances against colonialism, and the horrific destructions of World War II.

CHAPTER TWO

Social Networking and Entangled Attachments

Social networking among people who might be distant from each other in geography, culture, class, age, or other attributes often seems a phenomenon of the computer age, but it clearly long predates the Internet revolution. In the age of electricity, the growth of communications—mass publishing, faster and less expensive travel, telegraphy, telephone, and radio—created currents that allowed people to interact globally as never before. As has been seen, one vision of world harmony imagined a convergence of national states within rule-setting regimes such as the Hague Conventions and the League of Nations. A wider variety of non-state transnational alliances and affiliations, however, also coalesced to both bolster and challenge this form of internationalism.[1]

Social networks assuming non-state forms organized themselves around class, religion, gender, race, function, ideas, and perceived moral frameworks. They offered attachments that were transnational; that is, they pulsed above, below, and through the more formalized structures of national states, empires, and international institutions. Although today's concept of a "networked society" sometimes connotes a horizontal, nonhierarchical structure, my usage invokes the idea of social networks in a more flexible sense: they took hierarchical or horizontal shapes; they assumed forms with clear management structures or as loose associations of entangled attachments. Social networking came in all kinds of patterns.

The relationships between transnational attachments and the allegiances formed around national or imperial loyalties are complex.

Participants in transnational networks often proclaimed that they stood for universalistic goals articulated against the presumed particularism of national states and empires. Yet as this chapter elaborates, aspirations for universal betterment could also draw on an often unstated sense of ethno-national and imperial superiority. In both the international networks discussed in Chapter 1, and the transnational attachments discussed in this and following chapters, the universal and the particular generally intertwined, and each drew strength from their tensions and coproductivity.

The historical periodization for globalization, put forth by A. G. Hopkins and others, sees it quickening in the late nineteenth century and slowing from the 1920s into the post–World War II period before resuming its rapid pace. Such a trajectory well describes economic interconnections. When examining the complex matrix of transnational social networks, however, it may be difficult to discern such a metanarrative of accelerations and decelerations. Rather, one might posit irregular patterns where some entangled attachments wax while others wane, some social networks become denser while others atrophy.

This chapter tries to capture the irregularity and diversity of currents rather than to characterize their overall flow. It seeks to develop notions of connection and entanglement—and of blockage and disruption. The networks and attachments that are traced below constituted no single field of transnational vision; some ran parallel, some intertwined together, some pulsed in different directions, some seem simply incommensurable. In the terrain of the transnational, historical trajectory is not a singular but a plural thing.

Language and Photography

The most fundamental building block of communication—language—became one medium that attracted transnational reformers. Ludwik Lazar Zamenhof, convinced that language divisions reinforced nationalist ideologies that led to global conflicts, attempted to create a new international language called Esperanto. Growing up as part of a Yiddish-speaking Jewish majority in a Polish town (part of the Russian Empire) in which other groups spoke Polish, Russian, and German, he was inspired to devise and publish in 1887 the first book of Esperanto grammar. The idea caught on, especially with middle-class people engaged in cross-border commerce and tourism. The language spread over the next few decades, at first primarily in Russia and Eastern Europe and then into Western Europe, the Americas, China, and Japan. Esperanto's first world congress, held in 1905 in France, attracted 688 Esperanto speakers from twenty nationalities. The World Esperanto Association, founded in 1908 by a Swiss journalist, continued to hold yearly congresses. The language became so identified with internationalism that it received considerable credibility among delegates to the League of Nations, although France blocked any official use of Esperanto on the claim that French was already a universal language. As one historian writes, the Esperanto movement displayed not just "a commitment to an ideal language" but "a theory of the purpose of language."[2]

Esperanto rode a global wave of popularity during the 1920s, a time of deep disillusionment with nationalism and war and of energetic networking on behalf of cosmopolitanism and peace. Esperanto, writes one scholar, "helped generate an ideological framework of one-worldism."[3] But the movement also divided in the 1920s, one wing becoming closely associated with socialist circles. Both wings were generally distrusted by strong nationalists, and the movement came under fire during the 1930s in Germany and Soviet Russia, precisely the countries in which it had initially been the strongest. Adolf Hitler and Joseph Stalin both disparaged the language as associated with Jews and subversion. They worked to stamp it out.

Other new methods for enlarging communication proliferated during the late nineteenth century. Louis Braille, a young boy living in Paris who had lost his eyesight, devised a system of raised dots that allowed reading by touch and thus expanded the reach of the written word to the blind. Variants of this system spread during the mid-nineteenth century, and in 1878 an international congress in Paris adopted a standard system, which was finally codified for the English-speaking world in 1932.

Such projects for humanistic language reform represented the hope that new kinds of codes might forge common meanings across all kinds of borders, facilitating understanding and peace. In this sense, photography also ranked as one of the new potentially transnational "languages" that emerged in the late nineteenth century. French photographer and balloonist Gaspard-Félix Tournachon, who adopted the name "Nader," publicly dramatized the potential of aerial photography when he flew over Paris in 1858. A few years later he launched his huge balloon *Le Géant,* which was unsuccessful but inspired the global-flight fantasies of Jules Verne. Seeing and photographing the world from on high or by traversing previously unseen territory became a preoccupation among many explorers and armchair adventure seekers who had growing access to mass-produced books and magazines. Photography, then augmented by film, rapidly spread a language based on images.

The desire to understand the world through photography sparked a variety of significant projects in the late nineteenth century. Scottish photographer John Thompson published one of the most famous and influential early collections, *Illustrations of China and Its People* (1873), after a decade of traveling in the Far East. In it, he established some of the conventions of documentary photography.[4] *National Geographic* magazine published its first photo in 1889, and before World War I published many photo tours that brought images of the world to its growing numbers of fans. The first photos of Lhasa in Tibet, the North Pole, and Machu Picchu, and some of the earliest color photos of gardens in Belgium, for example, all appeared in *National Geographic*. France and Germany provided the early leadership in photographic techniques, and international conferences, such as the International

Photographic Exhibition held in Dresden in 1909, drew photographers from many countries into technical and artistic communities. Generally these early photographers saw themselves as capturing new kinds of information that would serve the transnational development of science, social science, and civilization.

Albert Kahn, a French photographer, banker, and internationalist, perhaps best exemplified the idea that his images from autochrome photography—a portable color process—could draw the peoples of the world together in mutual understanding. From 1909 until the onset of the Great Depression, when he met financial ruin, Kahn sent photographers to more than fifty countries and collected some seventy-two thousand images, which he called "The Archives of the Planet." The archive boasted probably the earliest color photographs of Egypt's pyramids and India's Taj Mahal. It showed daily life among Kurds, Vietnamese, Brazilians, Mongolians, Europeans, and North Americans. The color pictures were, and are, stunning but the assumptions behind them were perhaps even more arresting: Kahn hoped to deploy photography as a tool that, by representing human diversity for all to see, might promote greater familiarity and peace among the world's cultures.[5]

The semiotics of photographs, however, involved more complexity than simply broadening people's visions and promoting familiarity. Kahn may have hoped that photography could be a neutral symbolic language that enhanced mutual recognition, but the meanings of photographic images necessarily emerge from the variable and unstable constructions of both producer and receiver. Photography's new representations of the world thus advanced no single agenda.

Photographic technologies were developed and consumed most thoroughly, for example, within the hearts of empires, and they therefore often represented an imperial perspective. A multivolume set of 468 photographs, *The People of India* (1868–1875), published in London, accompanied the first census of India (1872) and land survey of India (begun in 1878). All represented efforts to categorize colonial

A photograph from Albert Kahn's "Archives of the Planet," ca. 1920, showing Angkor Wat, the famed temple complex in Cambodia. Kahn's archives consisted of 4,000 stereoscopic plaques, 72,000 autochromes, and around 183,000 meters of film. The archives were intended to promote peace by documenting the world's people. Five cameramen supervised by French geographer Jean Brunhes shot photographs in forty-eight countries on nearly every continent. (© Musée Albert Kahn—Départment des Hauts-de-Seine, Léon Busy, photographer [A35852])

inhabitants and make them legible to their rulers.[6] The Ottoman Empire also became an early supporter of photography, and Sultan Abdülhamid II used photography as one method of enhancing control over his territories.[7] Around 1907 in Russia, the photographic pioneer Sergei Mikhailovich Prokudin-Gorskii began to execute a photographic survey of the Russian Empire to be shown in color slide projections. The project brought him to the attention of Tsar Nicholas II, who then gave his project official sponsorship. From 1909 to 1912 Prokudin-Gorskii traversed the various regions of Russia and sought, through his slide show, to make the diverse landscapes and peoples more familiar to Russian audiences. The tsarist regime, like other imperial rulers, recognized that picturing the empire could help constitute it as a familiar and bounded whole.

Many of the photographic projects of empires famously projected images of domination—over land, animals, and indigenous people. Some seem designed to soberly inform people back home about new lands and the civilizing role of imperial institutions. Some clearly aimed primarily to entertain. Either way, photographs helped guide audience responses to encountering cultural difference. For example, exotic and often highly sexualized women were favorites on postcards; photos of white women displaying animal trophies pictured the domination of white prowess even over native masculinity; juxtapositions of traditional lifestyles with the machines of modernity—autos, cameras, record players—became stock favorites. As also reflected in the international institutions erected at the same time, the more the world became "one," the more its many hierarchies of difference—race, gender, region—were displayed in high relief.[8]

Laura Wexler's examination of the photos by American photojournalist Francis Benjamin Johnston of US imperial adventures at the turn of the century suggests how the artifice of photography seemingly presented the "real" while inflecting imperial mission with a sense of benevolent supremacy, or what she calls "tender violence." Similarly, the US photographic archive of the building of the canal in Panama projected such imperial visions. Ernest Hallen, the US government's official photographer of the canal's construction work, who provided an extensive, systematic record of the undertaking, favored techniques that emphasized grand panoramic and panoptic perspectives.[9]

The meanings of photographs, however, were never easily contained. In examining the early US colonial period in the Philippines, Vicente Rafael has found that elites in colonies often adapted the technology of photography to project their own self-confident emergence as leaders of protonations. Rafael writes that "images emerge at times from the archives that contain certain intractable elements, peculiar details, or distinct sensibilities that do not easily fit into the visual encyclopedia of colonial rule." An examination of imperial photographic archives of Samoa in the same period likewise finds uncertain views that seem inconsistent with a stereotypically imperial gaze. Esther Gabara shows how, in the hands of Mexican and Brazilian modernists of the 1930s, photographic conventions became distorted and "errant."[10]

Kahn died during the Nazi occupation of France. By this time national states had firmly embraced photography and its successor, motion picture film, in order to highlight difference and stoke ferocity and war. The propaganda machine honed by the Nazis revolved around the use of images and rested on the understanding that photography, while thoroughly constructed, could be easily taken for "reality" and could motivate and manipulate. Nazi filmmakers excelled at crafting images that could tap existing prejudices to augment hatreds, at shaping pictures of enemies that the state could then justifiably destroy.[11] And most other nations involved in World War II joined in the project of merging images into war making. What John Dower has aptly called a "war without mercy" in the Pacific fed upon a war of images. Photographers and filmmakers often borrowed and readapted techniques from each other along transnational networks and then used them for national ends.

The comparatively inexpensive technology of photography, let loose in a transnational world, both defied putative borders and also hardened nationalistic and imperialistic divisions. Although its images and symbolic languages produced currents that connected the globe, the meanings and effects that circulated in those currents, and remain embedded in photographic archives, proved variable and multivocal. Photography exemplifies the differentiated commonalities of this period.

Labor and Anticolonial Transnationalism

As telegraphy, postal services, mass publication, and photography accelerated global transmissions, activists espousing diverse causes could find new audiences. Transnational social networks proliferated. Sometimes entangled within the processes of state building and imperial consolidation and sometimes not, the outreach of transnational movements helped define many of the most significant global trends of the late nineteenth and early twentieth centuries.

Efforts to abolish slavery forged one of the most prominent of such networks. British abolitionists had convened a World Convention in London in 1840. From midcentury on, abolitionists from the Americas, the Caribbean, Europe, and elsewhere increasingly linked up to create a transnational antislavery movement.

Action on the level of national states remained all-important, and it would be misleading to suggest that national and imperial goals stood apart from the transnational antislavery cause. The many antislavery conventions and decrees during the latter half of the nineteenth century, after all, emerged from the specificity of national and local circumstances, such as grassroots resistance by slaves, the Civil War in the United States, variable economic changes favorable to free labor, and the triumph of liberal revolutions in particular countries. Antislavery objectives also became entangled in imperial justifications. By helping to structure a benign "civilizing" mission for colonial powers, antislavery campaigns could sometimes enhance discourses of national destiny and advance the universalistic rhetoric that dressed up assertions of imperial virtue. In the Berlin Declaration of 1885 and the Brussels Act of 1890, for example, colonial powers pledged to suppress slave trading and work toward abolition even as they were carving up parts of the world.

Transnational organizing, however, proved critical to stigmatizing slaveholding and to the longer legacies that antislavery campaigns produced. Moreover, as antislavery networks collaborated across the globe to collect and share data, other kinds of labor abuses came within their purview. Practices of contract labor, debt peonage, and trafficking in women and children, for example, often seemed analogous to, or at least on a continuum with, chattel slavery. The well-organized antislavery campaigns of the nineteenth century thus fostered collaboration among reformers on a range of issues and boosted the authority of a twentieth-century movement concerned with human rights more generally.[12]

As industrialization accelerated, attempts to improve working conditions for the burgeoning urban industrial labor forces also spawned an array of transnational efforts designed to combat what some called "wage slavery." Seeking transnational solutions to economic exploitation, labor advocates embraced the idea that workers had common interests that might supersede national loyalties. Many viewed the national state itself as a creature of the ownership class. In this vision, the goals of international peace and justice could not arise from cooperative bodies of national states until worker-led social democratic forms of governance had triumphed in every locality. Worker-based movements that tried to build transnational networks based upon class rather than nation, however, had goals that competed as much as they coalesced.

Jean Jaurès, leader of the French Socialist Party, emerged as one of the most influential leaders of the social democratic movement, which spread principally in Europe and the Western Hemisphere. In 1889 Jaurès helped found the Second International, a body that famously declared May 1 as International Labor Day. Associated with the Paris Exposition of that year, the gathering brought working-class organizations together around a vision that transcended states. Another meeting, coinciding with the 1900 Paris Exposition, brought two thousand delegates from sixteen countries and created an International Socialist Bureau (headquartered in Brussels) to serve as an informational clearinghouse for geographically scattered workers' organizations.

Between 1900 and 1914 Jaurès became one of the most influential advocates of working-class solidarity in the face of industrialization and rising nationalism. An electrifying speaker, at the 1912 meeting he proclaimed, "We are all opposed to those ready to deliver the multitudes to the bronze clutches of the demon of war. It is up to us, workers and socialists of every country, to make war impossible." His "Second International" met regularly until World War I, and Jaurès worked against the military draft and on behalf of general strikes in France and Germany that he hoped would force governments to negotiate with each other.[13]

Jaurès was assassinated by a nationalist in 1914 just as the Great War was beginning, but his messages continued to resonate internationally in the interwar era. Peace (between owners and workers and between nations), he had argued, was unachievable under capitalism. A socialism forged by cooperating trade unions and workers' cooperatives, by contrast, could create both a supportive political process in individual countries and a grand moral transformation. Although his Second International disbanded during the Great War, supporters reconstituted it in 1923 as the Labor and Socialist International. The Second International and its successor sought evolution, country by country, toward a transnational democratic socialist state that would express working-class interests and gradually seize ownership of production from private hands.

Attempts to build international labor solidarity, however, had competing advocates and agendas. The struggling International Labour Organization of the League of Nations, as already mentioned, tried to monitor labor reforms and empower labor unions within the existing order of national states. Socialist networks led by women such as the German Clara Zetkin spread globally from the 1890s on and generally concentrated on promoting sex-based legislation that would provide special workplace protections for women. International Women's Day, which began to be observed on March 8, 1913, emerged from efforts of socialists who wanted to honor and give greater visibility to the contributions of working women.

Anarchism and syndicalist doctrines also circulated globally. A number of factors may help explain the rapid spread of anarcho-syndicalist ideas at the turn of the century: the growth of inexpensive publication; the mass migration of Jews and Italians, two groups in which anarcho-syndicalist doctrines had become strong; the cross-border role of sailors, who spread the doctrines to port cities on many continents; and the influence of major syndicalist models, especially the CNT in Spain, the CGT in France, and the IWW in the United States. Some historians also suggest that the proliferation of dangerous occupations such as mining and sailing encouraged "virile syndicalism"—an aggressively anticapitalist masculinity that emphasized male bonding around acts of physical strength and violent resistance to authority.[14] Anarcho-syndicalism before World War I took on a local intensity especially in immigrant, urban areas of the United States and Latin America, and it also spread to East Asia through student and other exchanges. Campaigns against radicalism in many countries after World War I significantly weakened anarchism as a transnational movement, although the CNT in Spain grew stronger by successfully deploying general strikes to enlist support from much of the Spanish working class in the interwar period.

The Bolshevik Revolution in Russia in 1917 advanced yet another radical transnationalist vision. In 1919, in the midst of civil war in Russia, the Bolsheviks called for a "Third International" to be held in Moscow. Guided principally by Vladimir Lenin, the group formed the Comintern, a central governing body that would command a worldwide communist revolution. The Comintern's creation formalized the split, grown wider during the war, between pro-Soviet communist parties and those social democratic parties that had supported their nations' war efforts. A 1920 Congress of Peoples of the East, held at Baku, the capital of Soviet Azerbaijan, drew about two thousand delegates from workers' parties and anticolonial groups based in Turkey, Persia, Egypt, India, Afghanistan, Arabia, Syria, Palestine, Armenia, Georgia, Turkestan, India, China, Japan, Korea, and elsewhere. These delegates linked up to learn about the support for colonial self-determination sponsored by communist parties.[15] Africa's first two communist parties were formed in South Africa and Egypt in the early 1920s. By the early 1920s communist parties existed in most countries and continents in the world.

As Joseph Stalin began to emphasize "socialism in one state" in the mid-1920s, the Soviet Union's internationalist emphasis faded. Leon Trotsky had advocated building a transnational revolutionary movement, but his expulsion from the Soviet Union in 1928 and subsequent assassination in Mexico dramatized Stalin's nationalist turn. By 1934 Stalin accepted that communist parties would have to form "popular fronts" with social democratic parties in order to combat the rise of fascism, and the Comintern was disbanded in 1943. Meanwhile, Trotsky's followers had created a Fourth International in 1938, but their transnational movement kept splintering.[16]

Although there were persistent tensions between broader transnational connections and narrower national or ethnolinguistic loyalties, most communist or socialist labor-based movements tried to find ways to accommodate both. Lenin, for example, tried to solve the national question by establishing a purportedly federated Union of Soviet Socialist Republics (USSR). Many Marxists within the Austro-Hungarian Empire likewise imagined transforming the Habsburg monarchy into some kind of federation. Labor transnationalists, generally, spoke in universalistic terms but constructed their networks with a sensitivity to particular national loyalties.

In colonial territories the revolutionary ideology of communism, its appeal enhanced by resentments over the false promises of Wilsonian self-determination, created a transnational context that facilitated the growth of networks of anti-imperial resistance. Especially after the Great War, diverse homegrown movements drew strength from their leaders' global networks to challenge Western hegemonies. The Oriental Branch of the Workers' Communist Party, for example, operated both locally and across Asia. Trinidadian George Padmore's publication *The Negro Worker* (1928–1937) joined the advocacy of communism to anti-colonialism, and merchant seamen distributed its messages widely in Africa and elsewhere in the black diaspora.

The careers of three leaders within India's nationalist movement exemplify how anti-imperial transnational networks fostered campaigns for national self-determination. Narendra Nath Bhattacharya, known as M. N. Roy, was a transnational anti-imperial activist, a Bengali Indian revolutionary, and a political theorist. Roy had developed some of his revolutionary philosophy while in New York City, where he met his future American wife, Evelyn Trent. After traveling to the neutral nation of Mexico during World War I, Roy started what would become the Mexican Communist Party. Once the war ended, he accelerated his transnational activities, founding the Communist Party of India, serving with the Comintern for several years, and organizing to promote a revolutionary movement in China. With Trotsky's expulsion, Roy fell out of favor in Stalin's Moscow and left the Comintern and the Soviet Union. Once back in India during the 1930s, his continued commitment to transnational revolution landed him in prison, where, disillusioned by both Western democracy and communism, he began to work out his own manifesto for a future characterized by India's independence and a broad vision he called "New Humanism." His humanism, advanced as a universally applicable philosophy, emphasized scientific and critical approaches to knowledge mixed with an ethical grounding. Despite their substantial differences, Roy and Jawaharlal Nehru worked together to try to maneuver India toward independence.

Nehru had also been closely involved in transnational anti-imperial movements. In 1927 as a delegate from the Indian National Congress, he helped organize in Brussels an International Congress against Colonialism and Imperialism. Closely tied to Soviet goals, the Congress sought to connect labor movements with anticolonial leaders. Before World War II, Nehru established connections with liberation advocates in Egypt, Syria, Palestine, Iraq, and North Africa, many of whom already had established friendships with Mohandas K. Gandhi. It was Nehru who, in 1947, raised the flag of an independent India, espousing secularism and liberal, parliamentary democracy.

Gandhi's technique of nonviolent resistance to colonial rule had also gained him a transnational following. While in South Africa before World War I, he had joined with women in the large population of Indian laborers to successfully demand that the government recognize Hindu, Muslim, and Parsi marriages, which had been declared invalid.[17] Back in India, his famous Salt March campaigns of 1930–1931 brought wide attention to nonviolent resistance, and the currents from Gandhi's philosophy penetrated not only other anticolonial projects in Asia and Africa but also the often intertwined networks of Western peace activists. The War Resisters' International (WRI) and the Christian International Fellowship of Reconciliation (FOR) were only two of the many transnational organizations that helped popularize Gandhi's views among European and North American antidraft and pacifist groups before and after World War II.[18]

Gandhi and Nehru advocated the concept of *Vasudhaiva Kutumbakam,* or the world as one family. They envisioned India as a hub that could bind East Asia, South Asia, the Arab Middle East, and North Africa. The sufferings under colonialism would presumably forge bonds of sympathy that would radiate out to eventually include the world as a whole, nurturing a transnational consciousness as well as national self-determination.

Roy, Nehru, and Gandhi illustrate how India's nationalism and eventual independence became nourished within transnational networks that sought global solidarity among anticolonial movements. As Sugata Bose has written, "anticolonialism as an ideology was both

Mahatma Gandhi and Sarojini Naidu on the nonviolent "Salt March" of 1930. Gandhi and Naidu, along with eighty thousand other Indians, were arrested after this campaign, which protested the British tax on salt and British rule of India. Naidu was the first Indian woman to serve as president of the Indian National Congress. (The Illustrated London News Picture Library, London, UK/ The Bridgeman Art Library)

tethered by the idea of homeland while strengthened by extraterritorial affiliations."[19] Like other articulations of early twentieth-century universalist ideologies—whether generated from Britain, France, Germany, the United States, or the Soviet Union—Indian leaders saw little contradiction between their own embrace of nationalism and the transnational webs they hoped to anchor and orchestrate. They proposed their own nationalist struggle as the opening wedge toward a larger global order that they claimed would emphasize justice and peace over inequality and war.

Contacts among labor and anticolonial movements circulated in many directions. Irish revolutionaries built connections to labor movements in the United States; Sikh migrants in Canada kept in touch with anticolonial activists in India; nationalists from Southeast Asia established contacts with sympathizers from Africa and South Asia; Sen Katayama organized for anticolonial and communist causes in both Japan and the United States; the Paris-based Étoile Nord-Africaine connected Algerians and French supporters in agitating for independence of French North Africa; philosophical tracts and bomb-making manuals published in Paris or New York surfaced within resistance movements throughout the world. Just as national states organized international bodies and agreements, groups advocating workers' revolutions or those aspiring to throw off colonial rule and establish their own states (or non-states, in the case of anarchist-influenced movements) also forged transnational networks.[20]

Diasporic Attachments

The waves of migration (both coerced and voluntary) that characterized this period mixed populations throughout the world and nurtured the emergence of transnational networks that followed the paths of the various diasporas. Though characterized by no single pattern and having no consistent relationship to national identities, diasporic attachments based on perceived ethnocultural ties provided important carriers of globalizing currents.

Slavery had produced an African diaspora throughout the Atlantic and some of the Pacific world. As most countries formally abolished slavery over the last two-thirds of the nineteenth century, indentured or contract laborers from the Indian subcontinent, China, and elsewhere augmented ex-slaves as cheap labor used especially in agriculture. The global diffusion of laborers from Africa and Asia, along with the histories of colonialism in most labor-exporting areas, created a milieu in which diasporic attachments often intertwined with labor solidarity and anticolonialism.

"Pan-Africanism" emerged as one of the most significant currents of diasporic transnationalism. The African-American intellectual W. E. B. Du Bois powerfully articulated how Africans, even though geographically dispersed, could become part of an emergent black nationalism. In 1900 Du Bois addressed a Pan-African Congress to call for the integrity and independence of African states. This congress, convened in London by Trinidad-born barrister Henry Sylvester-Williams, would be the first in a series of congresses that brought together delegates from Europe, the West Indies, the United States, and Africa to oppose colonialism and racism. Yet while building transnational solidarity within the African diaspora, Du Bois also advocated equality for people of African descent within the individual nations in which they resided. He advanced the idea that African-Americans had to live within a "double consciousness," an awareness of the self as distinct from the persona that dominant groups might construct. "The problem of the twentieth century," Du Bois declared in his famous 1900 speech to the congress, "is the problem of the color line." The First Universal Races Congress met in 1911 in London to build support for a global struggle against racism.[21]

The end of World War I brought new Pan-African initiatives. A Pan-African Congress of 1919 convened in Paris to coincide with the

Versailles Peace Conference. Its delegates invoked Wilsonian self-determination and issued a proposal to turn Germany's former colonies in Africa into a new state, but the officials at Versailles largely ignored the effort. A fifth Pan-African Congress, held in New York in 1927, was primarily financed by Addie W. Hunton and the Women's International League for Peace and Freedom (WILPF), a sponsorship that underscored the overlapping goals of the Pan-African Congress and the WILPF, a transnational women's organization. Throughout the 1920s Du Bois, Hunton, and others consistently championed self-determination in Africa as well as equality for African-descended citizens in their own countries. Although few delegates from Africa attended international conferences during the 1920s because colonial administrations restricted their travel, groups throughout Africa formed to fight white minority rule and used new networks of communication to link their efforts to sympathizers elsewhere in the world. Padmore's *The Negro Worker,* his work as head of the Comintern's International Trade Union Committee of Negro Workers (before he renounced the Communist Party over its policies toward colonialism), and his labor organizing throughout Africa and the Caribbean during the Great Depression of the 1930s facilitated the spread of Pan-Africanism.[22]

Marcus Garvey espoused Pan-Africanism of a different kind. Born in Jamaica, where he founded the Universal Negro Improvement Association (UNIA) in 1914, Garvey brought a charismatic message of racial pride to the United States and built a huge following after World War I. From 1919 to 1922, Garvey's Black Star shipping line visited ports throughout the world and attracted enthusiastic supporters. By using black seamen as agents, Garvey established a global informational network that spawned branches of the UNIA in Africa, Australia, and the West Indies and throughout the Americas. At its height the UNIA had perhaps a thousand chapters in forty-three countries and territories. Like Du Bois and other Pan-Africanists, Garvey called for self-determination of African nations, but he rejected the assimilationist message of Du Bois's "double consciousness." Embracing race essentialism and racial pride, Garvey preached that America was a white country and that black people needed to return to Africa and establish nations based within their own race. He tried to promote a settlement in Liberia but was jailed on mail fraud charges in 1923. In 1927 he was deported back to Jamaica, as his movement faded. The UNIA's global influence fell as quickly as it had risen, but Garvey's uncompromising message of black nationalism and pride continued to influence the Pan-African movement on several continents.[23]

The writings of Léopold Senghor, who would become the first president of Senegal, and Martinican poet Aimé Césaire helped forge a related transcontinental intellectual movement called *négritude*. Meeting in Paris during the 1930s and linked to flourishing black arts and cultural movements in Haiti and in Harlem, black intellectuals from Africa and the Caribbean sought to build a common identity that rejected assimilation, turned *nègre* into a positive word, and asserted opposition to French racism. These intellectuals did not seek political independence from France so much as creation of a more inclusive, transnational culture based on equal respect. Just as French colonialism contained both a universalizing discourse of Greater France and a particularizing discourse related to race, so *négritude*'s critique of French colonial modernity also developed a "two-fronted response." One front embraced French citizenship in the French empire and the other articulated a cultural nationalism in which mythic black-African culture and soul stood opposed to the presumed dehumanization of Western modernity.[24]

In his examination of what he called the "Black Atlantic," Paul Gilroy uses ships as a central metaphor. The displacement of Africans to other continents brought an accompanying need to hang on to memories of distant places and to see the Atlantic Ocean as a connecting highway rather than as a barrier. The circulation of people, ideas, and arts within this Black Atlantic, through people such as Du Bois, Padmore, Garvey, and Césaire, Gilroy argues, formed a sense of nationalism even under conditions of the fragmented consciousness produced by geographical and cultural displacement. People in the African diaspora, he suggests, lived with instability and juxtaposition of identity long before the advent of the term *postmodernity* in the late twentieth century.[25]

Pan-Africanism as a transnational nationalism, of course, flourished not just on the ocean currents but on the new currents of the electrical age. Du Bois's writings and his newspaper, *The Crisis,* circulated widely; Padmore's *The Negro Worker* and Garvey's newspaper *The Negro World* constituted parts of their global networks. Other giant figures in the Pan-African movement also circulated their ideas and platforms within the new networks of travel and communication: During the 1930s some of the major activists in the Pan-African movement— C. L. R. James, Claude McKay, and Paul Robeson, all of whom embraced socialism and its anticolonial agenda—were prolific writers and artists.[26] Moreover, many Africans, some of whom would later lead postcolonial governments, participated in this transnational circulation. Kwame Nkrumah attended school in the United States, spent time in London, and became the first president of Ghana. Julius Nyerere studied in Scotland before he headed the newly independent nation of Tanzania and helped found the Organization of African Unity (OAU).

Diasporic allegiances that became influential in the late nineteenth and early twentieth centuries emerged in diverse formulations, each with distinct regional characteristics depending on the density of the diaspora and the power of the grouping with which it aligned. The Gadr movement, for example, took shape in San Francisco among Sikhs who sought to mobilize migrant groups in support of an anti-imperial, anti-British uprising in India. Irish nationalists mobilized their far-flung networks with a similar goal. Chinese *tongs* spread their influence throughout immigrant communities on several continents.

Pan-ethnic or pan-national movements, however, could prove ambiguous and even deceptive. Programs to promote "Pan-Americanism" and "Pan-Asianism," for example, claimed to construct broad regional identities, but they can also be seen as tools of expansionist national states. The respective attempts by the United States (after the 1880s) and by Japan (especially in the 1930s) to create geographically proximate spheres of influence provide examples of highly nationalistic programs dressed in the garb of regional imaginaries. Both the Pan American Union and the creation of Manchukuo expressed rich regional cultural circulations of ideas about moving toward modernity but came manifested politically as client state relations or as highly asymmetrical regional associations.[27] Populations of Slavs, Ottoman Turks, Germans, and Arabs, to cite more examples, also asserted transborder identities. These movements, too, often arose from regional cultural circulations but became creatures of expansionist states and empires seeking to justify boundary claims, border transgressions, or attempts to drive away outsider populations. Regionally based transnational appeals, of course, waxed stronger when confronted by the claims of oppositional networks (for example, in liminal areas in the Balkans and the Caucasus) and when they served as useful weapons within the geopolitical rivalries of national states.

The Jewish diaspora constituted another variant of transnational attachments. In 1900, 82 percent of Jews lived in Europe, the majority in Eastern Europe; by 1939 the number had shrunk to 57 percent, with the United States and, to a lesser extent, Palestine as newly important centers of Jewish life. Jews from this increasingly globalized diaspora, itself split into Ashkenazi and Sephardic branches, played important roles in many of the intellectual currents and social movements discussed in this book—internationalism, anarchism, socialism, pacifism, as well as in a variety of economic, artistic, and epistemic networks. Jewish transnationalism, often fueled in opposition to a global discourse of anti-Semitism, could combine feelings of loyalty to an ethnic identity, national attachments to particular countries, and a universalism that aspired to build tolerance for difference. Although linkages forged among often far-flung Jewish communities proved important to transnational networks of all kinds, there are few common threads among them. Jewish transnational linkages were both secular and religious; they strengthened both capital and labor; they both buttressed and undermined divisions marked by nationality, empire, gender, and racial identity.

The modern nationalist movement called Zionism, however, was one transnational impetus that may be discussed in very loose analogy with Pan-Africanism, as it sought to imagine and advance a national identity within a diasporic community that held no singular or specific territory except in various constructions of memory. A movement of highly varied roots and diverse histories that began in the late nineteenth century, Zionist groups constituted an "international nationalism" that advocated the establishment of a Jewish national home in Palestine. They gradually grew stronger in response to pogroms in Russia; to unfulfilled promises for a homeland that were made in the Balfour Declaration of 1917 and in the League of Nations' creation of a Palestinian mandate; to rising anti-Semitism in Europe during the interwar era; and finally to the Nazis' mass killing of Jews in the Holocaust. As with other diasporic groups, the longing for a grounded homeland and the transnational organizing in pursuit of that goal became bonding elements.[28]

Religious Transnationalism

Major world religions had all built strong transnational affiliations in the age that preceded the consolidation of national states. In the nineteenth century, however, state-building projects could rival and sometimes even tried to suppress such religious attachments. Moreover, the growing influence of scientific method, evolutionary thought, secularism, and Marxism seemed to challenge religious ways of knowing.

In this context of increasingly secular state building and scientific modernity, religious connections nonetheless continued to refresh themselves and even flourish. In fact, under competition from secular trends and from each other, Christianity, Judaism, Islam, Hinduism, Buddhism, Yoruba, and other groups all experienced revival and expansion. New modes of communication and the accelerating global flows of people and ideas facilitated the new energy. C. A. Bayly has argued that this period saw the consolidation of religion as a universal category of identification, and that "many modern nationalisms were themselves heavily influenced by emerging religious solidarities."[29] There were, however, always inherent tensions between religious claims to universalism and practices rooted in adaptation to local cultural traditions. The uniformities of religious doctrine came to be rendered in distinctive local ways—as differentiated commonalities.

From one perspective, Christianity could seem on the decline in our period. In the late nineteenth century Friedrich Nietzsche, son of a Lutheran pastor, articulated an influential disenchantment with Christianity, even as Karl Marx advanced a highly materialist view of the human condition. These and other philosophers challenged the basis of Christian belief from many directions in the generation before the eruption of the Great War. Then in 1914 an Orthodox-inspired killing of the archduke Francis Ferdinand, heir to the Austro-Hungarian throne and a devout Catholic, threw Europe into what became a devastating war that pitted Christian rulers against each other—the German and Austrian emperors against the British king, the Russian tsar, and finally the US president—and prompted extravagant rhetoric on every side about doing battle in the name of a Christian Lord. Just as the costs of war weakened Europe's states economically, the fighting took its toll on both the territories and the faiths of Christendom. The Russian Revolution of 1917 toppled the established Russian Orthodox Church. Persecuted Christian communities, especially of Armenians and others on the eastern frontier of the new Turkish republic, were scattered and killed as the old Ottoman Empire fell apart. Britain's hold on colonies became more precarious, and the Irish crisis pitted Catholics against Protestants. The dispirited generation that survived the devastations of the First World War emerged with all kinds of faiths shaken. After surveying the memorials to the dead from this struggle, Diarmaid MacCulloch writes, "The greatest casualty commemorated in this multitude of crosses and symbols of war is the union between Christianity and secular power: Christendom itself."[30]

Yet countervailing signs of Christianity's expansion also emerged, illustrating the contradictions of the age. From the middle of the nineteenth century appeared new visionaries, new excitements over End Times, a vibrant new Pentecostal movement in the United States, and— most importantly—an upsurge of Christian missionary fervor. Financed from private donations, Protestant missionary societies led efforts to "civilize" people around the world by saving their souls, spreading literacy (to facilitate Bible reading), and instructing people in the virtues of monogamous marriage and disciplined labor. Christianity reached into every continent.

The Salvation Army, for example, was founded in 1878 in England and grew into a worldwide network of schools, hospitals, and other institutions. Initially looked upon with suspicion by state authorities, it was later seen as a helpful tool in controlling "dangerous" populations. The Salvation Army constructed both Britain's urban poor and the "heathens" and "savages" in Britain's empire as populations in need of the social salvation it offered. Becoming an imperial force that discursively linked together both domestic and colonial social threats and remedies, the Army became active throughout the globe. It was called upon, for example, to reeducate ex-convicts in places as far-flung as Japan, Australia, South Africa, French Guiana, and elsewhere.[31]

Social-gospel Protestantism furthered the global evangelical movement. The American Student Volunteer Movement for Foreign Missions (SVM), founded in 1886, famously promised "the evangelization of the world in this generation." The SVM movement, allied with the Young Men's Christian Association (YMCA), quickly spread to Great Britain and to other countries of Western Europe and developed chapters in Syria, Egypt, China, India, and across the globe.[32]

The late nineteenth-century famines, especially in India, China, and other mission fields, assisted evangelization, as the sensational coverage of these tragedies spurred missionary activity, boosted circulation for the new missionary magazines, and prompted heartrending appeals for donations to support Christian relief efforts everywhere. In the United States, the *Christian Herald* carried out the most dramatic campaign, using the relatively new medium of photography to show graphic images of people in various stages of starvation.[33] Such images, while meant for philanthropic purposes, also worked to underscore the superiority of Christian civilizations and to suggest the need for imperial interventions. Moreover, missionaries and other humanitarian activists often invoked ideals of a shared humanity in their appeals while remaining blind to the ways in which Western imperial policies had contributed to the very calamities that altered social and ecological patterns and thus disrupted food production and availability.

By the time of the World Missionary Conference in 1910, Protestant Christianity had become a rapidly growing global network incorporating many church leaders in non-Western areas. As the faith expanded, its meanings and practices became ever more diverse. The African prophet William Wadé Harris, for example, defied colonial boundaries in 1913 to lead a transborder revival movement in West Africa that gathered perhaps one hundred thousand conversions. Harris, educated in a mission school in southeastern Liberia, spread an indigenous Christianity into areas not previously tilled by European missionaries. He urged his converts to abandon their nature spirits, which had failed to protect them from colonial conquest, and to embrace the Christian God, who could restore their sovereignty and bring access to needed knowledge and technology. Preaching accommodation with most Westerns ways but also upholding the custom of polygamy, Harris was responsible for the largest conversion to Christianity on the African continent. When Western missionaries later arrived in areas of West Africa, they were often astonished to find Harrist churches flourishing. Indeed, especially from the 1920s on, indigenous rulers and prophets throughout Africa carried out vigorous campaigns to found their own Christian churches independent of European interference.[34]

The influenza epidemic of 1918–1919 promoted the transnational growth of Christian divine-healing churches. The teachings of Faith Tabernacle Congregation, which formed in 1918 in Philadelphia, found their way to Ghana, an area also populated by many indigenous healing cults. Through pamphlets and correspondence, Faith Tabernacle's leaders promised to heal people of influenza at a time when medical authorities had neither the knowledge nor the supplies to adequately treat hard-hit populations. In Ghana, colonial authorities banned native healing cults as "witchcraft" but allowed Christian healers. As word of successful cures circulated, Faith Tabernacle's evangelism spread to include Britain's Apostolic Church and stretched into Côte d'Ivoire and Togo to become forerunners of the large Pentecostal movement that would continue to spread even after Faith Tabernacle itself declined in the mid-1920s.[35] Pentecostalism, which had its modern roots in Britain and the United States in the late nineteenth century and emphasized healing, speaking in tongues, and a direct relationship with God, became one of the most dynamic global movements in Christianity in the twentieth century.

William Wadé Harris (center) with singers and fellow missionaries after a mission in the coastal town of Assinie in the French colony of Côte d'Ivoire, 1914. Prophet Harris led a mass movement that spread Christianity throughout West Africa in the early twentieth century. (Archives of Société des Missions Africains, Rome)

Catholics also stepped up their involvement in social issues by accelerating a global missionary effort. Pope Leo XIII's encyclical *Rerum Novarum* (1893) placed Catholicism behind attempts to ameliorate industrialization's excesses. It championed fair wages and legal protections for workers. And in the 1920s, Pope Pius XI adopted worldwide outreach as a priority. He founded new mission centers around the globe, endorsed vigorous national churches under indigenous leadership, and consecrated six Chinese bishops and a bishop in Japan and in Vietnam—the first non-Western bishops since the eighteenth century. In addition, Catholic missionaries constituted one of the largest groups of French men and women working abroad, although they often had conflicted relationships with imperial administrators of the determinedly secular Third Republic. French imperial policy in Indochina, Polynesia, and Madagascar, for example, emerged in the crucible of discordant religious and secular goals, and indigenous communities were sometimes able to work the dissension to their own advantage.[36]

The transnational religious networks in this period all intertwined with their members' other affiliations—national, imperial, racial, regional. For example, in many Christian mission fields, missionaries tended to keep to their own, with ethnic and national affiliations trumping ideals of Christian unity. Social separation from racially different "native" converts was pro forma almost everywhere, and missionaries also broke down into national groups. British missionaries in Asia and Africa often found American Christians too zealous, too egalitarian, and too uncultured—the same attitudes that marked an anti-American discourse outside of the mission field as well.[37]

As Christian missions tried to "uplift" indigenous people, they developed the kinds of ambiguous relationships to colonial states that so often marked "contact zones." The Salvation Army and other mission efforts based in Britain became an important arm of policy at home and abroad. The American YMCA similarly functioned during World War I as an arm of state military power. It ran the programs for the troops sent to France and conducted anti-Bolshevik espionage in the new Soviet Union. Missionaries abetted colonialism by schooling their converts in their own social conventions related to monogamous marriage, hygienic rituals, work habits, and gender roles. Often working in volatile and insecure areas, they frequently favored forceful colonial rule as a way to facilitate order, progress, and conversion.[38]

The instabilities and injustices of colonial rule, however, could also place religious conversion at odds with the economic and political structures of empire. In China, the US YMCA's goals to improve economic conditions led some missionaries to criticize colonial powers and the foreign merchants who seemed to exploit the very people they had pledged to serve. Moreover, missionaries developed expertise in native languages, and some cultivated a sympathy based in cultural understanding. As missions involved themselves in education, health, and the preservation of languages, the basis for a locally generated articulation of ethnic identities flourished—and sometimes bolstered anticolonial movements. If missionaries could not avoid being a part, sometimes even an appendage, of an imperial presence, some nevertheless sought to ameliorate, critique, and at times actively resist it.

Moreover, the indigenous Christians who assumed positions of local leadership brought even more complexity to the fraught intersections between transnational religion and colonialism. The ambiguous historical memory surrounding Anglican missionary Bernard Mizeki provides an example. Mizeki was born in present-day Mozambique, converted to Anglicanism in Cape Town, and was dispatched to Rhodesia as a "native catechist" in the 1890s. After being stabbed by opponents in 1896, his body reportedly miraculously vanished into air. The site of the Mizeki miracle in present-day Zimbabwe came to symbolize both a despised colonial collaboration and also a growing cultural nationalism fed by annual pilgrimages with special meaning for trans-African Anglicanism.[39] Missionaries, in short, could both embody and also mediate the global inequalities of the imperial age.

Korea exemplified another twist on the intersection of anticolonialism and Christianity. After Japan seized their country in 1910, Korean Christians fused their faith with Korean national identity and developed it into a symbol of nationalist resistance against the Japanese occupation. This association helped set the stage for the later robust growth of Christianity in Korea.

As Christian revivalism spread missionaries around the world, assisted by Western economic expansion, Islam experienced a parallel surge designed to push back and halt Christianity's spread. The growth of European spheres encroaching into India, Southeast Asia, and Africa spurred Pan-Islamic networks, and the new forms of publication and communication reinforced bonds of attachment on all sides.

Indeed, as Islam expanded in West Africa and, like other religions, adapted to local variations, some groups found special success by embracing the new technologies that colonialism helped introduce. Sheikh Ibrahim Niass, for example, used radio to spread his Tijani Sufi revivalism in the areas of Gambia and Senegal, and his network expanded to become one of the most important religious forces in West Africa. Roads that were improved to enhance imperial commerce also extended the reach of Muslim scholars. A Tijani dissident, Yacouba Sylla, inspired the rise of the Yacoubist movement, which became particularly powerful in Côte d'Ivoire.[40]

Transnational networks may have proved an especially congenial structure for the spread of Islam, or at least that has been an influential argument advanced since the 1970s in the scholarly work of Ira M. Lapidus. Lapidus and the others who have endorsed this view argue that the concept of a network provides a powerful "root metaphor" in a civilization that has struggled to sustain its identity under the onslaught of colonial political administrations. In this view, transnational interactions among Muslims became part of a network of practices animated by powerful symbols—the Quran and the mosque. These Islamic symbols became the focus for personal loyalty, ritual, and sacrifice in a sprawling territory controlled by mostly alien political jurisdictions.[41]

Pilgrimages helped reinforce such transnational ties of practice, and they created a common loyalty to specific and highly symbolic places. Pilgrimages, of course, may be found in all transnational religious affiliations, as they help bring diverse localized practices and beliefs into a more unified sense of community and orthodoxy. But the Hajj (pilgrimage to Mecca) proved especially important for the extensive Islamic networks that reached from western Africa, across the Middle East and South Asia, to Indonesia.

The Hajj had provided, writes Sugata Bose, a "key integrative element in the economy, religion, and culture of the Indian Ocean in the precolonial era," but the introduction of steamships and railways further consolidated its importance to the Islamic world.[42] The opening of the Suez Canal in 1869 and the offering, by British and Dutch steamships, of regular Hajj trips helped forge Pan-Islamic links among Cairo, Mecca, and Indonesia, which was emerging as the most populous Islamic country. Ottoman Sultan Abdülhamid II positioned himself as a defender of Islam against Christian encroachment and completed the strategically important Istanbul-to-Baghdad railway and the Istanbul-to-Medina railway, which also made the Hajj somewhat easier. The sultan also dispatched emissaries to many distant lands to spread Islam.

The rise of Egypt as a major crossroads within the Ottoman Empire, as a result of the Suez Canal, posed challenges for the sultan and for Pan-Islamic movements generally. The opening of the canal accelerated the movement of trade, people, and culture and drew many parts of the world together. It also facilitated the rising hegemony of European states in the Middle East and in Africa, which colonial powers began to partition in the 1880s.

The mixture of Islamic and Christian influences under colonialism brought clashes but also borrowing and accommodation. Even as European encroachment and technologies changed caravanning patterns in northwest Africa, for example, Islamic law continued to structure and facilitate networks of trade and cultural exchange in that region.[43] With the demise of the Ottoman Empire after World War I, the British imperial authorities and the Saudi state gained greater territorial influence over Mecca and Medina, Islam's second holiest city. Still, Muslim networks proved adept at crossing seas and forging religious connections that state boundaries could hardly contain or control. Stronger colonial rule from the West often enhanced the oppositional appeal of Islamic practices.

Islam was split along lines of doctrinal disputes, and different movements within Islam all had transnational reach. The largely Sunnibased Salafi movement, for example, called for a return to traditional Islam that would accommodate the kind of technological and scientific modernizations taking place in Europe. From the mid-nineteenth century into the twentieth, writings by the main figures of the Salafiyya circulated especially among intellectual elites and influenced anticolonial and nationalist movements, particularly among Arab Muslims. Such Pan-Islamic appeals, closely linked to calls for Muslim societies to modernize in order to free themselves from European colonial rule, provided a basis for transnational connections as well as for militant anti-Western nationalism. At the same time, often propelled by rivalry with each other, Shi'i elites and the Naqshbandi Sufi orders also, in their own ways, promoted Islamic revitalization across and within national boundaries. All of these revitalization quests bore the imprint of both universalism and sectarianism.

Although the symbolism of the Hajj played a major integrative and symbolic role in Pan-Islamism, the numbers of actual participants remained comparatively small in this period. Before World War II, overseas pilgrims rarely surpassed 100,000. The peak year, 1927, registered around 132,000, but the global economic depression brought sharp declines thereafter. Pilgrimages were made easier by new transportation, but European imperial regimes generally regarded them with suspicion. Worried that pilgrimages might spread politically subversive ideas along with infectious diseases, colonial regulations over the Hajj proliferated, and international sanitary regulations closed key ports. Calcutta (Kolkata) was closed as a pilgrim port for thirty years, for example, after an outbreak of plague in 1896. Only in Dutch-ruled Indonesia did a colonial officer, Snouck Hurgronje, advocate facilitating well-run pilgrimages to Mecca. Hurgronje, a noted Dutch Orientalist, believed that a religious accommodation with Islam would facilitate Dutch rule and would reduce, not increase, political radicalism.[44] Moreover, splits within Muslim communities during the Hajj always had the potential to rip away at Pan-Islamic solidarity. The Wahhabi ascendancy in Saudi Arabia sometimes sparked hostility from Shi'i and Sufi pilgrims.[45]

With the rapid spread of Christianity and Islam, reform movements also reshaped Hindu, Buddhist, and Confucian traditions. As in Islam, many reform leaders called for a return to traditions that emphasized elements consistent with adapting to modernity in order to more effectively challenge outside imperial powers. Perhaps partly to counter the appeal of Christianity and Islam, these faiths became more systematized in terms of doctrine, ritual, and organization. They even took on proselytizing attributes, and they also fused with national or protonational visions. The Young Men's Buddhist Association, for example, modeled itself on the YMCA and played a role in China, Burma, and elsewhere by promoting national strengthening against European influences.

Swami Vivekananda well illustrates the intertwined spread of transnational religious impulses and nationalism. A disciple of the nineteenth-century mystic Ramakrishna, Vivekananda traveled India as a "wondering monk" and then proceeded on a world trip, visiting China, Japan, Canada, the United States, England, France, and Italy. Arriving in Chicago for the 1893 World Parliament of Religions, held in conjunction with the Columbian Exposition, Vivekananda managed to get himself accepted as a representative of India and received growing acclaim for his speeches. Presenting Hinduism as an international force that encompassed toleration for all religions, he also proclaimed the spiritual superiority of the East (especially India) over the materialism of the West. While in the West, he had reportedly remarked to a friend that he hoped to return home and "send an electric thrill" through "India's national veins."[46] Indeed, he returned to India in 1897 to be hailed as a prophet of Indian nationalism. His enthusiastic reception in the West, where he sometimes came to symbolize India's worth to the rest of the world, established him as perhaps the most important representative of Indian culture. Swami Vivekananda remained a singular figure both in the transnational spread of Hindu teachings of Vedanta and yoga and also in the creation of a sense of Indian nationalism that informed Gandhi and others.

Theosophy also stretched globally even as it promoted Indian nationalism in the 1920s. Like Vivekananda's teachings, Theosophy probably spread in the West in the context of a particularly Orientalist vision of India. Annie Besant, a British socialist who campaigned for democratic self-rule in India and was elected president of the Indian National Congress in 1917, embraced Theosophy and headed the Theosophical Society. Theosophical views, which embraced a kind of mystical spiritualism, helped popularize ideas of human community and essential religious unities, even though they also accommodated prevailing views of racial hierarchy.[47]

Localized religious traditions could also spread globally within specific diasporas. Wherever the African slave trade brought Africans, for example, religious practices came along, adapted, and even flourished. Specific groups of Africans, especially throughout the New World, tried to preserve and pass on beliefs and rituals. The religious culture of Yoruba, for example, thrived as *Candomblé* in Brazil and Santería in Cuba.[48]

Within major religious affiliations, transnational conversations around proper gender roles seem at least superficially similar in this era. Some Christian and Islamic reformers (women and men), for example, propounded education for women on the maternalist grounds that women's moral education was essential for nurturing future male leaders. Encouraging motherhood and modern housekeeping within the moral framework of a religious tradition dovetailed with the goals of those who advocated nation building, literacy, sanitation programs, and other attributes of modernity. Religious transnationalism, in fact, provided a powerful (though certainly not the only) framework for the women's networks that emerged in the late nineteenth century.

Worlds of Women

As with other transnational movements and affiliations, women's networks varied widely in their goals and cannot be seen as taking shape independently from other movements. Gender-based women's networks were affiliated with groups associated with labor, anticolonialism, socialism, racial solidarity, and religion, and with epistemic, artistic, and professional communities. Clearly, there was no single "women's movement" generated from any single place. Rather, there was a robust current of diverse "women's movements" flowing from multiple locations. With such variation, transnational identifications along lines of gender sometimes undercut and sometimes reinforced other demarcations of difference based on ethnicity, nationality, class, religion, and region.[49]

Many causes rallied relatively elite women who could marshal the resources to travel internationally. The more formalized transnational organizations of women were therefore heavily based in Europe, European settler colonies, and the United States. Most transnational networks, however, emerged simultaneously with local activist groups, each helping give shape to the other. Campaigns for suffrage, for a larger role in civic life, for control of prostitution and alcohol, for birth control, and for special protections for workers were a few of the strands within the larger current of women's connections.

Local and national politics provided one context for the growth of the suffrage movement, but transnational organizing offered another essential ingredient. In the United States and Great Britain, declarations advocating women's civil and political rights (along with access to higher education and to professional service) had become influential—and controversial—by the middle of the nineteenth century. The writings of Mary Wollstonecraft and John Stuart Mill had wide dissemination, first in the English-speaking world and then in translation, as did the Seneca Falls Declaration of 1848. Suffrage leaders in the United States, Britain, and France established in 1888 the International Council of Women, the first lasting transnational women's organization. Socialist groups formed the International Suffrage Alliance in 1902. Before World War I, Finland, New Zealand, Australia, and Norway granted voting rights to women (although aboriginal women were restricted in some Australian states). The important roles that women played during World War I in many countries provided additional impetus to suffrage. Denmark, Sweden, Canada, Soviet Russia, the Baltic states, Germany, Poland, Czechoslovakia, Hungary, the Netherlands, and the United States embraced women's suffrage during or just after the war. In Britain, women were granted a parliamentary vote, although fully equal suffrage did not come to Britain until 1928. Other countries, such as Burma, Turkey, and Ecuador, gave the franchise to women during the 1920s. As agitation for suffrage spread, victories seemed to beget more victories.[50]

Drawing inspiration and tactics from their globalized networks, movements for suffrage and other rights for women broadened their scope in the interwar era, expanding in Western Europe, in the old Russian, Austro-Hungarian, and Ottoman empires, in Egypt, Turkey, India, Japan, and Latin America. The First International Women's Day Celebration Conference, held in Canton in 1924, highlighted women's activism in China. One of the leading Egyptian feminists, Huda Shaarawi, famously returned from a women's conference in Rome in 1923, stood on the railroad step, drew back her veil, and received applause from the crowd of women onlookers. As founder of the Egyptian Feminist Union and its president from 1923 until 1947, she championed greater independence for women as well as national independence for Egypt. US and Cuban feminists pressed the Pan American Union to establish an Inter American Commission of Women (Comisión Interamericana de Mujeres) in 1928. Transnational peace activist Rosika Schwimmer fled postwar Hungary in 1920 for the United

States, where although the Supreme Court barred her from becoming a citizen because of her highly visible involvement with the feminist peace movement, she continued her activism. In 1934 Turkey enfranchised women in national elections, a measure that radiated through Islamic networks.[51] Transnational organizations carried some of this global activism among women, while books and ideas also helped sprout local initiatives that were independent of larger organizational structures. Modest reformist approaches and bold transgressive acts both found encouragement within the formal and informal transnational circuits that women were forging.

For many women who struggled to gain the right to vote, national suffrage campaigns constituted less ends in themselves than means by which other social concerns might be addressed. Women in many countries led reformist causes associated specifically with women's issues. Josephine Butler led efforts to protect prostitutes in England and the British Empire, and Ghenia Avril de Sainte-Croix carried on Butler's work in France and within the League of Nations during the interwar era. Transnational efforts aimed at protecting women from becoming the victims of male vice and sexual exploitation.

Members of the Woman's Christian Temperance Union (WCTU) argued that greater political involvement by women could help protect the home by alleviating the brutalities arising from the evils of alcoholic drinks and prostitution. The WCTU, based in the United States, became one of the largest transnational women's movements, extending itself along currents of Christian connections and, mostly, within the zones of Anglo-American cultural influence. WCTU members believed that the United States was superior in its drinking habits to most of the rest of the world. Indeed, temperance crusades had successfully lowered alcoholic consumption in the United States. Moreover, the WCTU held that Christianity, efforts for peace, work against violence against laborers, and opposition to both prizefighting and animal cruelty would advance globally along with women's rights

Huda Shaarawi (center) and the Egyptian delegation to the Ninth International Woman Suffrage Conference in Rome, 1923. Shaarawi was the force behind the Egyptian Feminist Union, the first explicitly feminist organization in Egypt. The Union merged feminism with advocacy on behalf of anticolonial nationalism and Islamic modernity. (C. C. Catt Collection, Bryn Mawr College Library, Special Collections)

and temperance. Basing their arguments on biological essentialism, WCTU members advanced the view that women, as mothers, were natural homemakers and peacemakers, while men spread militarism and exploitative profit making. Women, in effect, were represented as the mothers of the human species and as custodians of international morality and well-being. Ian Tyrrell's global history of the WCTU traces the work of some of the thirty-eight global missionaries the WCTU dispatched to recruit women worldwide.[52]

Empowerment of women as a means to combat militarism was a common theme among transnational women's groups. Calling for a halt to conflict in Europe, an international group of women met at The Hague in 1915 and established the Women's International League for Peace and Freedom. This group quickly widened its mission to fight colonialism and racism as well as militarism, and it became one of the few interracial organizations of the interwar era—a time when views of strict racial hierarchies were still strong.

Birth control became another cause of transnational advocacy. Drawing upon European women physicians who advocated use of the vaginal diaphragm, Margaret Sanger promoted birth control in the United States and gained both acclaim and notoriety worldwide. After she met Sanger in New York in 1919, for example, Baroness Ishimoto (later Katō) Shizue returned to Japan and formed a birth control league. When Japanese authorities refused to grant Sanger a visa to visit, Sanger booked a ship to China, docked in Japan on the way, and received visitors in her stateroom. Under pressure, authorities finally permitted Sanger to undertake a speaking tour, and Ishimoto accelerated her efforts to spread Sanger's message. In the late 1930s, however, the nationalist, pro-natalist stances associated with Japan's growing militarism (as in Germany) stalled the country's prewar birth control movement.[53]

Calls for women's empowerment had an ambiguous relationship to empire building. Sometimes supporters of women's rights from the West interlaced their advocacy with imperial justifications, often pointing to practices such as sati (self-immolation), foot binding, and harem as evidence of the backwardness and injustice that colonial uplift might remedy. The harem especially became construed in much of the West as the very antithesis of respectable notions of family order and as a sign of a degenerate society that only imperial authority could stamp out.

At the same time, women in less powerful colonized territories often recognized that they were constrained through both imperial and gender inequalities. In this sense, feminism (a term that appeared in

Margaret Sanger and Ishimoto (later Katō) Shizue (side by side, center), and other advocates of birth control in Japan, 1937. These two women worked in their respective countries and also globally to elevate the status of women and to give women more power over planning their families. Katō, who lived to age 104, was one of the first women elected to the Japanese Diet after women received the vote in 1946. (Sophia Smith Collection, Smith College)

various languages in Western Europe in the late nineteenth century) and anti-imperial causes could also go hand in hand. Moreover, women's advocates from colonies could call on women from the metropole to support their causes and give them international visibility. In the 1880s and 1890s, for example, India's Pandita Ramabai appealed to networks in England and the United States to press her opposition to Hindu customs related to child marriage and sati. She also converted to Christianity. Such women's and Christian networks helped her finance her Mukti Mission, established in 1889 for the education and training of poor women, especially widows. Still, Indian feminism did not arise out of a transnational network of women so much as it sprang from local grievances and traditions and then tapped into broader networks. And these could be fragile. Pandita Ramabai's feminism so disquieted some of her British missionary sponsors that they came to see her as heretical.[54]

Global travel consistently undermined the idea that Euro-American women activists were essential in bringing greater women's equality to the rest of the world. When American Carrie Chapman Catt decided to "survey the status of women" by a global trip around the world from 1911 to 1913, she found both the expected and the unexpected. In many places she saw the disempowerment and even isolation forced upon women and commented upon women's plight in clearly Orientalist terms. But she also traveled through places, such as Rangoon, Burma (now Myanmar), where matriarchal customs meant that women voted in local elections, held property, could choose and divorce their husbands, and controlled much of the retail trade. In some places in Southeast Asia, she witnessed the decline of women's power as the influence of Islam and Christianity spread. In the end, she wrote that her trip provided "an experience so upsetting to all our preconceived notions that it is difficult to estimate its influence upon us."[55] Women's networks entangled unpredictably within the uncertain currents of transnationalism.

Transnational organizations to improve the status of women became somewhat less visible over time, especially in the West. Older women dominated these movements, and younger women seemed reluctant to join the formal associations that championed suffrage, pressed purity causes, and frequently advocated a variety of religious or political agendas.[56] Younger, particularly urban, women found attractions within another, quite different, transnational current—consumerism. "Modern girls" popped up on every continent in the early twentieth century. Like the organized transnational women's movements with which they occasionally overlapped, these "modern" women asserted an independent spirit and sought new freedoms. But they rejected the nineteenth century's world of women, one that often assumed values found in homosocial bonds, gender essentialism, and domesticity. Instead many "modern girls" gravitated toward a jazzier version of femininity that looked toward heterosexual companionship, a sporty and androgynous look, and a revamped vision of family life. This book's final chapter will examine "modern girls" and their involvement in an array of transnational "codes" spawned through consumerism. The bonds they developed were less those of affection based on gender than those woven through acts of purchase and self-presentation in an age of mass media.

The variety of aspirations projected in global women's movements reflected differing ideas about proper or natural gender roles. Definitions of masculinity and femininity and of proper sexuality, of course, varied widely around the world. As global networks intruded upon localized habits, the production of perceived gender differences and of sexual behaviors could undergo change and challenge, not always in predictable ways. Discourses of masculinity generally infused imperial ideologies, as a rhetoric of benevolent paternalism mixed with the threat of military force. Many women's organizations, as we have seen, participated in this masculine projection of empire, endorsing an extreme version of domesticity counterpoised against a presumably rational and assertive manliness. On the other hand, the new global connectivities, even in imperial realms, also provided networks within which people on both sides of colonial divides could meet, question prevailing social values, and develop alternative affiliations. In transnational space, feminists and same-sex unions might find nourishment for their opposition to rigid gender or sexual norms. Cosmopolitanism could thus challenge the very discourses of masculinity that were embedded in imperial and other hierarchical relationships. Issues of gender expectations and realms of intimacy, as

Ann Stoler has elaborated, lay not outside of imperial and global politics but often at their heart.[57]

⁓

In this increasingly networked world, aesthetic currents associated with music, literature, and art may have produced some of the most intangible, yet enduring, attachments. Realism, impressionism, cubism, art nouveau, surrealism, Dadaism, and neoclassicism all drew together aesthetic movements that developed a global semiotics and, often, cosmopolitan circuits of collaborating artists and intellectuals. Paris seemed to generate an intellectual avant-garde. Its status as a transnational gathering place provided fertile soil for cross-cultural attachments based within globalized artistic communities of many kinds.

It would be impossible, however, to map all of the transnational affiliations and intellectual currents that developed in this era.[58] This chapter has tried to suggest examples rather than provide a comprehensive accounting, and to advance several central arguments. First, transnational affiliations almost invariably harbored tensions between universalistic and particularistic claims and goals. Second, realms of the transnational, the national, the imperial, and the local were not distinct; most people lived in them all at the same time. Global currents and the individuals involved in them shaped localized variations and vice versa; transmission lines ran in diverse directions, and the frictions among them often proved mutually constitutive.

CHAPTER THREE

Exhibitionary Nodes

As popular representations of the world's geographic and human diversity spread within the increasingly dense transnational currents of the age, collecting and categorizing became a mania, as both science and entertainment tried to tame, order, and make legible the world's vast differences. The tradition of collecting "curiosities" and of assembling specimens from around the world, of course, well predated the late nineteenth century. Collectors in this era, however, displayed a distinctive faith that the sum of their assemblages would produce a system of universalized knowledge that would transcend geographical bounds. Most collectors and exhibitors saw the "facts" of their collections as building a unifying system. In Britain, writes Thomas Richards, "the administrative core of the Empire was built around knowledge-producing institutions like the British Museum, the Royal Geographical Society, the India Survey, and the universities," and collections of data promised to rationalize the empire, and the world, by ordering them into "categories of categories."[1] Such enthusiastic faith in collections of facts and artifacts emerged from a confluence of romanticism, evolutionary ideas, bureaucratic methodologies, and the rapid shrinking of time and space.

Who, however, collects what, and what is collected? Who establishes categories, and what gets categorized? The answers to such questions help map flows of power and constructions of hierarchy that once masqueraded as naturally ordained.

The mania for collection both shaped and reflected the transnational currents and power dynamics of the age. The taxonomies created within collections ordered the world's presumed differences—in national capacities, in racial and sexual characteristics, and in animal and plant hierarchies. They were implicated in structuring imperialism and in asserting national and class advantage. Collecting, cataloging, and exhibiting can assert (or simulate) control. Yet the more these exhibitionary nodes linked into broad global networks, the less their meanings could be carefully channeled. The exhibiting and collecting of this age certainly projected dominant hierarchies, but they also represented the messier attributes of "contact zones"—realms of transnational connection where what was taught and what was learned could be neither tightly disciplined nor unambiguous.

World's Fairs

World's fairs in this period perhaps best reflected the exhibitionary spirit of the age. They presumed to present tours of the world, but each was a tour confined to a constricted space, locality, and time. Fairs were shaped within the politics of individual large cities vying for attention, and they mostly represented the world as imagined by their sponsors, usually Westerners. They opened and then closed within several months. But despite their seemingly local and ephemeral nature, world's fairs constituted one of the most important nodes in the transnational currents of this period. Fairs became major cultural enterprises of global significance because their representations projected powerful imaginaries about the world, its diverse cultures, and its interconnectivity and divisions. They often left behind catalogs, collections, iconic buildings, networks of people, and memories that continued to structure perceptions of world "realities." A world's fair offered a simplified and comprehensible scale to both those who attended and those who learned indirectly about its exhibits.

A series of world's fairs stretched over the century that followed the famous Great Exhibition in London in 1851, better known as the Crystal Palace Exhibition. The idea was simple: if masses of people could not traverse the actual world, then glimpses and bits of that world could be assembled and represented to them. To showcase whatever city and country served as host, each fair attempted to contrive a compelling attraction that could both educate and entertain.[2]

The dozens of small and large fairs—held mostly in the West and deeply implicated in the emerging colonialist order—conveyed multiple meanings and by no means advanced any unified view of the world. Yet their projected imaginaries about the state of the world's peoples and history illuminate two of this book's prominent themes. First, the fairs mixed images of national and cultural particularism with expressions of universalism. They provided structured representations of the new imperialism of the age—a time of nationalistic excesses and decidedly hierarchical visions—but cast these visions as a harmonious coming together of disparate parts. Universal peace was a prominent theme in most of the exhibitions, but so, of course, was nationalism. Secondly, discourses of rationality often coexisted with, and even helped give definition to, a spectacularity associated with the emergence of mass mediated culture. The fairs mixed the modernist impulses of reason and classification together with projections of fantasy and spectacle.

Prince Albert, Queen Victoria's husband, who championed London's Great Exhibition of 1851, predicted that it would provide a new starting point from which all nations would thenceforth be able to direct their exertions. In a way he was right, not because it actually sparked the evolutionary global advancement that he envisioned but because it set a broad model for how visions of progress in future fairs and public spaces would be designed, articulated, and debated. It foreshadowed the themes of particularity/universalism and reason/ spectacle.

The Great Exhibition was held in Hyde Park in London in a huge iron and glass "Crystal Palace" designed by Sir Joseph Paxton, a specialist in greenhouse construction. The mixture of hard iron and translucent glass provided an apt metaphor for the fair's juxtapositions of materiality and fantasy. The Crystal Palace established four categories that would come to be used in most fairs of the future: Manufacturers, Machinery, Raw Materials, and Fine Arts. Within these four areas stretched thirteen thousand exhibits from countries all over the world. Six million visitors (some crowding in on affordable "Shilling Days") attended, and the exhibition produced a surplus of revenue that, into the future, funded some of the great British museums and enterprises fostering science, design, and natural history. Celebrating the prospects for progress in both nation and world, the exhibits highlighted but at the same time claimed to efface the boundaries of nation, culture, and class.

The dominant messages of the Great Exhibition of 1851 featured the transformative impact of machinery, powered by raw materials, inspired by industrial ingenuity, and executed by skilled labor. The exhibits, of course, showcased products from Britain and its empire above all, but its larger goal seemed to project the cornucopia of goods that free trade could offer. Looms, appliances, reapers, and a host of other innovations hummed paeans to the Industrial Revolution and to global exchange. National technological advancement and international prosperity became seamless.[3]

The Great Exhibition exemplified and foreshadowed future discussions about whether such material "progress" enhanced or debased good taste and the dignity of work. Perhaps to temper the projections of power and industry, the Great Exhibition showcased print culture and "correct" design principles, displays that merged machinery into traditions of artisanry and early nineteenth-century design reform. Exhibits presented labor as ennobled in this new mechanized world. Dedicated artisans could lend their skills to modern industrial technique—if only consumers could be schooled, through such displays, to exercise sound aesthetic judgments.[4]

Visitors to the Crystal Palace encountered specific visions of how industrialization promoted a civilizing process, and of how improved standards of living might elevate personal morality and public taste. The huge glass hall hosted major concerts featuring the world's largest organ, showcased the famous tightrope walker Charles Blondin, displayed arts and architecture from ancient Egypt through the European Renaissance, held aeronautical and motor exhibitions, and exhibited various scenes from the natural world. A yachting event, which would evolve into the America's Cup competition, was held in conjunction with the Great Exhibition. Such spectacles of machine and of human achievement merged with exhibits of exquisite small-scale designs, such as those found in Sheffield knives and silver scissors, in the lace designs devised by women, in fine French porcelain, and in the printmaking arts. The Crystal Palace thus seemed providentially poised to have a positive moral and material effect on a world waiting to be reformed through the presumably enlightened conquests that many in the West believed would characterize the global expansion of commerce.

Displays from other nations brought this first modern world's fair its greatest distinction. Visitors looked with wonder at the array of agricultural products and raw materials from around the world—herbs, grains, spices, fruits, coal, and clay. From India, especially, the gorgeous jewelry, shawls, and silks highlighted an unsurpassed tradition of skilled artisanry. The global dimension of such displays fit well with the fair's larger themes of how free trade, skilled labor, and design could complement each other.

On the other hand, by implicitly mapping the world to represent differences in the physical, economic, and cultural characteristics of its nations and peoples, the Palace exhibits extended ambiguous messages. In the words of one guidebook, the displays presented not only "the different industries of nations, but that of centuries."[5] India's goods were presented as the products of a romantic and timeless tradition, as the magical offerings of an "unchanging East." Ethnographical models of

India's artisans presaged the practice, in future fairs, of highlighting living showcases of human "types" from around the world. Themes of exoticism and Orientalism, suggested in the clay and wood-carved models in the Crystal Palace, would later morph into "real" anthropological displays enacting Western evolutionary science. In this sense, the "premodern crafts" provided a foil to complement and define the "modern" of British industry. But there was also the suggestion about the capacity of Britain to regenerate premodern lands while incorporating their cultural strengths. In the world of the Crystal Palace, cultural and economic exchange simultaneously destroyed and created boundaries among peoples.

For many visitors and commentators, the Great Exhibition captured a moment of optimism; reason and awe seemed to shape the wave of the future. Not everyone, however, was swept away. The exhibition touched off wide-ranging debates over the role of machines and their effects on humans. The uplifting messages of the Palace met other commentary that insisted that laborers would be losers in the spreading system of industrial capitalism. William Morris famously refused to enter the Palace. Karl Marx, among others, argued that the exhibition displayed a deleterious commodities fetish that would undermine dignity and good taste even as it rendered workers subservient to the needs of capital. Machines, many charged, would make slaves of their operators and undermine the nations who exalted them. The fair, in the words of Jeffrey A. Auerbach, was "a protean event with numerous possible meanings."[6] It not only disseminated a positive vision of a national identity based upon capitalism, free trade, and British destiny, but prompted a public debate over competing visions. The kinds of debates and ironies surrounding the Crystal Palace event would echo in subsequent global exhibitions.

The Crystal Palace had not been the first grand industrial exhibition in Europe. A series of French exhibitions, since 1798, had attracted international comment and admiration by featuring progressive techniques in agriculture and technology. In just a single decade before 1851, Berne, Madrid, Brussels, Bordeaux, St. Petersburg, Lisbon, and Paris had all featured exhibitions. But the Crystal Palace set a new standard by opening to international exhibitors from the entire world. In its wake, others were quick to emulate, as numerous cities and countries tried similarly to put themselves in the vanguard of the globe's material and moral progress. One huge building had contained the London extravaganza, but the increasingly grandiose fairs after 1851 became vast campuses in which distinctive architectures punctuated the presentation of cultural difference even as orderly design principles worked to harmonize them.

A General Exposition in 1863 in Istanbul and another in 1869 in Cairo, celebrating the opening of the Suez Canal, were among the few held outside of Western Europe. They showcased both the Ottoman Empire and Egypt as modern nations on the European model. Writing of Cairo in 1869, the newspaper *Nil* boasted that foreigners would see the old city in a new light as the "Paris of the Orient," with "balls, concerts, vaudevilles, circuses, ballets . . . first-class hotels luxuriously furnished, entertainments and feasts."[7] From 1851 to the outbreak of the First World War, such extravaganzas and their breathless media coverage appeared somewhere on an average of every two years.

Paris alone hosted an Exposition Universelle approximately every eleven years—in 1855, 1867, 1878, 1889, 1900, and more after World War I, culminating in the spectacular 1937 exhibition that offered 250 acres of interior space. The 1878 fair, which boasted what was then a record-breaking territory of sixty-six outdoor acres, introduced new practices that future fairs would embellish. An "Avenue des Nations," resplendent with specimens of architecture from countries on every continent, seemed to offer a more extensive tour of the world than a single building could simulate. Moreover, where fine arts had played a minor role in the London Crystal Palace, the Paris expositions gave them highest prominence by emphasizing the French theme that successful

The Eiffel Tower at the Paris Exposition, 1889. Electric lights lit up the night and announced an exciting new age in which darkness, literally and symbolically, could be rolled back. (Library of Congress)

manufacturing should depend on its integration into a tradition of fine arts. This fair attracted thirteen million paying visitors, and its promoters claimed it had been a financial bonanza in terms of the revenue gained from enhanced trade.

The 1889 Paris Exposition Universelle, a centennial celebration of the revolution of 1789, expanded upon the themes of technology, the arts, and colonialism. Being part of the Third Republic's strategy to construct a more exalted national identity and imperial agenda, the fair is most remembered for its signature gateway—the strange and then-controversial iron Eiffel Tower, the tallest building in the world (until 1930). As with previous fairs, the architects of the 1889 exposition sought to represent the finest of French culture as well as the latest in machinery.

The world presented in the shadow of the Eiffel Tower again became a harmonious offering of difference. The American display introduced consumer innovations such as Thomas Edison's phonograph. Mexico's national pavilion, built to suggest an Aztec palace, announced the modernizing and "whitening" goals adopted by the regime of Porfirio Díaz. The Colonial Exhibition, one of the most popular exhibits, displayed France as the master of a far-flung empire that was spreading French civilization throughout the world. The Algerian and Tunisian exhibits were housed in extraordinary hybridized palaces intended to rival the lavish displays Britain had developed of India and to flaunt the wealth and accomplishment of French colonies. A *village nègre* enclosed some four hundred indigenous peoples in a live display. One visitor wrote that "the ingenious French have established colonies of savages whom they are attempting to civilize. They are the genuine article and make no mistake."[8] European fantasies about harem life turned belly dancers into the most popular and profitable attraction, drawing some two thousand spectators a day. Encounters with non-Western artistic traditions often inspired: Claude Debussy reportedly borrowed forms from the Théâtre Annamite in reworking his distinctive musical style; Paul Gauguin adapted a Japanese cloisonné-style separation of colors into his postimpressionist paintings.[9] "Exotic" subjects, it seemed, could offer creative gifts.

Americans, bidding for world recognition, also built fairs to advertise their power, ingenuity, and visions of future international leadership. At the US Centennial International Exhibition in 1876 in Philadelphia (celebrating the signing of the Declaration of Independence), some ten million visitors were treated to a spectacle that held special importance for a country whose citizens, living in a vast territory relatively insulated by two oceans, could seem removed from the wider world. The official name of the exhibition was the International Exhibition of Arts, Manufactures, and Products of the Soil and Mine. In its two hundred buildings, including an iron-and-glass Horticultural Hall designed to recall the Crystal Palace, the Centennial celebration brought together exhibits from thirty-seven nations and proudly showcased America's specialty products. A screw-making machine, a telephone, a typewriter, and Hires root beer exemplified American inventiveness, and a Women's Building began the tradition followed in future world's fairs of celebrating the role and accomplishments of women, while safely segregating them from the male mainstream. The fair opened with a ceremony that switched on the impressive Corliss steam engine, which powered all of the other machines at the fair. Li Gui, the Chinese emissary who was interested in how Western technology might contribute to "self-strengthening" measures in China, was in awe. "Nothing can be done without machines. . . . All the universe seems to be the macrocosm of the machine," he wrote in the travel account of his around-the-world visit.[10]

If machinery impressed a visitor from the East, however, the exhibitions from Japan and China proved among the biggest hits for Americans. A fascination with Asia and Asian markets had burgeoned after Commodore Matthew Perry's visits to Japan in 1853 and 1854. The commercial treaties the United States subsequently signed with Japan and China spurred hopes for expansion of the trading highways that had long characterized the Pacific region. Japan erected its own separate building to show its finest traditions—intricate bronzes, showy lacquer work, artful screens, and elaborately carved figures and furniture. China's pagoda-style display featured elaborate screens, urns, and vases. The Japanese pavilion, especially, touched off an enthrallment with the arts of the "Orient." Over the next few years a generation of American art collectors and scholars, such as Ernest Fenollosa, Edward S. Morse, and John LaFarge, would travel to Japan and elaborate a common nineteenth-century hope that the "feminine" arts of the East would marry the "masculine" industrial machinery of the West (especially North America) to complete the foreordained evolutionary course of civilization. Although some people in Asia talked about foreign devils and some people in the United States championed exclusionary policies that restricted most Chinese and Japanese immigration, this philosophical and aesthetic stance emphasized the civilizational gains that could be derived from the Pacific exchange's "marriage" of different cultural traditions. Influenced by the stylistic simplicity of Japanese open-plan and screen-wall construction at the 1893 fair in Chicago, Frank Lloyd Wright pioneered the sleek form-follows-function look of modernist architecture.

As with its predecessor in England in 1851, the Centennial Exhibition prompted expressions of awe but also of disgust and fear. One of its architects wrote of his joy at seeing that the "restless, happy crowds are flitting from point to point, and the whole looks like a fairy-land, an incantation scene, something that we wish would never pass away." But Japanese commissioner Fukui Makoto wrote, "Crowds come like sheep, run here, run there, run everywhere. One man start, one thousand follow. Nobody can see anything, nobody can do anything. All rush, push, tear, shout, make plenty noise, say damn great many times, get very tired, and go home." Henry Adams wrote to a friend: "I have registered an oath never to visit another of these vile displays. The crowd there was appalling and there was a great deal of sickness and alarm—Much typhoid is caught there and if they are not lucky, they will have yellow fever."[11]

The famous White City of the Columbian Exposition in Chicago in 1893, however, eclipsed the Philadelphia Fair in its scale, didactic ambition, spectacle, and controversy. Civic boosters allied with scientists, educators, and business interests to design elaborate displays that, presumably, would teach Americans (and foreign visitors) about the world. Opening during a severe economic downturn that threatened the stability of the social order in the United States, the fair followed the pattern of previous fairs by projecting a nationalistic confidence, unity, and ambition even as it emphasized the language of international harmony.

Like previous international fairs, the Columbian Exposition emphasized both industrial and moral progress. An array of American-made farm machines revolved around a huge globe at one end of Agricultural Hall. Full-size models of Pullman cars and locomotives presented the railroad as the harbinger of global prosperity. Elevators, pneumatic conveyors, models of ocean liners, affordable carriages, Westinghouse dynamos, long-distance phones, electric trolleys, mechanized street cleaners, Singer sewing machines, and steam-powered newspaper presses—all boasted of US ingenuity and positioned the country in the vanguard of the globe's future interconnectedness. While Westinghouse's incandescent lighting system illuminated the entire fairgrounds and its buildings, General Electric's three-ton searchlight and the seventy-eight-foot shaft of colored lights called the Edison Tower of Light demonstrated the dawn of the electrical age.

Amid these technological marvels, this so-called White City expanded upon a practice that would become a standard element for future fairs. It convened a World Congress of experts on almost every conceivable topic to advance theories promoting "progress, prosperity, unity, peace, and happiness." The Congress became a gathering place for the variety of new professions that, as Chapter 4 will show, were forging transnational epistemic communities. The exposition's grounds themselves became a demonstration, for example, of how new expertise in health and sanitation could turn a polluted and sickly urban environment into a City Beautiful. Cuban travel writer Aurelia Castillo de González looked past the United States' burgeoning imperial pretensions to praise a vision of modernity that, if imported to Latin America, she claimed would prevent imperial encroachment by showing an adoptable model of a well-planned, well-engineered, and more harmonious future.[12]

In addition to the promise of technology and the uplifting potential of applied expertise, evolutionary science was another structuring principle of the White City. The Smithsonian Institution's anthropologists avoided a seemingly random collection of interesting things and instead carefully constructed an allegorical and moral lesson about civilization and its advancement. The presentation of "racial types" and of evolutionary classifications purveyed the dubious concept of "race" and aimed to educate viewers in the emerging racial science of the day. Some races ("Anglo-Saxons") were represented as destined to lead the world while lesser races represented throwbacks in evolutionary time who needed to either die out or be tutored. The theme of purification in the White City extended from sanitation facilities to urban planning to racial science.

On the entertainment-oriented Midway, sensory temptations became associated with darker "races" who contributed song, dance, and titillation. Here, erotic female dancers and exotic cafés tempted the Americans who flocked to Chicago from cities and from farms. Little Egypt's dancers, with bare midriffs and semitransparent skirts, presented movements that American slang labeled the "hootchy-kootchy" and brought outrage from purity crusader Anthony Comstock.[13] White Western viewers, for whom racial difference might have raised repulsion based on fears of racial or biological contagion, could relish the exotic from the safety of a White City. Although Ottoman sultan Abdülhamid II donated 1,819 photographs depicting the Ottoman Empire's natural beauty, architectural grandeur, and modern institutions, representations of Orientalist fantasies undoubtedly proved more memorable to most visitors.

The lavish spectacle, the scale of production, and the complex mixture of lofty education and bawdy entertainment combined together with a hawkish consumerism to mark the Chicago fair as quintessentially American. The fair featured soon-to-be-ubiquitous products such as postcards, hamburgers, soft drinks, and a Ferris wheel, named for George Washington Gale Ferris Jr., a Pittsburgh bridge builder who sought to create a huge metal landmark that would surpass the Paris Exposition's Eiffel Tower.

Like the fairs before it, the Columbian Exposition prompted debates over national identity. An appeal by African-Americans to construct an exhibit in the White City was denied. Women, again, had a separate building, but African-American women were similarly barred from it. Such racial exclusion prompted a series of protests and spurred African-American leaders to greater action.[14] Critics elaborated other familiar laments—the fair was too crowded, too elitist, too bawdy, too open, too restrictive. The fair projected clear themes involving technological, scientific, national, and racial destiny, but the precise meanings accorded to these themes invited discussion and controversy.

The Chicago fair foreshadowed America's arrival as a global power, and in 1898 the spirit of expansive and racialized nationalism manifested itself in foreign policy. Taking on the once-great empire of Spain, the United States embarked on what Secretary of State John Hay called a Splendid Little War, which sparked its experiment in overseas colonial acquisition. The government of Republican William McKinley justified as a war measure the annexation of Hawai'i, a territory increasingly dominated by US sugar interests. As Spain withdrew from its three-centuries-long hold on the Philippines, McKinley concluded that America's civilizing mission necessitated its colonial control over that Pacific archipelago, long an entrée to the coveted China market. In the Caribbean, which US strategic planners had slated to become an "American Mediterranean" that guarded a hoped-for Panama Canal route, the United States gained Puerto Rico as a colony and in 1903 subjected both Cuba and Panama to protectorate status.

The sense of power and colonial destiny that accompanied these imperial moves became deeply embedded in the series of extravagant US World Fairs held in Omaha in 1898, Buffalo in 1901, St. Louis in 1904 (to commemorate the Louisiana Purchase), Portland in 1905, Seattle in 1909, San Francisco and San Diego in 1915, and Philadelphia in 1926. All of these fairs, promoted by local city boosters for profit and regional status, celebrated America's emergence as an imperial and global power and introduced the nation's new colonial subjects to its increasingly skeptical citizens. The theories of racial inequality and hierarchy, advanced by physical anthropologists, appealed to dominant white interests in both political parties. As Lee D. Baker writes, "Southern interests marshaled the anthropological discourse on racial inferiority for propaganda and Jim Crow legislation, while Republican interests used the anthropological discourse on race to demonstrate that the inferior races of the Pacific and the Caribbean needed uplifting and civilizing."[15] These American imperial fairs also fed on models from perhaps the greatest world fair of all—the Paris Exposition of 1900.

The Paris Exposition of 1900, which attracted some fifty million people, displayed colonialism at its most confident peak. A decade and a half before World War I would plunge Europe into a nightmare of debt and self-doubt, this turn-of-the-century exhibition emphasized the prospects for global peace and commercial uplift that so many Europeans then believed would provide the major themes of the twentieth century. The Eiffel Tower, built for the earlier fair, was painted yellow and bedecked with electric lights. Previous decades had seen a rise in labor organizing, strikes, and industrial strife, but the fair of 1900 projected confidence in industrial capitalism and in the mutual advancement that commercial connections might bring. In this greatest of all world's fairs, previous fair themes stood out in even bolder relief: capitalism, colonialism, and world peace wove together in an expanding arc called progress.

A Musée Social at the 1889 Paris Exposition had become celebrated for hosting international discussions related to the "social questions" raised by industrial civilization. The Musée Social's organizers for the 1900 fair, building on the model of 1889 and the Chicago fair's congresses, gathered experts together to exchange scientific information on subjects as far-ranging as fisheries, publishing, dentistry, hypnotism, philately, and public health and medicine. Their special interests, however, centered on how to deal with the insecurities of the industrial age. They sought ameliorative examples from various countries and groups. Subsections formed on protection of child workers, regulation of work conditions, wages and profit sharing, workers' and employers' associations, farm credit, workers' housing, workers' cooperatives, savings and insurance institutions, sanitation, temperance, slums, and poor relief. The industrializing nations contributed a range of models— from Germany's extensive state-provided accident and old-age insurance, to Italy's workers' cooperatives, to French displays of voluntary mutual aid organizations, to America's representations of "model" corporations and enlightened capitalism. The Paris fair offered a congress on "women's works and institutions" that discussed equal gender rights but mostly concentrated on expanding educational opportunities and on according special protections to women and child factory workers. The gathering accentuated the maternalist impulse in women's growing international networks by emphasizing women's special role to elevate and protect the less fortunate.

The fair thus facilitated transnational discussions about how to arrange the roles of the state, of labor, and of private capital. But it presented, as Daniel Rodgers writes, "no agreement on how an effective counterforce to the world of iron might be constructed. State paternalism, private paternalism, mutualism, socialism, maternalism: the shorthand phrases led toward different configurations of power and policies."[16] The Paris fair presented a kind of smorgasbord, with no one configuration for organizing the new industrial society seeming dominant.

The colonial area within the 1900 fair stretched farther than any previous one, with even more fantastical architecture representing the pasts and futures of colonies. In the fair's conference halls and art nouveau palaces appeared no hint of the struggles and suffering from European or colonial wars, of strikes or social conflicts. Colonies seemed places of newly ordered bounty, indebted to the know-how of colonizers: the Dutch East Indies were present in three pavilions; nearly twenty French colonies or protectorates had their own displays or buildings; Americans showed off their "civilizing" missions in Cuba and in Native American mission schools. Other nations offered additional cultural and architectural contrasts: Russia contributed nine pavilions employing over three thousand people; Serbia constructed a Byzantine mansion with a display of silkworm cocoons; the Ottoman government, which had not participated in earlier Paris fairs, featured a huge neo-Islamic pavilion with a bazaar, workshops, café, military museum, and theater performing vignettes from Turkish life.[17]

The Paris Exposition of 1900, its successors in the 1920s, and the Paris Colonial Exposition of 1931 featured displays of humans as their most popular attractions. The nineteenth-century fairs had showcased colonial craftspeople and servers, but the idea of exhibiting humans blossomed as teams of anthropologists and entertainers illustrated the ideas of racial evolution that were sweeping the West. Joseph-Arthur de Gobineau's *Essay on the Inequality of Human Races* (1853), which advanced ideas of biologically rooted racial hierarchy, reached the heights of its popularity during the first two decades of the twentieth century in both the United States and France. In line with this racialized view of the world, peoples from throughout the globe began to be imported and displayed alongside the plants and animals that were already standard fare. Humans became, in effect, zoological exhibits—and profitable ones. These "human zoos" became living catalogs of evolutionary categories, projecting tropes of primitivism and narratives about the history of the world.

Such exhibits easily slid into entertainment and demeaning caricature. The more exotic the display, the more audience it attracted. One Egyptian visitor criticized the absence of any modern Egyptian industry or intellectual contributions. An Egyptian novelist portrayed a visitor to the fair as being so embarrassed by the performance of two female Egyptian dancers that he left in shame.[18] British guidebook writer Alex M. Thompson praised the "multi-coloured dwellings of the various Asiatic and African natives. . . . Here one may sit and take tea or coffee, served by men of strange tropical nationalities, whose faces look as polished as your fire-grate at home, while . . . the 'Danse du Ventre' drones."[19]

Embracing the practice of human display, Americans at the St. Louis Fair also introduced their new colonial subjects to visitors. The largest and most popular proved to be the "Philippine Reservation," occupying a huge and lavishly arranged area that surpassed anything the British had shown for India or the French for Algeria. In the Reservation, anthropologists carefully structured the diverse people from the Philippine Islands (numbering some twelve hundred) into representations of race evolution. The progression of "primitive" peoples morphing into well-dressed and disciplined "modern" constabularies provided a visual demonstration of progressive colonialism. This theme would structure US world's fairs until the 1930s. Moreover, with each new fair in America, the exotic enticements of the Midway (soon called the Joy Zone) became ever more substantial and garish. The always popular *danse du ventre* was promoted at the San Francisco fair in a huge painting that featured a mechanically driven rotating belly.[20]

In all of the early twentieth-century fairs, colonies had their own buildings and identities, each hiding the militarized brutality, the greed, and the cultural destruction that was part of colonialism while emphasizing commercial and moral progress. British decision makers in India, for example, accorded an increasingly larger presence to lavish Indian palaces filled with opulent produce. These huge palaces exemplified the wealth that India had brought to England and also sought to show that British rule had brought progress and prosperity to India. By contrast, the epic-scale famine and poverty in the British colony had no visibility. Similarly, Australia, Canada, New Zealand, and South Africa rivaled each other to establish national distinctiveness and to show the material and cultural accomplishments attained under white rule. Decimation of aboriginal peoples had no place. France carefully crafted structures representing each and every colonial possession, with Algeria, Tunisia, and French Indochina having special visibility. Portugal, Belgium, Holland, and Japan all joined in the celebration of imperial uplift, as their displays of colonies such as Brazil and Angola, of Congo, of Indonesia, and of Formosa and Korea, respectively, grew in grandeur in each fair during the 1920s and early 1930s. Out of sight remained the violence that extracted colonial abundance.

As fairs became increasingly structured to celebrate empire, they became more and more associated with large and successful imperial powers. Spain, Germany, Russia, Austria, and other countries grew less enthusiastic about participation in fairs, and the internationalist mission of fairs became less convincing. Fairs thus simultaneously offered festivals celebrating interconnectivity and also became venues for hardening divisions among nations.

Fair-displayed colonialism and internationalism contained another central paradox: fairs supposedly celebrated human unity, but effective displays depended on highlighting differences among the world's peoples. Even as fairs supported a romanticized, one-sided vision of colonialism, the separate and lavish fair buildings fostered the constructions of distinctive colonial identities.[21] Even after the fairs, these constructions (architectural as well as cultural) often had substantial impact in the colonies. By bringing together leaders from both metropole and colony to plan and execute displays, fairs helped consolidate disparate, and independent, ethno-nationalistic identities. Moreover, the humans who were exoticized in colonial exhibits gazed back at the gazers and made their own meanings. What they might have seen or learned is hardly well documented. After the close of the fairs, some lingered outside of their homelands; some returned. But the impact of their views, as varied and particularized as they might have been, must have reflected a new awareness of cultural differentiations and fostered nationalisms of their own.

This paradox is illustrated by the instability of lines between white and nonwhite worlds at the 1900 Paris Exposition, where American commissioners sponsored a display on Negro Life in the United States that challenged some of the primitivist tropes so prevalent elsewhere. Organized by the African-American sociologist W. E. B. Du Bois, an array of photographs showed the world of middle-class black Americans—professionals, writers, experts—whose intellectual and cultural sophistication challenged the color line that colonialism inscribed.[22]

During the depression decade of the 1930s, the overt justifications for colonialism waned, opposition to racism grew, and human displays in colonial pavilions mostly ended. In the New York fair of 1930, for example, the theme of "Democracy" helped banish the nation's most overtly imperial displays. Still, the Chicago Fair of 1933–1934, the 1937 Paris Fair, and the New York Fair of 1939 retained many of the structural elements of past shows: the displays of self-confidence about progress, commerce, and empire; the promise of science and technology; the lavish use of electrical power for astonishing illuminations and efficient transportation; the vision of a union between art and technology. Coming in the midst of economic depression and international turmoil, this staged optimism about the future seemed more and more contrived. Moreover, the depression seemed to give a further boost to Midway entertainments. The Chicago fair's Midway featured a large dance hall, in which two hundred taxi dancers danced with visitors for a dime; a Lido theater with notorious fan dancing by Sally Rand; a Midget Village, "freak shows" in an Odditorium, an Oriental Village that boasted a Slave Mart, Flea Circus, and Monster Snake Show. The fair tradition was increasingly being given over to carnival and spectacle, still passed off as internationalism.[23]

At the Paris Fair of 1937 a two-hundred-foot mural consisting of 250 painted panels depicted the "spirit of electricity" from the Greeks to the present. Harmonizing with this theme, the United States featured its Depression-era electrical power projects (dams, rural electrification), and the Soviet Union presented electrical projects as the soul of communism. Yet in another part of the fair, Pablo Picasso created a very different mural, showing not progress but the destruction that German aircraft had rained upon the Spanish town of Guernica in a bombing raid on April 26, 1937. The growing horror of the Spanish Civil War augured greater trouble to come. As Jay Winter writes, "the two murals encapsulated the collision between hope and despair which created massive fissures in the 1937 expo itself."[24] Within a few months, both the fair and the Spanish Republic would end. And not too many months after that, the site of the fair's Tower of Peace, which stood taller than any nation's pavilion and had been inspired and sponsored by French pacifist veterans of the First World War, would itself host Hitler's military might.

Incongruities thus haunted the 1937 fair. The Spanish Republic's building stood near to the one in which the Pontifical States celebrated the fate of Catholic martyrs in Spain. The massive pavilion of Nazi Germany, designed by Albert Speer as a monument to the country's national grievances and renewed power, faced off against an imposing Soviet building topped by a seventy-five-ton monument to industrial and farm workers. Behind but also facing the German edifice stood the Land of Israel Pavilion, a Zionist statement erected by the Jews of Palestine. The League of Nations had a pavilion, and so did the Japanese, whose invasion of China had so clearly illustrated the impotence of that body.

Representations of empire were greatly diminished and moved to the periphery. The Indian representative had wished to come with national, not colonial, status, so India had no presence at this fair. Although French officials still displayed their own colonialism as the spread of republicanism, other nations no longer featured colonies and human zoos. Even before 1937, at the 1931 Colonial Exposition in Paris, the United States had allowed parts of its colonial empire—Alaska, Hawaii, Puerto Rico, the Virgin Islands, and Samoa—to represent themselves for the first time at a foreign exposition. Although the Eugenic Society sponsored a beauty pageant to feature the "Best Colonial Marriage," the days of colonialism and its optimistic portrayal at world's fairs were clearly waning.

World's fairs have been described as vehicles of local and national pride, as conveyors of ideals of peace and internationalism, as structures embedding colonial hierarchies, as opportunities for sharing expertise and cultural exchange, as places where newly consolidating and "modernizing" states could project their self-definitions, as sites where colonial subjects cultivated their own national imaginaries. They held all of these, often conflicting, meanings. Modernity, as represented in the world of fairs, emerged as more complicated than the fair boosters might have initially imagined.

The simultaneous meeting and separation of different cultures at world's fairs played out especially visibly in architecture and art. Many fairs presented arresting visual experiments in integrating Islamic influences into Western buildings and using Western styles to inspire the neo-Islamist forms that were often readapted back into the design repertoire of their host countries. Classical influences appeared strong at the Columbian Exposition and the Paris Exposition of 1900, but the Exposition Internationale des Arts Décoratifs et Industriels Modernes, held in Paris in 1925, pronounced the primacy of Art Deco with its internationally eclectic influences. The Antwerp Fair of 1930, the largest held outside of Britain and France, presented an imposing Congolese pavilion but built it in an Orientalist mode because the architects deemed African architectural forms too modest to be used for anything other than decorative motifs. The art gallery for the 1931 Paris Exposition, which became the Permanent Museum of the Colonies (today called the Museum of African and Oceanic Art), displayed art from the French colonies and also works by acclaimed French artists such as Paul Cézanne and Gauguin. These two, of course, had themselves derived inspiration, in both style and subject, from non-Western art. Such pastiche represented a world in motion and an eclecticism that drew from the contradictions between transnational and particularistic influences.

As nodes of transnational circulation for forms and ideas, fairs became spaces of complex cultural exchange. The physical and intellectual architects of fairs joined the world together even as they separated its parts. They showed that cultural contacts produced both attraction to and repulsion of difference. By mashing together incongruities and by trying to order world cultures whose interrelationships were disorderly, the fairs simultaneously constructed and deconstructed their messages. Despite the intentions of promoters and exhibitors, the modernity revealed in the fairs showed itself as unstable and highly contingent. Designed as tours of the world, fairs ended up representing something much more complicated—the chaotic look and feel of twentieth-century modernity.

Museums

World's fairs were part of what Tony Bennett calls an "exhibitionary complex" that manifested itself even more solidly in the bricks and mortar of museums.[25] Museum professionals circulated in global networks, borrowing ideas from their counterparts in other countries and using international connections to build their collections.

German ethnologists in the late nineteenth century created the most important museums in the world in Hamburg, Berlin, Leipzig, and Munich. Their ethnographical exhibits, which became globally influential, projected the same kind of universalism and particularism that infused other imperial visions of the era. Well-traveled cosmopolitans, these ethnologists celebrated a unitary humanity and believed that only a museum could display and rationally compare the world's rich human varieties. At the same time, their museums were designed to celebrate the roles that they, their cities, and their still-consolidating nation had assumed as leaders of the new scientific internationalism. Not overly imperial in their late nineteenth-century displays, the museums nonetheless depended for their collections on the emerging imperial order and participated in pushing the "ethnographic frontiers" into areas that seemed the most exotic and "savage." If "otherness" had not been the initial vision of the global science of ethnography, it increasingly became its underlying frame.[26]

Many of the great public museums that had taken shape during the late eighteenth and early nineteenth centuries were restructured in the late nineteenth century around the (sometimes conflicting) goals of advancing scientific research and teaching the public the newest findings of natural history. London's celebrated Natural History Museum, for example, opened in 1881, and a new curator, William Henry Flower, tried to make it an important teaching institution by reorganizing its original displays into scientific lessons about evolution in the natural world.[27] London's Natural History Museum, together with the modern scientific museums in Berlin and other major capitals of Europe, established models that were broadly influential worldwide.

As in Europe, the new museums claimed to embody transnational intellectual and professional currents even as they became central symbols of imperial and national pride. Most proudly asserted both global vision and local distinctiveness. The great Latin American museum collections from this period, for example, took shape as a nationalist discourse produced within the transnational networks of curatorial expertise. Hermann Konrad Burmeister, a Prussian naturalist, directed the Museo Público in Buenos Aires for thirty years after he was hired in 1862. Ladislau Netto, a Brazilian trained at the Musée d'Histoire Naturelle in Paris, led the Museu Nacional do Rio de Janeiro. German-born Hermann von Ihering headed the Museu Paulista in São Paulo. All worked to research the geological formations of the Southern Hemisphere and to display its creatures, especially the whales from the southern seas and its huge, extinct glyptodonts.[28] A Dutch medical practitioner, J. W. B. Gunning, migrated to the Cape Colony in the late nineteenth century, became first director of the Staatsmuseum (later renamed the Transvaal Museum), and compiled one of the first surveys of birds of South Africa. The establishment of major museums in far-flung locations in this era exemplifies how the analytical scales of nation, empire, region, and world are best understood in interaction with each other.

In this period major museums began to separate collections for study from those for public exhibit, boosting the capacities for both. Research collections expanded as most museums became sponsors of transnational expeditions. The American Museum of Natural History, for example, sponsored fifty-seven collecting parties during its peak years 1929–1930. Latin American museums avidly collected fossils that provided significant evidence of paleontological connections among the continents of South America, Africa, and Australasia.[29] At the same time, exhibitions became more exciting through better taxidermy and the spreading practice of placing specimens against high-quality, naturalistic dioramas. Displays of huge ocean mammals might hang from ceilings; the reassembled bones of enormous extinct land creatures might amaze visitors. Like the world's fairs, museums boasted their science and rationality but also cultivated the kind of spectacularity needed to attract audiences.[30]

Sometimes sensationalist displays went to extremes. Robert Peary in 1897 shipped six Eskimos to New York to be studied at the Museum of Natural History, where they were confined in a cellar. Upon the death of one man, the museum mounted his skeleton for display and refused to relinquish the bones to a son, Minik, who had also been captured and who ultimately died in New York of influenza in 1918.[31]

If the ability to assemble museum collections signified power, then the sacking of other people's collections loomed also as a highly symbolic challenge. The Old Imperial Garden and Palace in Beijing (Yuanming Yuan), for example, stood as one of the greatest collections in the world in the mid-nineteenth century. Not a public museum in the Western tradition, the invaluable antiquities and art held in its temples, galleries, and halls gave it great symbolic importance. Its gardens contained exquisite reproductions of famous landscapes from southern China. In 1860 French and British troops went on a looting and burning rampage, plundering Yuanming Yuan while grabbing valuable items as trophies of conquest. The goal, of course, was to humble and punish the Chinese, spread a sense of despair, and weaken the Qing court. The scar made a lasting impression on the Chinese. "Hence, for a long time to come," writes Young-tsu Wong in *A Paradise Lost*, "while appreciating the marvels of Western science and technology, they were somehow reluctant to sing praises of the moral values of the West."[32] Within China, Yuanming Yuan had once seemed the center of the world; the destruction of its collections signaled the world's reordering.

Collecting Plants

Botanical gardens also displayed the "world" to visitors and depended upon new links of global trade. Exchange of plants and of gardening aesthetics, of course, long predated the 1870s. Missionaries, traders, and travelers had become inadvertent or intentional conveyors of plants. Horticultural practices spread along with European colonizers who sought solace from strange lands by importing familiar plants arranged in familiar landscapes. Horticultural and acclimatization societies, as well as farmers in settler colonies, became imperial intermediaries. Hoping to improve the land or to introduce more profitable practices, they borrowed and adapted, sending specimens through imperial networks from one continent and context to another. Even before the middle of the nineteenth century, many Mogul gardens became Anglicized; botanic gardens and associated museums took shape in Melbourne, Calcutta, Ceylon, Trinidad, New South Wales, Hong Kong, and Canton. France established the famed Jardin d'Essai in Algiers to provide a laboratory for acclimatization efforts, and its horticulturalists subsequently experimented with Chinese yams, bamboo, and other plants that might complement those that could be grown in France.[33]

The networks of people who specialized in plant and animal exchange and in acclimatization both decreased and increased biodiversity. Gorse, a tough fire-resistant evergreen brought to New Zealand and Australia from Western Europe as a wind and fire break, proved highly invasive and choked off other species. Introduction of the carp from Germany to Nebraska, according to one historian, was "on par with the destruction of the buffalo ... one of the most significant, federally provoked environmental catastrophes in the United States."[34] By contrast, new connections also spawned an ever-widening array of adaptations and gave rise to new horticultural aesthetics and new commercial products. American horticulturalists domesticated a scraggly plant from Mexico and renamed it the poinsettia after the American diplomat who had acquired it. Varieties of reddish poinsettia plants, perfected by a German-American grower and his Hungarian-born horticulturalist in California, became a Christmas-season phenomenon. An American dryland plant specialist, Thomas Kearney, adapted Egyptian cotton to cultivation in the deserts of California and Arizona to produce the "Pima" cotton (named for the Pima Indians who lived near Kearney's research station outside of Yuma) that became so widely used in the early twentieth century. The experimental station run by Louis Trabut at Rouiba, Algeria, forged connections with US plant breeders to help adapt figs and dates for growing in California and sisal plants for use in the dry lands of Algeria.[35]

Some collections followed networks of empire and allied themselves to specific imperial projects. Kew Gardens, for example, became one of the premier sites of botanical collection and experimentation.[36] The curators at Kew together with the Horticultural Society of London created an unrivaled collection of plants from China by sending expeditions into the hinterlands from the colonial garden in Hong Kong. (Specimens of Chinese tea plants became the basis for tea plantations in India.) Kew also established relationships with botanical stations throughout the empire, with Colonel David Prain becoming director of Kew after having been superintendent of the Calcutta Botanic Gardens, an important research center of tropical botany, and one of the authors of the thirty-seven-volume botanical survey of the empire.[37] Kew became not only a collector but also a disseminator: between 1863 and 1872, Kew sent over eight thousand plants a year abroad. And the professionals at Kew established their preeminence over the methodology and taxonomy of botanical classification into species.[38]

Botany, of course, had been an adjunct to medicine even before it became an adjunct to commerce. Kew tried to play a key role in facilitating the production of quinine, which was found to be effective against malaria and could, therefore, facilitate European expansion into Africa and elsewhere. In the early nineteenth century, Peru had tried to outlaw the export of the cinchona seeds and saplings that produced quinine, but smugglers managed to circumvent restrictions. A race to develop effective cinchona plants that could be grown in colonial plantations shadowed the larger late-nineteenth-century "Great Game" for empire. In this contest, Kew's mission was clearly imperial, as the garden's transnational network allied with the British state to develop this all-important tool.

Both in its medicinal and in its commercial aspects, the global trade in quinine helped strengthen imperial power. Half of the quinine production in Bengal, for example, went to the Governments Medical Stores, and in Madras almost all of it did. The royal near-monopoly on this vital drug greatly enhanced the leverage of the British Raj.[39] British successes in quinine cultivation, however, paled in comparison to the Dutch. More successful than Kew in nurturing plantation-adaptable cultivars, the Dutch developed quinine as a lucrative crop in their East Indies colonial possessions. By the 1930s, Dutch plantations in Java produced most of the world's quinine. Within a generation, the Peruvian plant had given rise to a global commodity chain upon which all kinds of imperial and transnational interactions depended.

Other botanical gardens besides Kew also refined methods of plant collection and made the previously strange more familiar. For example, the German-Russian Carl Maximowicz, a botanist who traveled around the world and then focused on studying the flora of Japan during the 1860s, became head of the Botanical Garden of St. Petersburg in 1869. From this position he gained the funds to employ teams of Japanese collectors to develop the institution's collection, the oldest and most prominent botanical garden in Russia.

If some gardens represented imperial interest, however, other collections emerged less from any alliance with a nation-state or empire and more from a desire to advance specific commercial, civic, or scientific projects. A brisk exchange of plants among arid regions in Australia,

Hawaii, South Africa, California, and elsewhere, for example, transformed local horticultural practices in all of these places and stimulated local adaptors to create botanical collections as a way of publicizing newly available species. Civic boosters in turn-of-the-century San Diego established Balboa Park, where the irrepressible horticulturalist Kate Sessions plotted out an array of plant borrowings that she hoped would transform the look of southern California while still being sensitive to its arid climate. Huntington Library and Gardens, established by Los Angeles railway magnate and developer Henry E. Huntington in the early twentieth century, developed a famed Desert Garden, one of the oldest collections of cacti and succulents brought from trips to Central and South America and elsewhere. A British naturalist gathered one of the most impressive private collections of orchids, bromeliads, and palms at his Jardín Botánico Lankester in Costa Rica in the 1940s. Improvements in transportation and horticultural practices allowed many private nurseries, now both famous and forgotten, to make a business in the global marketing of seeds and exotic plants, especially flowers. During the 1920s to 1940s, British plant hunter Frank Kingdon-Ward captivated readers with accounts of his exploits. His widely selling *Plant Hunting on the Edge of the World* (1930) celebrated the ways in which brave plant collectors discovered strange and exotic lands and tamed their natural offerings into familiar taxonomies and potential products. Plant prospecting and acclimatization could provide parables of the interconnected world order and its hierarchies.

Plant collection and distribution depended on global collaborations that bridged cultures and on establishment of interactive networks. Local people, after all, held access to information on the whereabouts, the characteristics, the possible propagation techniques, and potential uses of plants that might be unfamiliar to outside collectors. Even if the cultural traditions within which plants were understood seemed haphazard and unsystematic to those schooled in European taxonomies, the local oral or written descriptions could prove invaluable.

British collectors who roamed the interior of China in the late nineteenth century, for example, complained about, but always used, Chinese gazetteers. Most hired Chinese collectors to assist them in areas that could turn hostile to Western foreigners. If Orientalist assumptions inflected the writings of Western collectors, their observations and practices also disrupted easy generalizations. The multiethnicity of China's regions, the deals that had to be negotiated in different locations, the ways in which even the presumed appropriation of knowledge forced hybridization—all illuminate the creation of co-productive global networks being born within the structures of unequal power.[40]

Collecting Animals

In this age of connectivity, collecting and displaying animals also expanded rapidly. Although traveling menageries of exotic animals had provided common forms of entertainment and entrepreneurial activity for centuries, animal collections in zoological parks eclipsed the appeal of menageries in the latter half of the nineteenth century, and new "scientific" zoos became expressions of the comprehensive, systematic, and global collecting that characterized the age.

Jean Delacour exemplified the transnational networks forged through collecting. He created what many regarded as the finest private zoo in the world, and his career illustrates the shift of zoos from private collections to public institutions. Especially renowned as a collector of rare birds, Delacour assembled an array of noncarnivorous animals, such as gibbons, gazelles, kangaroos, flamingos, and cranes, on his estate, Château Clères in Normandy. Owning perhaps five hundred different species of birds, he erected aviaries for smaller birds and took special care of the most rare. On his annual expeditions between 1922 to the late 1930s, especially to tropical lands, he gathered live specimens and distributed them to other collectors—some thirty thousand birds and eight thousand mammals were divided among Paris, London, and New York. Delacour published the most significant handbooks on birds for Southeast Asia and elsewhere. In 1939, on the eve of World War II, his estate was burned, and he fled to New York to work for the Bronx Zoo, the American Museum of Natural History, and eventually the Los Angeles Museum. After World War II, he labored to restore his chateau and zoological park at Clères and, upon his death, left it to the state of France.[41] Zoological parks, and aquariums, like world's fairs, natural history museums, and botanical gardens, sprang from a transnational exchange of expertise, even as they were also propelled by national, local, or personal pride in their construction.

Zoos spread as part of the transition from a rural, agricultural world to an urban, industrial one. They grew fastest in countries caught up in these changes. By 1903 a guidebook to Europe could describe sixteen zoological gardens in Germany, four in Britain, and four in France; zoos had opened also in Antwerp, Amsterdam, and Rotterdam. Under the leadership of the Bengali scientist Ram Brahma Sanyal, the Calcutta Zoological Gardens distinguished itself both in its animal displays and its research. The first zoo in the United States, whose founders looked to European models, opened in 1874 in Philadelphia. Many other US cities followed—Kansas City, Baltimore, Providence, St. Louis, St. Paul—as civic boosters incorporated zoos along with botanical gardens into designs for new municipal parks. An official National Zoological Garden opened in Pretoria in 1916. In Europe and elsewhere, zoos often emerged from private collections (as in Delacour's case) sustained by private patronage, while in the United States they emerged from civic movements to create public parks. World's fairs began to add zoos, and these sometimes became permanent. The 1931 exhibition in Paris that housed a display of exotic animals, for example, became the basis for the zoo in the park of Vincennes. In the early twentieth century, professional zoos that tried to

"Paradise," a wildlife panorama constructed for Carl Hagenbeck's Tierpark outside of Hamburg, 1908. Opened one year earlier, the Tierpark showed animals (and often people) in extravagant, "realistic" settings and influenced the look of zoos throughout the world. (Hagenbeck-Archiv, Tierpark Hagenbeck)

project a conservationist mission could be found throughout the world.[42]

Such collections turned animals into representations of both the interconnectivity of the globe and its regional diversities. Carl Hagenbeck's famous Tier-park that opened outside of Hamburg in the early twentieth century advanced new models, influential internationally, of intertwining botanical gardens, natural history displays, and animal exhibits to create broad representations of other parts of the world. Using rows of tiered enclosures in which moats and screens remained invisible to the public, the Tierpark offered an African and an Arctic "panorama" featuring animals in their "natural" habitat. After the opening of Hagenbeck's sensational exhibits in 1907, visual simulations of natural landscapes through panoramas and other features became the obligatory backdrops for animal collections and for the displays of humans *(Völkerschauen)* that Hagenbeck also featured.

Infused with the age's mania for taxonomy and distinguishing themselves from the menageries of an earlier era, zoos claimed the status of scientific displays that would encourage research and educate the public in biology and natural history. In fact, their displays increasingly offered the veneer of science more than its substance. According to the analysis of Eric Baratay and Elisabeth Hardouin-Fugier, the argument for the scientific utility of zoos was widely advanced, but actually zoos were far outpaced in scientific achievement by universities and museum laboratories.[43]

Zoos struggled to balance science with spectacle. One elephant, after all, would attract more visitors than even the most complete and careful array of small mammals. Urban dwellers had become accustomed to being entertained by circus animals, traveling menageries, and exotic creatures in pubs and public parks. World's fairs also conditioned expectations of exotic sensationalism. Zoos had to compete, and the tension between scientific education and audience appeal was difficult to manage. Albert Geoffroy Saint-Hilaire, director of Paris's Jardin d'Acclimatation in the late nineteenth century, tried to advance the scientific agenda that his father and grandfather had pursued but felt forced, when faced with bankruptcy, to add sensational ethnographic exhibitions—of Nubians, Eskimos, Argentine gauchos, and dwarfs whom he named the "kingdom of Lilliput." Ota Benga, an African Pygmy, was exhibited at the Bronx Zoo briefly in 1906, but zoo directors generally tried to avoid the ethnographic displays of live people that had become so popular on world's fair midways. Most zoos never resorted to the diving horses and water-sliding elephants featured at Coney Island and other amusement parks, but zoos nevertheless steered a wobbly course between science and showmanship. When the National Zoo of the United States was established in 1889, it proclaimed its goals as both "the advancement of science" and "the recreation of the people."[44]

Zoos were often supported, in part, by visitors' fees, and one way that they attracted audiences was by simulating familiar miniworlds. They did this in a number of ways. Projecting a politics of hierarchy, zoological collections positioned the collector and audience as master over all creatures—the outrageously exotic and the commonplace, the huge and the tiny, the fearsome and the timid. They structured memorable, if biologically erroneous, lessons about social hierarchy. The lion, for example, was the "king" of beasts. They often projected a sentimentalized view of animals. Largely urban zoo-goers, after all, had little direct experience with animals and found them most interesting when they were anthropomorphized. Cages and confines became larger so they could house animals in "families" whose activities were then described to match the prevailing assumptions about human emotions and gender roles.

The explosion of zoos, large and small, created a surge in demand for "exotic" animals (zoos of the period seldom contained common farm animals). In response, dense transnational networks formed to facilitate trade in animals from distant lands, a trade that depended heavily on the growth of commercial infrastructure, such as the Suez Canal, and on colonial power. Such networks included entrepreneurs, shipping companies, local administrators, and local procurers who brokered trades, found reliable assistants, and mediated cultural misunderstandings of all kinds.

Hamburg became one of the most important nodes for animal collecting. Carl Hagenbeck, whose father had been a fishmonger in that city, began to buy animals to build his local menagerie while still a teenager and quickly branched out to broker animals throughout the world. Teaming up with some Italian explorers in the 1860s, he arranged a huge shipment of African wildlife—elephants, giraffes, ostriches, lions, hyenas—that attracted widespread publicity and made him famous. By the mid-1880s he and his family had orchestrated the collection and dispersion of over a thousand lions, three hundred camels, one hundred and fifty giraffes, tens of thousands of moneys and birds, and thousands of reptiles. His animal business became part of a larger entertainment empire that included traveling circuses and ethnographic exhibits as well as his Tierpark, which opened in 1907 and became celebrated for its "natural" settings with background panoramas.[45] In his animal-trade business, Hagenbeck also supplied the kinds of "curious" human specimens he displayed in his own circuses and zoo in Hamburg. Charles Reiche, a German immigrant to New York City, set up a similar animal-trade business near Hanover, contracted agents in Egypt and Ceylon, and supplied much of the US market. German animal dealers, in fact, dominated the global wildlife trade until World War I.[46]

After the Great War the German networks began to fall apart. Germany lost its colonies; its shipping companies suffered from the war; hoof-and-mouth disease prompted new regulations on animal importation. The expansion of demand by private collectors, amusement venues, and zoos, however, continued. A new generation of animal collectors, especially the American Frank Buck, turned collecting into a celebrity career. Buck capitalized on the decline of the German networks and spent his career gathering animals from South Asia and the East Indies. Zoos also got directly into the act, as animal-hunting expeditions brought favorable publicity. The US National Zoo's director, William M. Mann, himself headed expeditions to collect animals in Tanganyika, the Dutch East Indies, and Liberia. Seeking both publicity and animals, however, Mann's trips mainly garnered the former. On the trip to Batavia (now Jakarta), his wife's journal recorded that the group found "almost as many animal collectors in towns as animals."[47]

One of the people Mann hired in Borneo, Liang Gaddi Sang, exemplifies the global nature of animal collecting. Born in Borneo but living mostly in Siam, Gaddi was employed at various times by the governments of Malay and Siam, the US Fish Commissioner, the Crown Prince Leopold of Belgium, and the British Museum.[48]

The proliferation of zoos and the huge global trade in birds, mammals, and fish destroyed living creatures at an almost incomprehensible rate. To collector networks, natural abundance seemed limitless. If four animals died for every one successfully transported for display (and many more died once they entered their permanent confinements), most animal traders calculated only the financial loss. In fact, the huge decline in populations of certain birds and mammals could even provide new justifications for zoos, which began to emphasize preservation despite the appalling death rates that the animal trade and confinement in most zoos produced.

As the transnational circuits of animal collectors and traders became more ruthlessly efficient and threatened certain species, they generated global organizations aimed at curbing abuses. The numbers of transnational groups and agreements devoted to preservation multiplied, especially in those very countries whose citizens were most active in the destruction. During the nineteenth century, animal protection societies grew in many European and American cities, and their leaders became part of a transnational network of reformers, some of whom also embraced vegetarianism and extended their animal protection societies into colonial areas. In 1903 British and American naturalists established the Society for the Preservation of the Wild Fauna of the Empire to foster preservation in Africa. T. Gilbert Pearson, a founder of the National Audubon Society, formed the International Council for Bird Preservation in London in 1922.[49] A 1930 international convention prohibited killing certain kinds of whales, and in 1933 a Convention Relative to the Preservation of Fauna and Flora in Their Natural State was adopted.

The transnational circulation of ideas about natural preservation, however, also intertwined with discourses of nation, empire, and race.

Hunters and hikers concerned with maintaining vigorous lifestyles often spearheaded efforts to establish game reserves and national parks in order to regularize rules of use. In Africa, India, and elsewhere in the colonial world, such reserves turned indigenous hunters into "poachers" on European-controlled hunting lands. In these areas, animal hunting became an important recreation for imperial officials, who collected personal trophies or built collections for imperial natural history museums. Preservation therefore often had an adverse effect on the self-sufficiency of indigenous peoples and particularly on their nutrition. Preservationists frequently invoked their special interest in the advancement of science. After considerable international pressure to protect the dwindling gorilla population and enable the work of scientific expeditions, for example, King Albert of Belgium established in the Congo in 1925 the National Park Albert, the first national park in Africa. In colonial areas, facilitating hunting and science often went hand in hand with racial restriction.

Romanticized attachments to natural settings and animals commonly constructed preservation efforts as necessary to promote national and racial destiny. In the early twentieth century in California, Germany, South Africa, and elsewhere, eugenic societies and preservationists had overlapping constituencies. The creation of national parks in Africa provides an example. Although game reserves had been established in South Africa before World War I, the upsurge of Afrikaner nationalism after the war spurred new aesthetic and practical arguments for the creation of a larger national park. Kruger National Park, which restricted use by black Africans, was created in 1926 as a white space in which white tourists could reimagine and nostalgically celebrate their ancestors' settlement of the wildlife-rich territory.[50]

Collectors and exhibitors devised fairs, museums, gardens, and zoos as nodes that they hoped might, in some tangible form, represent "the world" to viewers. Often these forms of collecting blurred together. Fairs featured museums, zoos, and gardens that sometimes became more permanent institutions. Zoos grew to feature gardens, and gardens added zoos. All exhibitions claimed to advance science, instruct visitors about the world, and entertain, even though such goals often ran at cross-purposes. Many of the conventions developed in these exhibitions also intersected with the worlds of amusement parks, movies, and popular fiction. Such collections, preponderant in the West but following networks of imperial power and trade into many other areas of the world, attempted to establish categories, to universalize knowledge, and thus to control representation. Constructed within imperial and evolutionary visions of the world, they often projected interlocking sets of hierarchies: "Civilized" Europeans who embraced science, machinery, and progress stood in evolutionary progression over primitives who would slowly change or die. The rational order imposed within gardens tamed nature's apparent anarchy. Humans stood as the masters of the animal world.

Still, networks forged by acts of collecting had more complex characteristics than simply the production of hegemonies. Collectors came from all kinds of origins and roamed the world out of all sorts of personal and sponsored motivations. Collections, after all, could be assembled in diverse places, and they could travel and change over time. Even fairs, static in time and place, involved dense webs of exchange. People, plants, animals, objects, and ideas were all on the move and, perhaps, on the move again. Adventurers, wealthy patrons, eccentrics, corporate enterprises, diverse institutes, and governments relied on global exchanges to produce their assemblages. Collecting and displaying thus involved not only dominion but myriad interactions that, on many levels, shrunk the world.

⌒

These institutions of display—fairs, museums, botanical and zoological gardens—illustrate the mutually constitutive discourses of nation, empire, and world. Imperial and national rivalries and glory propelled institutions and elites not just to draw from but also to outperform their peers. But each node of exhibition and collection took shape within and depended upon transnational circuits of expertise and acquisition. Exhibitionary nodes also, as has been seen, combined rational classification with spectacle. They drew from the latest of scientific knowledge and technological invention but merged these wonders into the emotional pleasures honed in amusement parks. Great halls exemplifying hierarchies of classification and the disciplinary structures of professionalism were interspersed with exotic temptations projecting the unstable meanings and ambiguities compatible with porous social formations. Both reason and spectacle proved central to the cultural circulations that produced new global imaginaries. No single projection could necessarily contain or control the cacophony of cultural meanings that became a feature of the era.

CHAPTER FOUR

Circuits of Expertise

The collection of data and the sharing of technical expertise, so important to exhibitions, were hallmarks of the transnational professional associations that emerged in this era. The new professionals of the late nineteenth century generally embraced a scientific, positivistic faith: if sufficient data on a particular question could be collected, the information could then be ordered, analyzed, and used to solve problems in the natural and social worlds. In this great task, the divisions of religion, ideology, and even national loyalties might be put aside as specialists constructed common understandings of statistics and science. Nature might be engineered for human benefit; the social sphere might be reordered to eliminate gross injustice; epidemic disease might be eradicated. The new professionals, who energetically worked to build transnational epistemic communities, generally embraced the idea that global evolutionary progress could be guided by the authority of their expertise.

In the late nineteenth century, international congresses of several scientific disciplines (mathematics, statistics, chemistry, philosophy) began to meet, and many launched projects to compile international catalogs or bibliographies. At the same time, the opening of universities in Western Europe to foreign nationals contributed to transnational encounters, as did the spread of translation and publication. Through these professional connections, specializations in old and new disciplinary categories reordered the sciences, social sciences, and humanities.

Those who constructed circuits of expert knowledge claimed they could assemble observations from around the globe and extend their expertise by using far-flung networks in which localized "facts" could be compared, tested, confirmed, and connected together. Experts in the colonizing West often appeared to dominate the circuitry, but many leaders and intellectuals throughout the world also embraced ideas about improvement through science and expertise. The allure of transnational science emerged partly out of self-defense against more technically advanced opponents and partly from fascination with the idea of a universal scientific project.

Many governments encouraged their citizens to embrace transnational science and technology. The Great Reforms of Tsar Alexander II in Russia during the 1860s and 1870s sought to wed Russian nationalism to Europeanization, and midcentury Ottoman rulers also launched Tanzimat, a modernization campaign centered on military strength but also assuming broader scope. The Meiji government in Japan embraced the introduction of Western science and sent its famed forty-eight-person commission led by Iwakura Tomomi to visit the United States and the major cities of Europe during 1871–1873. This Iwakura mission produced sixty-eight volumes of diaries, documents, commentaries, and special reports designed to assess practices in the West and their applications to Japan. In China after the Taiping Rebellion, the Qing rulers and educated elites encouraged translations of basic scientific texts, such as Joseph Edkins's *Primers for Science Studies* (1886), later published as *Primers of Western Learning* (1898).[1] King Chulalongkorn of Siam embraced administrative and architectural Westernization. The Porfiriato in Mexico had its ruling elite of *científicos*. The positivists who shaped the Brazilian republic in 1891 placed the motto "Ordem e Progresso" (Order and Progress) on the country's new flag. The Japanese victory in the Russo-Japanese War of 1905 held global significance to those who aspired to resist or best Europeans through technological acquisition and adaptation. In the interwar era, nationalist leaders in India, Korea, and elsewhere sought to blend Western science and technology with their distinctive heritages. Build-

A Japanese rendering of the departure from Yokohama to the United States of Japan's first extensive foreign mission, headed by Prince Iwakura Tomomi, Ambassador Extraordinary and Plenipotentiary, in 1871. Iwakura's mission, which was gone for nearly two years and studied practices that might help Japan to modernize, visited cities in the United States, Western Europe, Russia, Egypt, South and Southeast Asia, and China. (Private Collection/The Bridgeman Art Library)

ing upon and learning from transnational communities of expertise was a global phenomenon—a "shared developmentalist project" that transcended discursive boundaries of East versus West and blurred lines between programs that could be called capitalist, corporate, socialist, statist, or some version of "national strengthening."[2]

As these examples suggest, there was a tension between transnational professionalism and national or imperial goals. Disciplinary specialization did not rule out national distinctions, and different national groups sought recognition for their particular models in the production and dissemination of knowledge. The tensions of nationalism, however, could be mediated through the circuits of experts who, even if anchored in national institutions and different cultural styles, might study in foreign universities, travel to world congresses, and exchange views through international journals. The effects of such mediating circuits were neither predictable nor uniform. As Peter Wagner writes, "Transnational orientations could take the form of intellectual interaction, either to widen and refocus debates, or to gain a stronger position for an individual approach within the national field."[3]

Transnational epistemic communities thus could undermine national projects through hybrid borrowing or reinforce them through the hardening of differences—or they could do both at once. Louis Pasteur's breakthroughs in bacteriology, for example, boosted French national prestige, facilitated its colonial strategy, and fostered transnational research networks. As in other realms of interaction, claims to universality and to national and imperial distinctiveness often fit together. Indeed, a country's highest expression of nationalism often arose from the claims to universality embedded in its scholarly discourses.

Even as scientists imagined globalized circuits of knowledge, they constructed discourses of difference. Michael Adas has shown how in the West the use of machinery came to be an indicator of the "measure of men," the most important indicator that supposedly marked the superiority of the West over the rest. Africans, for example, were widely represented as incapable of developing a technological civilization, and Westerners who found archeological evidence of massive architectural and engineering feats, as in present day Zimbabwe, wrongly attributed such ruins to the influence of outsiders. One of the most common tropes in Western imperialist accounts involved showing some small wonder of technology (a rifle, a phonograph, a camera) to preindustrial people and describing their astonishment.[4] The acquisition of Western science and technology became an important marker of progress in the narrative that dominated professionalism.

Western historians, themselves privileging scientific and technological measures as the truest gauge of human achievement, once took for granted that modern knowledge had begun in the West and had then diffused into "backward" regions. This story of the spread of enlightenment was itself related to justifications for the colonial project.

Postcolonial critique has, however, challenged such premises. In their counternarratives, some scholars have represented networks of science and technical expertise as purveyors of abstracted and often inappropriate "imperial knowledge" that vied with more contextual and localized knowledge. Such scholarship may imply a global/local dichotomy in which the global was the imperial enemy of the local.

Other postcolonial scholars, however, have emphasized "coproduction" between the transnational and local realms. They argue that even in a world of vastly unequal power and of racial and imperial hierarchies, good science depended on co-constructed circuits that could accommodate the experimentation, comparison, and collaboration that transnational connections facilitated.[5] As participants in building circuits of expertise on radio waves, for example, the Bengali scientist J. C. Bose, the Italian inventor Guglielmo Marconi, and the Serbian-American Nikola Tesla were all important to the late nineteenth-century transnational breakthroughs in research.

This chapter builds on the framework of coproduction. If circuits of knowledge often projected imperial and hierarchical assumptions, localized interactions also altered both findings and implementations. Even as scientists tended to endorse the idea of a common transnational language and methodology, differentiated and coproduced expressions on the ground often reshaped their sense of commonalities. While keeping in mind asymmetries of power when analyzing epistemic currents, then, the discussion that follows emphasizes the themes of coproduction and differentiated commonalities.[6]

Scientists, Surveyors, and Engineers

In 1870 a proponent of the idea that the earth was flat bet five hundred pounds sterling that no one could scientifically prove the earth's curvature in a body of water. British naturalist and professional surveyor Alfred Russel Wallace rose to the challenge. He set up an experiment along six miles of the Bedford Level, in Norfolk, demonstrated a discrepancy in heights of objects at each end, and was judged the winner. The outcome, however, only further energized the flat-earth proponent, who denounced and sued Wallace for years into the future.[7] Flat-earthers, who retained a transnational group of supporters, could not accept the world as a globe, despite the repetition of this "Bedford Level Experiment" in many other places on into the twentieth century.

The theory of a round earth, of course, had predated Columbus's voyage, and one might have expected that the famous explorations of the seventeenth and eighteenth centuries would have worn down beliefs about a flat earth. But scientific revisions of deeply rooted "truths" about the makeup of the world never gain easy acceptance.

The global spread of new scientific methods created backlash and uncertainty everywhere. What might be the implications for humans of a round earth? Or of the accumulating evidence confirming an evolutionary view of biology, another view with which Wallace was associated? Could science (with its view of how the earth and its creatures slowly evolved over far more than seven days) be reconciled with the

Bible or the Quran or other spiritual systems? Despite the storms of controversy raised by such questions, prevalent even (or especially) in those areas in the forefront of scientific discovery, confidence about the reliability of scientific technique spread rapidly. Scientists (the word *scientist* was coined in the 1830s and widely used by the late nineteenth century) created webs of understandings and techniques that sought to corral the world's natural systems into arenas of specialized knowledge tamed for human use. Guided by emerging professional standards and goaded by naysayers, expertise became transnational.

To comprehend the earth in scientific terms required extensive mapping and surveying with scientific techniques such as Wallace had employed. Although the mapping of trade routes had long been commonplace, the latter half of the nineteenth century brought precision mapping on a different scale than before. In this period, experts explored and surveyed the last remaining unmapped areas of the world in the name of science and usually of empire. New techniques of triangulation produced very large-scale field surveys, and such scientific surveys often included the accumulation of detailed data on the people, animals, plants, and natural features of a region.

The scientific expeditions that surveyed and described the remaining "unknown" world produced heroic figures, especially in those national states and empires that might reap benefits. Britain's Great Trigonometrical Survey of India, for example, became one of the celebrated attempts of the early nineteenth century to create a vast archive of knowledge for imperial purposes. Then, between 1863 and 1885, Britain hired native Indians to measure and map the million-and-and half square miles of the trans-Himalayan region. Code-named "pundits," these mappers took the disguise of pilgrims and risked their lives and health to record accurate measurements of the territory, which technically belonged to China. On his first surveying trip, Nain Singh walked twelve hundred miles recording his measured steps by using specially constructed rosary beads; he subsequently won international fame and awards from the Royal Geographical Society. Pundit Sarat Chandra Das wrote two books and inspired the character of Hurree Chunder Mookerjee in *Kim,* Rudyard Kipling's famous novel about the Great Game in Central Asia. The pundit known as Kinthup (or K.P.) returned to India after four years of harrowing danger, during which he and his colleagues mapped the course of the Brahmaputra from its source into India. Although their activities had remained secret during the mapping, these and other pundits soon became highly acclaimed because their technical contributions had significantly enhanced survey techniques and their endurance epitomized imperial greatness.

European expeditions into sub-Saharan Africa also took advantage of local expertise. In trying to settle a dispute over the origin of the Nile, for example, Richard Francis Burton relied upon Arab informants while his rival John Hanning Speke relied on Ugandans. Their competition erupted into high drama when Speke shot himself in advance of a public showdown with Burton. Henry Morton Stanley's attempt to settle this controversy would explode into one of the most sensational stories of the late nineteenth century.[8]

Land surveys and scientific commissions proliferated in the late nineteenth century, as the ambitions of national states intertwined with the discourses of expertise that sought to make the whole world legible. Only governments could afford the expense that extensive triangulations entailed, and only national states had the compelling interest in developing systematic and uniform statistical information. Both Russia and the United States, for example, commissioned scientific surveys to map and consolidate knowledge about their inland empires. John Wesley Powell, who would later serve as director of the US Geological Survey, famously explored the Colorado River and Grand Canyon in the 1860s. Various US biological surveys, which preceded the creation of the Fish and Wildlife Service Bureau in 1939, were likewise guided by scientific agendas. Russian surveyors gathered information on Siberia, as well as bordering lands in Central Asia and Tibet. Napoleon III created the Scientific Commission of Mexico to "lift up this unknown world and deliver it from chaos." This commission (1864–1867), which coincided with the ill-fated French attempt to establish an empire in Mexico under Maximilian, floundered in its extravagant ambitions but did issue a lavish sixteen-volume report along with important reference works on the botany and zoology of Mexico. Mapping the most inaccessible parts of the world became "global sport in both Norway and Sweden," as competing explorers ventured north of Siberia across the Northeast Passage, north of Canada across the Northwest Passage, into Central Asia, and also entered the race to the South Pole.[9]

Colonial administration heightened the need for surveys of land and people, and each colonial power adopted some form of expert commission to collect and evaluate information on acquired territories.[10] The United States carried out extensive data collection in the Philippines after 1898. In these reports, the array of landscapes and peoples that characterized the various territories of the archipelago came to buttress the views that ranked peoples of the world into a racial hierarchy according to skin color, physical features, type of agricultural practice, and gender norms. The modernizing elites in Manila also had a stake in such surveys, as they worked to assert their own capacities for scientific administration and for larger degrees of self-governance. Even though surveys were legitimating tools of colonial states, they often attracted help from subjects who were engaged in their own nation-building and career-enhancing projects.[11]

International agreements such as the many boundary-drawing treaties of this period—for example, the Anglo-Afghan Treaty of 1875, the Canadian-US agreements, and the post–World War I territorial settlements made at Versailles—also depended on more accurate, common maps. The idea that the entire world could be "known" provided a strong pillar not only of the age's confidence in measurement but also of the conviction that the world, through science, might converge into a unified, if hierarchically ordered, whole. Mapping projects provide clear examples of how nationalism, imperialism, and transnationalism often stood not in opposition but as codependents.

As empty spaces on world maps became filled and calibrated, the history of humankind through archeology likewise became a field for global, rather than simply local, knowledge. More precisely, local knowledge interacted with and helped to shape emerging transnational disciplinary practices. German archeologists were especially important in this late nineteenth-century development. Alexander Conze became the first to include photography in reports of archaeological excavation; Carl Humann, an important developer of scientific techniques of excavation, worked throughout the Ottoman Empire and cooperated with archeologist Osman Hamdi Bey, founder of the Istanbul Archeology Museum. Teobert Maler, born of German parents, came to Mexico with an Austrian army supporting Maximilian, stayed to become a citizen of Mexico, conducted a survey of Palenque for Harvard's Peabody Museum, and devoted his life to archeological study of the Mayan civilization. Heinrich Schliemann, who had traveled to California and made a fortune in banking during the Gold Rush, conducted significant but also highly sensationalized digs to uncover the sites of Homer's Troy. In the decades before World War I, Germans developed a keen interest in the Bible as a historical text and, consequently, in Middle Eastern archeology.[12] Worldly scientists illuminated natural and human history, but their activities also often led to the plundering of local sites, the alienation of artifacts, geopolitical positioning, and even hucksterism in the name of science. The careers of these German explorer-scientists suggest the globality of this new age of investigation, as well as the uneven pace of identifying professionalized disciplinary practices.

Such examples tend to confirm that surveying and archeological missions often bent scientific knowledge toward the purpose of Westerners. Naming is one way of claiming; controlling representation (in geographic space as well as in historical time) is the most profound form of power. Still, the new cultures of professionalism were not simply one-way impositions. Building transnational circuits of knowledge rested on local expertise and on various degrees of coproduction. Moreover, globe-trotting professionals might become ever more cosmopolitan as they cultivated their abilities to thrive in unfamiliar terrain or to succeed as cultural mediators.

Engineering, often considered to be applied science, became one of the most hallowed professions in this instrumentalist age. Sandford Fleming, a Canadian born in Scotland who was a member of over seventy international societies, a surveyor and mapmaker, a champion of the Prime Meridian reform movement, and a facilitator of the transoceanic cable line across the Pacific, saw his profession of engineering as a neutral peacemaker in the social turbulence of the industrial era. In 1876 he wrote that engineers were not usually "gifted with many words" but that they did battle against "nature in her wild state" in order to "smooth the path on which others are to tread." "It is their privilege to stand between these two great forces, capital and labour, and by acting justly at all times between employer and the employed, they may hope to command the respect of those above them equally with those under them."[13] Moreover, the amazing technical feats associated with construction of the Suez Canal in the 1860s and the Panama Canal in the early twentieth century became emblematic of the claim that engineering could draw the world geographically closer together. Civil engineers working on projects such as canals, roads, and bridges were among the most active professionals to form transnational networks that were both personal and professional.

Although this ideal of the politically neutral engineer skilled in universally useful techniques circulated widely, many of the huge turn-of-the-century projects employed laboring people in ways that could scarcely "command respect" from all. The building of the Panama Canal, for example, orchestrated one of the largest, most global labor mobilizations in modern history. With jobs and compensation scales arranged according to race and nationality (West Indians received the most perilous assignments for the lowest pay), the tens of thousands of imported workers from every continent paid a huge, generally overlooked price in life and limb, even as engineers reveled in accolades. Other colonial construction projects assembled similarly global workforces, not to serve the uplifting goals so often proclaimed in professional circles but to drive down costs in the increasingly globalized labor market.[14]

As engineers did battle against "wild nature" and sometimes against cadres of laborers, their efforts were almost always justified within an entangled rationale linking service to the world with service to empire and nation. The case of India provides an example. Under the rule of both the East India Company (EIC) and then the British crown, India became a laboratory for experiments in the application of scientific and technical expertise. The construction of canals, irrigation works (for agriculture), and railroads was central to the British conception of imperial development, yet this transportation infrastructure necessitated large numbers of civil engineers who could develop methods suitable to local conditions. Before the EIC relinquished its rule of India to the crown in 1858, it had established engineering colleges at Mumbai (Bombay), Roorkee, Calcutta, Roona, and Madras. The heavy emphasis on state-directed engineering projects accelerated in the latter half of the nineteenth century (an emphasis that ironically emerged simultaneously with Britain's highly visible public promotion of laissez-faire theories). The Famine Commission of 1880 especially pressed for a range of applied specialists, operating on the village level, and suggested that their success would be a test of imperial benevolence. After more end-of-the-century famines, the new viceroy, George Curzon, proclaimed that the advancement of practical science would be his highest priority, and he created a Board of Scientific Advice that lasted until 1924. The model of state-sponsored engineering schools and ambitious projects, pioneered in India, came to be replicated in Britain itself and elsewhere in the empire. Indian graduates became part of a broad transnational network of experts from everywhere on the globe who shared ideas about technical training and infrastructure development.[15]

Britain, the United States, France, and Germany each adopted somewhat different models for the training, credentialing, and employment of engineers. More important than such differences, however, was the proliferation throughout Europe and colonial areas of technical schools, each with specializations relevant to the respective extractive and industrial strengths of each area. National and imperial rivalry thus fueled the transnational spread and exchange of technical practices. Building canals and railway beds, regulating river flow, and draining wetlands for agriculture all fit the export-oriented goals of colonial powers and often fit within the modernizing visions of elites outside of Europe as well. By the early 1880s, for example, most irrigation engineers in Egypt were Egyptians schooled in the techniques of the École Polytechnique in France, and the surplus of Egyptian-trained experts served throughout the region for decades.[16]

China's technical education likewise arose within the context of both transnational networks of expertise and nation-building imperatives. The Chinese "self-strengthening" movement, launched after the second Opium War, emphasized military technology, engineering, and basic science. The Fuzhou Naval Yard, one of the most important industrial sites in late-Qing China, hired foreigners to teach many of the technical courses related to ship building. Similarly, the expansion of its Jiangnan Arsenal, which focused on training related to technology and machinery, by 1892 produced forty-seven kinds of machinery under the supervision of foreign technicians and successfully produced rapid-firing machine guns for China's coastal defense. New schools, encouraged by the Chinese government, embraced Western science and emphasized engineering, even as increasingly more Chinese students also studied abroad. Although China's defense industries faltered in the face of the country's declining resources and defeat in wars, they exemplify how important access to transnational networks of experts became in helping to determine which countries flourished and which floundered in the late nineteenth century. In the late 1920s and early 1930s the Nationalist government in China worked with German experts to try to shift industrial infrastructure away from treaty ports to presumably less vulnerable interior locations, but this program also stalled as war approached.[17]

Japanese scientists worked very successfully to join transnational scientific circles. Self-confidently embracing attributes of modernity, the state promoted participation in technical and professional conferences, issued the extensive reports of the Iwakura mission, and sponsored student study outside of Japan. Japan's scientists made special contributions to the science of seismology, among other fields.[18] Japan's modernizers and scientists did not regard such transnational participation as Westernization, because they sought to import Western practices not as a coherent entity but as piecemeal adaptations. The newspaper *Nihon,* published on the day the new Japanese constitution was announced in 1889, stated, "We esteem Western science, economics and industry. These, however, ought not be adopted simply because they are Western; they ought to be adopted only if they can contribute to Japan's welfare."[19] The overlap between transnational circuits and state-building projects could hardly be better expressed.

Engineering projects often focused on controlling water resources. Hydroelectric dams proliferated in the late nineteenth century, especially in the United States, Scandinavia, and the Alps, as a result of improvements in turbines and transmission lines. An era of large-scale dam building began in earnest with the construction in 1931 of Hoover Dam, which was completed in the United States in 1936 and thought to be the largest man-made structure in the world and a marvel of modern engineering. Other monster-size dams followed: Shasta Dam in

California and Grand Coulee Dam in Washington. Meanwhile, American engineers were helping lead the construction of the Dneprostroi Dam in Ukraine, Soviet Union, in the late 1920s and early 1930s. General Electric Company manufactured the dam's first huge power generators. At the time of its construction, the Dneprostroi Dam claimed to be the largest in Europe. France completed the Kembs Dam in 1932 on the Rhine River, which had been a site for hydroelectric power since the late nineteenth century and would become thoroughly regulated by a dam-and-lock system after World War II. Uses of the Rhine (but unfortunately not its protection, until more recently) lay in the hands of engineers of the Rhine Commission, which, dating back to 1815, was the oldest multistate commission in Europe. In China, engineers for the Nationalist government, inspired by foreign models, as early as the 1920s began plans for a huge dam at Three Gorges on the Yangtze River (a plan ultimately carried out after 1989).[20]

Created under President Franklin Roosevelt's New Deal, the Tennessee Valley Authority (TVA) most fully reflected the vision of top-down planning for the kind of huge projects that technocrats everywhere began to associate with modernization and progress. The TVA married the promise of engineering a system of dams to regulate an entire river system with the hope of engineering human health and prosperity on a broad regional scale. Dams could bring both flood control for agricultural development and inexpensive electrical power for accelerated industrialization. Farmers and workers, region and nation would all supposedly benefit. The TVA model became globally influential, and in the next few decades millions of people would tour its system. TVA's head, David Lilienthal, popularized the idea that dams would bring progress to any country whose wild rivers were "waiting to be controlled by men." His writings were translated into many languages.[21] Although most of the large dam-building projects in the developing world, influenced by the TVA model, came after World War II and often with financing from the World Bank, American, Soviet,

Nazi, and other dam-building undertakings during the 1930s confirm the importance of a transnationally influential developmentalist project not necessarily tied to particular forms of national states. From the late nineteenth century on, for example, German engineers had been reshaping the Rhine, and under the Third Reich they drained marshlands to the east while also advancing ideas about reshaping both the landscape and its people. Each state, of course, manifested the commonality of water-related developmentalism in somewhat different figurations.

Despite the disruptions associated with the First World War and the waning prestige of the German academic institutions that had often taken a lead in professionalization, the interwar era became the heyday of transnational professional associations, especially in the natural sciences. Under the auspices of the International Research Council, formed in Brussels in 1919, international unions were formed for astronomy, biology, chemistry, geophysics, and physics in 1919, and for geography, radio science, mechanics, soil sciences, and microbiology in the 1920s. In 1931 the Research Council regrouped as the International Council of Scientific Unions (ICSU), headquartered in Paris, and continued to foster its networks. The Comintern also sponsored its own transnational professional circuits, the most important of which advocated the complementary scientific nature of the biological and physical sciences.

Walking the line between robust universalistic scientific communities and the hierarchies of empire seldom came easily outside of Europe. Most Indian scientists, for example, had experienced second-class status in British scientific and administrative circles. In 1876 Mahendra Lal Sircar consequently had helped launch the Indian Association for the Cultivation of Science (IACS), a group independent from colonial authority that eventually affiliated with the physics and chemistry department at Calcutta University. The group ultimately produced scientists who received global recognition, such as the 1930 Nobel Prize winner C. V. Raman, the first Asian scientist so honored. P. C. Ray, one of the great chemists of the turn of the century, who had been heavily influenced by developments in Germany, insisted in 1918 that "the Hindus had a very large hand in the cultivation of the experimental sciences" and wrote his monumental *A History of Hindu Chemistry* (1902–1909) to carefully document the scientific heritage of his nation, which remained under colonial rule.[22] Prominent Indian scientists, such as Ray's student Meghnad Saha, went on to advocate national advancement through the use of science for industrial promotion. Even when seeing science as wedded to particular national goals, however, Indian scientists such as Saha asserted the belief that science, as a transnational endeavor, should stand above particularity and draw the world together. Saha wrote that "rivalry amongst nations should give way to cooperative construction and the politician should hand over his functions to an international board of trained scientific industrialists, economists and eugenicists who would think in terms of the whole world."[23] Muslim and Hindu scientists sometimes formed distinct groups with different goals, but Rabindra Narayan Ghosh, who wrote on the use of scientific method, felt that cultural unity could be found in technological achievement. Without repudiating religious backgrounds, he taught, people could find common ground in scientific rationality.

The scientific and technical endeavors of this period were thus not necessarily Western impositions foisted on the unwilling. Although unequal and frequently in service of empire, professional circuits could generate sparks of transformative innovation from diverse locations. Ashis Nandy has suggested, for example, that the creative brilliance of Indian mathematician Srinivasa Aiyangar Ramanujan, who persistently resisted the kinds of proofs demanded by Cambridge professors and instead invoked Hindu deities as the agents for his mathematical breakthroughs, may have stemmed from the rich cultural cross-fertilization in his own life.[24] Epistemic currents, in short, became stronger as their architects became larger in number and more varied in background.

Agricultural and Forestry Sciences

The devastating waves of famine from the 1870s through the turn of the century, particularly in India and China, elicited calls for greater agricultural expertise. These "late Victorian holocausts," to use Mike Davis's term, seem linked to ways in which colonialist policies were changing both the global and the local economic orders. Still, governmental elites and agricultural experts from America and Europe generally promoted the idea that Western science and engineering were the solution, not the problem. Blind to ways in which interaction with the West could often devastate the complex social and economic networks that supported native production and land tenure systems, agronomists allied with engineers to build circuits of knowledge that promised to boost yields, control floods and erosion, and eliminate pests. George Curzon, for example, inaugurated a large number of experimental farms and agricultural colleges in India; a contingent of missionary–soil scientists from the United States went to work in China; Western hydrologists advised how to drain marshland and convert deltas in India and Southeast Asia into farms for rice export. As agricultural experts helped plantation agriculture spread throughout the world, more and more people became enmeshed in labor and commodity markets.[25]

Although Western agricultural experts in the early twentieth century generally worked to enhance the profits earned by export commodities, global networks could also facilitate an optimal mix of new and old practices to enhance self-sufficiency. In the Kigezi district of southwestern Uganda, unlike in much of the colonial world, local farmers rejected colonial land policies and cash cropping yet adapted new soil conservation practices that they layered onto precolonial customs. Their careful and limited interface with networks of agrarian expertise enabled them to produce farm surpluses even as population grew.[26]

As with agricultural science, the rise of a science of forestry accompanied the growth of colonial power. In many parts of the world, forests were common property, or at least different groups of people had access to different uses of the forest. However, as traditional ways broke down under the globalization of markets, forestry experts increasingly made a case for systematic, top-down intervention to curb the rapid clearing of land and the avarice for extractive products. The claim that experts backed by the power of states would make wiser use of resources than would local people bolstered arguments for standardizing and even commercializing forestry practices.

Interventions in forestry, like those in agriculture, had various effects. Some changed the land in dramatic and irreversible ways by developing methods of intensive use that contributed to deforestation globally. Forestry science could easily work against local groups who lived in or depended upon mixed forests. US timber experts, for example, devised methods of systematic logging in the colony of the Philippines. In German East Africa, one study concludes, "scientific forestry" was neither rational nor efficient but simply served the needs of colonial extractive industries. Colonial forestry experts in Southeast Asia became both advocates and facilitators for the huge rubber plantations that came to dominate land use there. Throughout the colonial world, European demands to make space for plantations of sugar, rubber, pineapples, and other commodities took down mixed forests and the lives of people who depended upon them.[27]

In other cases, transnational experience helped forestry experts grasp the important interrelationships between forests, healthy environments, and culture. The early nineteenth-century German biogeographer

Alexander von Humboldt profoundly influenced nineteenth-century visions of the tropics. Born in Prussia but living for extensive periods in the Americas and Paris, this influential transnational figure had addressed the deleterious consequences of cutting trees from mountainsides. Of even more significance for forestry was the work of George Perkins Marsh, the American scientist and US ambassador to Italy from 1861 to 1882. Marsh's influential books *Man and Nature* (1864) and *The Earth as Modified by Human Action* (1874) examined the global interrelationships among forests, wildlife, watersheds, and healthy communities. His work influenced the German-born Australian acclimatizer Ferdinand von Müller, who championed horticultural connections between California and Australia and helped develop exchanges of seeds and plants, including the Australian eucalyptus varieties that became so widespread in California.[28]

Professionalized forestry services often emerged as transnational coproductions. British colonial officials made tropical forests in India a training ground, and Indian foresters subsequently helped shape forest services in New Zealand, Ceylon, Kenya, Nigeria, and elsewhere. Gifford Pinchot, the founder of the US Forest Service who had previously studied at the French forestry school in Nancy, developed the conservation doctrine of "wise use" that became widely influential in Canada, Australia, and South Africa. The forest services of the major colonial powers watched each other closely and exchanged practices.

The science of forestry thus branched in several directions—toward greater exploitation, toward enhanced sensitivity to ecological interactions, and toward coproduction of practices among colonial and local experts. As in the case of other professionalized circuits, transnational interactions became critical in shaping policies, practices, and debates that historians have too often studied only within the framework of national or imperial histories.

Science in the Social Sphere

In the nineteenth century, close observation, careful documentation, and creative experimentation rapidly changed ideas about the natural world. Alfred Russel Wallace traveled through what is now Malaysia and Indonesia in the late 1850s and early 1860s, collected 125,000 specimens, and carefully observed the differences in their characteristics. He formulated ideas about natural selection and evolutionary theory that his friend, Charles Darwin, was also developing from his famed five-year voyage (1831–1836) on HMS *Beagle*.[29] This revolution in the way scientists thought about the natural world, together with convictions about the efficacy of applying scientific techniques, dovetailed with influences in what came to be called the "social" realm. In the late nineteenth century, the influence of what has been called "social Darwinism" mixed with philosophies such as August Comte's "positivism" to influence a larger milieu that forecast evolutionary social improvement through the application of professional expertise.

Daniel T. Rodgers's *Atlantic Crossings* details how the development of industrial capitalism in Europe and North America prompted a transatlantic exchange designed to address common social problems. Intellectuals and practitioners of newly emerging professions such as political economy, sociology, and education addressed questions of public sanitation, vice, labor codes, currency, poverty, housing, disability, and old age. They also debated the role that central governments should play in redressing social ills. Could transnational groups of experts create a "social science"?

Such exchange, of course, did not mean agreement on specific matters, nor did it encompass only Western Europe and the United States. The many transnational conversations that developed over how to tackle social problems certainly did not move toward programmatic cohesion. German social insurance plans introduced in the 1880s, for example, provided an influential model that stood in sharp contrast to experiments with worker's cooperatives or to the more private, corporate-dominated welfare systems developed in the United States. The Soviet government in the interwar period advanced very different socialist models that attracted leaders of Marxist parties to Moscow for study and exchange. But even if particular models varied, the transnational epistemic disciplines now calling themselves "social sciences" did foster some common sets of referents and generally shared the conviction that the whole world, in effect, could become a giant laboratory for experiments in social improvement.[30]

This cross-fertilization of social science networks reached far beyond the Atlantic community, as modernizers in the Ottoman Empire, Japan, China, and Latin America also participated. The Meiji government in Japan after 1870 and the Turkish government of Mustafa Kemal in the interwar era, for example, carefully studied and adapted an array of international models that addressed social problems. Moreover, discussions of social policy often traveled within imperial networks affected by local conditions and also by what Ann Stoler has called the "politics of comparison" among empires. Leaders of the new Soviet Union in the interwar era proclaimed their ability to re-engineer a new social order and even to create a New Man. International conferences, world's fairs, travel, student exchange, and mass publishing created circuits that brought leaders together from around the world.

In the spirit of science, independent fact-gathering organizations burgeoned, especially in the United States. Before World War I, new institutions such as the Russell Sage Foundation, the Brookings Institution, the National Industrial Conference Board, the National Bureau of Economic Research, and the Twentieth Century Fund sought to propel an intellectual revolution based upon the practical application of expertise.[31] The League of Nations enshrined the fact-gathering mentality in its various agencies, especially those dealing with labor and health. Although there was a growing chorus of dissenters who warned against the hubris and inherently antidemocratic tendency of the enshrinement of technocratic expertise, apostles of the new age paid as little heed to the naysayers as did natural scientists to flat-earthers.

Social scientists were especially involved with educational experimentation, and "industrial education" provided one of the important new transnational models during the early twentieth century. Programs of industrial education fit well with the emerging colonial order. The Hampton Institute and the Tuskegee Institute, for example, pioneered industrial schools in the southern United States, in the US colony of the Philippines, in Haiti under US military occupation, in the protectorate of Cuba, and as part of US missionary efforts in Africa. Between 1901 and 1909 German authorities attempted to implant Tuskegee structures in Togo in order to boost cotton production for export. In the early 1920s, well-publicized commissions financed by the Phelps-Stokes Fund encouraged developing industrial education in Africa. The recommendations from these commissions found strong backing in the British colonial office and from John Dube, the president of the South African Native National Congress (later the African National Congress) and James Aggrey of the Gold Coast, who lionized Booker T. Washington's program of educational and economic development. Afro-Cubans also generally welcomed a close connection with Tuskegee because it brought broader awareness of Pan-African ties and allowed them to adapt Tuskegee's models to suit their own aspirations for upward mobility. The links between educational strategies directed toward American Indians, African-Americans, and colonial areas suggest the complex transnational intersections among progressive-era faiths in social science expertise and Christian social-gospel ideas. They also suggest how practices that transnational professional currents carried around the globe might express both Western colonialism and also the anticolonial goals of empowerment that challenged it.[32]

Racial Science

As encounters with racially different people multiplied in this shrinking age, it is hardly surprising that ideas about race figured prominently in all social science discussions. Examined transnationally, no broad brush can paint a characterization of the knowledge systems about race that prevailed from the mid-nineteenth to the mid-twentieth century. For brevity, however, one might tease out four dominant threads: a missionary discourse, a physical anthropology discourse, a discourse of culture, and a discourse exalting race mixture and local empowerment (given various labels, such as *indigenismo*). All four circulated transnationally; they also often blurred and emerged in shadings. All could be found both as justifications for empire and as elements of anti-imperial arguments. But these four competing, and sometimes overlapping, views of the role of race helped construct the language and the understandings of social science and of world history that have long shaped discussions of the past and the present.

The missionary-inspired imperial discourse, especially prevalent in the mid-nineteenth century, held out hope that racial others could be saved and transformed; that all characteristics of their culture could be purged and replaced by enforcing a universalized morality and discipline. William Holden, a British missionary among the Xhosa in Kaffraria, wrote that by breaking the power of chiefs and placing the Xhosa in educational and labor camps, British overseers could guide "the black races ... to the highest state in the civil and ecclesiastical world." The American founder of the Carlisle Indian boarding school, Captain Richard H. Pratt, put it more succinctly: "Kill the Indian, and save the Man." The violence suggested in such views (and demonstrated in colonial warfare) dripped with sentimentality about the essential equality of humankind. People could be coerced, in effect, into joining the Christian "brotherhood of man."[33]

The "science" of race that emerged in physical anthropology toward the turn of the century did not so much replace such views as layer another set of coercive justifications beside them. If races were, in effect, different competing species, as many social Darwinists argued, then the progress of humanity depended upon the more robust and powerful race taking firm control over others and, in time, dominating the genetic pool. The "race-suicide" theories, which seem to have sparked particular panic among Anglo-American elites, propelled pro-natalist policies directed at the "better" races and policies of destruction or sterilization or draconian control directed at the "lesser." As Theodore Roosevelt proclaimed, "With much of the competition between the races reducing itself to the warfare of the cradle, no race has any chance to win a great place unless it consists of good breeders as well as of good fighters."[34]

Late nineteenth-century scientists (especially biologists and anthropologists) and medical doctors who wrote in terms of "racial type" usually presented racial mixing as degeneration within the human species. They also tended to represent successful nations and states as being ideally coterminous with racial composition. Such notions emerged especially strongly in settler colonies such as the United States, Australia, South Africa, and parts of South America. In these locations, becoming a "white" country seemed so pressing precisely because it was so problematic. Success in creating a white citizenship seemed to forecast national destiny in a "survival-of-the-fittest" world.

As Warwick Anderson and others have pointed out, however, the white body was not a stable signifier, and its biological definitions proved flexible according to location. Whiteness was frequently discussed as a matter of blood and heredity, but it was less a category of origins than a cultural category that connoted health, responsibility, and efficiency. Although *white* was an imprecise term, it nevertheless proved a useful marker in designating progress, along with a particular conception of masculinity, against its "nonwhite" opposite. To "whiten" a population also involved marginalizing, and often feminizing, nonwhite groups that were deemed to be "inefficient" or "degenerate." Racial science, empire, and global commerce all marched hand in hand to create a doctrine of "whiteness" and a racial justification critical to acquiring cheap labor.[35]

In Argentina, Chile, Mexico, Brazil, and elsewhere in Latin America, schemes to "whiten" the population through immigration became a major goal of national state building. As Juan Bautista Alberdi, the famous mid-nineteenth-century Argentine political theorist, put it in 1852, "gobernar es poblar" (to govern is to populate). As the science of race became increasingly elaborated later in the century, Alberdi's dictum seemed ever more urgent. The director of the Museu Nacional do Rio de Janeiro at the turn of the century joined other influential members of the governing elite in proposing that Brazil convert its population from black to white.[36] In Latin America, various incentive programs to attract immigrants from Europe, as well as proposals to "whiten" through modernization and efficiency, drew from and reinforced a discourse of racial hierarchy.

As some late nineteenth-century reformers sought to improve their nations by whitening, many others pursued an associated program. What if professional interventions, with assistance from state power, could strengthen the body politic by improving and standardizing *individual* white bodies? Regeneration not just of the national body but of its individual members might mean that strong white bodies would no longer be confined to temperate climates but could master the tropics and inherit the earth.

As social Darwinists regarded the ultimate triumph of white races throughout the globe as both assured by survival of the fittest and at risk if fitness were not maintained, eugenics became a transnational conversation propelled by organized networks and institutes. Francis Galton, a cousin of Charles Darwin, is regarded as one of the founders of eugenics—the idea that, because of the heritability of physical and intellectual characteristics, humans could be improved by scientific breeding. Eugenic ideas, important to the construction of states and empires, traveled rapidly within elite circles who wished to "better" their populations by preventing interracial unions and by barring the reproduction of those whose supposedly inheritable conditions (such as epilepsy, "feeble-mindedness," even alcoholism) rendered them undesirable. An international literature, circulating especially in the West, sounded alarms about a decline in fertility among European peoples, especially after the huge losses in population associated with World War I, and about the need to "strengthen" populations. This concern reflected anxieties about race and about how the growing participation of white women in public areas and workplaces outside the home might adversely affect reproductive rates.

Eugenics, however, was a big tent, and its supporters by no means all saw the world alike. One branch of eugenics (stronger in the United States, Britain, and Germany) assumed that biology and reproduction controlled destiny. Two Californians, Eugene Gosney and Paul Popenoe established the Human Betterment Foundation in 1928 and published *Sterilization for Human Betterment* (1929). Their book and other publications, which advocated eugenics through sterilization, circulated throughout the world and proved especially influential in Germany. California and Sweden became leaders in eugenic sterilization programs—many involuntary. British settler populations in Kenya in the 1930s also adapted eugenic ideas and created a vigorous movement. Although widely supported by the medical profession in Kenya, the push for racially based eugenicist policies in Kenya failed after the British colonial office refused to back it.[37]

In the Third Reich, official promotion of public hygiene, racial doctrines, and doctors' interests in medical experimentation mixed together to create a system designed to cleanse the fatherland through increasingly horrifying practices of eugenic medicine. German legislation passed shortly after Adolf Hitler seized power led to sterilization of two to four hundred thousand people. The Nazi state financed a eugenics institute, employed Hereditary Health Courts to decide on sterilization, traced the genealogies of "criminal types," and set up a racially based welfare state that targeted Jews and others who were deemed unfit for life under National Socialism. The horrific medical experiments at Auschwitz and the mass killings of Jews and other "undesirables" emerged from these ideas about "bettering" humanity through elimination of "unfit" breeders.

Historians have tried to explain how such extreme exterminationist practices emerged in Germany. Some have argued that German anthropology in the nineteenth century embraced a tolerant, humanistic, and internationalist agenda, while Anglo-American and French variants saw races ranked within an evolutionary hierarchy. In the early twentieth century, however, Anglo-American cultural anthropologists began to leave behind the physical measurement of "racial type" and accentuate the pluralism of cultural traditions. Indeed, the German-born Franz Boas and his cultural anthropology students at Columbia University saw themselves as continuing the older humanistic Germanic tradition. Germans, however, moved in the other direction—toward a more nationalistic view that became absorbed with biologically based theories of race and with "scientific" ways to measure racial distinctions.[38]

Studies have emphasized several factors behind this turn. Even in the nineteenth century the Prussian state had imagined a long-term colonial project in Eastern Europe, and the image of inferiors in the East came to figure commonly in culture. Empire building in East Africa, especially the brutal war against the Herero people from 1904 to 1908, further contributed to a racialized vision of the nation (just as similar colonial wars fueled racial ideologies in other imperial states as well). World War I, however, proved especially critical in the development of racial ideology in Germany, for a number of reasons. First, anthropologists in Germany gained access to POW camps during the war and worked on the classification of POWs to develop a "science" that ranked humans hierarchically according to racial attributes. In addition, the great fear of typhus triggered disinfection campaigns that identified socially marginalized groups such as Jews and Eastern Europeans as vectors of disease. Campaigns for health took on an exterminationist rhetoric, as the desire to eliminate dangerous germs and pests, displaced onto their presumed hosts, justified eugenic purification.

Moreover, racial discourses everywhere intersected with representations of masculinity, and post–World War I Germany developed a particularly romantic image of white soldierly masculinity. Embodied in the heroic figure of General Paul von Lettow-Vorbeck, the commander of Germany's African soldiers in the successful East African campaign, the image of the white German soldier in strong command of obedient black troops contrasted sharply with the image of "disorderly" African troops that Allied armies had used against Germany, particularly in the Ruhr Valley. Representations of the "white hero," and of black Africans as either dutifully subordinate or frighteningly threatening, fed interwar intersections among discourses of masculinity, race, and nation. Although Hitler embraced a less gentlemanly masculinity than that represented by the popular general, Nazi culture also emphasized a strong identification between restoration of "Aryan" masculinity and national strengthening. Finally, of course, in the economic environment of the 1930s Hitler was able to play upon an acute sense of national grievance against both the Versailles settlement and the economic order, a grievance blamed on all kinds of outsiders, but particularly Jews.[39]

As eugenic thinking careened to extremes in Germany, other groups of pronatalist eugenics professionals (stronger in Romance-language and Far Eastern areas) emphasized the need for ameliorative social conditions and decried coercive and grimly deterministic assumptions. The rifts between rival groups of eugenicists, different varieties of which were all connected to transnational networks, surfaced in international eugenics conferences in the interwar era. There was ongoing debate over whether racial and national regeneration should focus primarily on improving the genetic pool or on improving the surrounding environment. Different professions and people in dissimilar circumstances, of course, had different stakes in the answer.[40]

As "scientific" racism and eugenics built different constituencies, the meaning and significance of race was meeting important transnational challenges. In 1911 the Universal Races Congress, held in London, assembled fifty people from Asia, the Middle East, Europe, and the Americas to promote interracial harmony. Speakers at the conference endorsed both human universality and racial difference; they both reinforced and also denounced the idea that history was fundamentally a story of "races." This gathering had no specific outcome and was multivocal on the race question, but it did provide intellectual space for plurality and for dissenting voices of various kinds.[41]

Moreover, dominant voices within the profession of anthropology, which had once promoted the idea that humans could be arranged into clearly defined hierarchical categories, began to doubt that race defined any foundational set of characteristics. Franz Boas, as has been mentioned, moved away from the precepts of physical anthropology, with its stress on the biological grounding of racial difference. Arguing that difference was rooted in culture, not in characteristics such as skin color or skull size, Boaz and other cultural anthropologists redirected part of the discipline of anthropology away from its racialist orientation. Boas's many influential students working in the interwar period and after included Alfred L. Kroeber, Margaret Mead, African-American folklorist Zora Neale Hurston, Mexican anthropologist Manuel Gamio, and Brazilian sociologist Gilberto Freyre. In an article in the *American Anthropologist* in 1915, Kroeber advanced a list of professional principles that included "the absolute equality and identity of all human races and strains as carriers of civilization."[42]

As this culturalist view broke from the grim determinism of race essentialism, programs for "whitening" populations as a mark of social improvement lost scientific justification. But emphasizing cultural difference could still support policies of imperial coercion in order to promote the cultural transformation of the less powerful. Boas's pathbreaking book *The Mind of Primitive Man* (1911) represented primitive cultures as less complex and more intuitive than civilized ones, and the word *primitive* in popular usage came to be the antonym of *modern*, underscoring otherness and representing a gaping chasm of difference. A vogue of things "primitive" swept the West, influencing transnational artistic and cultural styles. Josephine Baker, costumed in a skirt of artificial bananas, enchanted Parisians with her seminude *danse sauvage;* Art Deco styles (often adorned with a line representation of Baker's facial features) became a worldwide sensation after Paris's Exposition des Arts Décoratifs popularized ethnic artistic forms. Antimodernists from various parts of the globe visited Mabel Dodge Luhan's dwelling in New Mexico, where they embraced the native and Mexican heritages and advanced the view that indigenous people lived lives superior to those in the modern industrial order. The appeal of primitivism rested partly on the idea that it represented a disappearing way of life. In most professional social science circles, "primitive" remained a condition that was headed for extinction in a shrinking and modernizing world.

Other social scientists inverted the paradigm of racial difference that remained so powerful within professional communities in the white West. While still presenting social science as a topic very substantially concerned with race, intellectuals such as José Vasconcelos Calderón in Mexico and Gilberto Freyre in Brazil articulated the idea that racial blending enhanced, rather than degenerated, a population. Vasconcelos, one of the most important intellectuals associated with the Mexican Revolution and Mexico's first minister of education, promoted Mexican nationalism around the idea that his country's racial mixture

A detail from Diego Rivera's *The Tarascan Civilization,* 1942. This mural, which decorates the Palacio Nacional in Mexico City, honors the work, artistry, and learning of pre-Hispanic Mexico. Rivera and the other great muralists of Mexico endorsed racial equality and helped to build Mexican nationalism around pride in its indigenous past. (Palacio Nacional, Mexico City, Mexico/Giraudon/The Bridgeman Art Library)

had produced a superior "cosmic race." Freyre, likewise, argued against the idea that Europeans had made the major contributions to Brazilian society. Instead, he saw Brazil's future as coming out of the mixing of Portuguese, Africans, and Indians. He pronounced that Brazil's "racial democracy" was perfectly consistent with evolutionary progress.[43]

Pride in racial mixture implied a new respect for local indigenous cultures and a rupture with ideas of racialized social Darwinism. A movement called *indigenismo* profoundly affected transnational discussions about race throughout the Western Hemisphere and elsewhere. Spread globally especially through the visual arts in the dramatic interwar murals of Mexican painters such as David Alfaro Siqueiros and Diego Rivera, *indigenismo* dignified the historic contributions of indigenous and mixed-raced people and foregrounded them in narratives of national and civilizational progress. This kind of antiracism often found support in and traveled through transnational communist networks, which viewed racism as a barrier to working-class solidarity.

Challenges to the hierarchical, biological view of race thus came from diverse sources. Cultural anthropology challenged its scientific claims. Some intellectuals embraced indigenous influences as part of a rejection of industrial modernism. Communist parties often built class solidarity around programs to advance racial equality and anticolonialism. The transnational currents concerned with the role of race in social science thus ran in no single direction, but each drew enhanced energy from the messy, crisscrossing nature of their networks.

Municipalization of the World

Networked professionals devoted to improvement in the social realm turned attention especially to the late nineteenth century's burgeoning cities. The prevalence of cities, of course, varied widely. In 1900 nearly 40 percent of Western Europeans lived in cities or towns of over five thousand people. Although much of Africa had no settlements at all of this size, recent research has nevertheless emphasized the long-ignored importance of Africa's urban history. Some cities (especially in Europe and America) arose as major productive centers; others (such as Shanghai, Calcutta, or Buenos Aires) became significant points of distribution. A few cities, such as Chicago, boasted both industrial and commercial might. Urban elites, in any case, drew their wealth and status from a globalizing economy, and cities themselves became symbols of new transnational economic interrelationships. Industrialization and commerce, wherever in the world they appeared, spurred the quickening pace of urban life and linked cities together. These new "global cities" offered a cosmopolitanism accentuated by diverse streams of immigrants who came through in transit or who swelled their neighborhoods as resident laborers, traders, and entrepreneurs.

Most cities exhibited similar patterns. Urban living conditions accentuated divisions between rich and poor and between majority and minority ethnic groups. Inadequate water supplies and sanitary systems raised the specter of disease, which could easily slip from poor and crowded areas to threaten the health of the powerful. Upper and middle classes, no matter the region or nationality, tried to confine criminality and vice to separate zones, even as some profited from and might themselves frequent these areas. Such divisions became even more apparent in the outposts of empire, where merchants and administrators from the metropole carved out privileged sectors in which they could separate themselves and try to replicate familiar landscapes and customs. In cities, women very often made claims on public space and found both new freedoms and new perils. Consumer goods, advertising, amusement parks, sports clubs, bars, coffee shops, and movie theaters rearranged the ways people lived together. Labor radicals, anticolonial activists, bohemians, and dissenters of all kinds could find gathering places and exchange ideas, as could those transnational elites who occupied the often classical-style banks and mercantile houses. From whatever vantage point, cosmopolitan urban life with its mix of ethnicities seemed to embody both the promises and the dangers of the age.

Cities often became not just polycultural spaces but also environmentally polluted. Smokestack industrialization, particularly in urban areas close to belts of mining and smelting, belched particles that darkened skies, poisoned waters, and sickened populations. Industrial areas concentrated around certain cities in England, Belgium, Germany, Pennsylvania and Ohio in the United States, Russian Ukraine, and Osaka in Japan, and to a lesser extent in South Africa, India, South America, and Australia.[44] Such conditions prompted appeals—crafted within transnational conversations—to reorganize space, create sanitary systems, and curb industrial smoke and effluents.

Berlin and New York boasted that they led the way in electric lights, which flooded the windows of stores and made dark streets less treacherous. But electrification by no means came just to the largest cities. In the early 1870s, ten thousand gas lamps had illuminated Denver, Colorado, for example, and these were easily converted to electricity; boosters dubbed Denver America's "City of Light," without irony, and claimed that no city in the United States had better public and private lighting systems (although Buffalo, New York, and others also claimed this status).[45] Municipal lighting became an emblem of progress, of public safety, of enlightenment. Names such as the "Great White Way" and the "White City" resonated within the racial coding of the day. The transformation of localized electrical systems of the turn of the century into the large regional "power pools" of the 1920s, together with the multinational stretch of utilities companies (especially American), served national advantage and also defied national boundaries in favor of transnational connectivity. Analogizing electricity to modernity, T. P. Hughes writes that "modern electric systems have the heterogeneity of form and function that make possible the encompassing complexity [of modern life]." Energy consumption soared.[46]

It is hardly surprising that cities converged in some of their basic structures. Networks of communications and transportation, after all, emulated each other, and the many world's fairs served as nodes to showcase new international practices. In addition, expertise in urban planning, like that in most other professions, took on a transnational character, and planners embraced the idea that there could be a universalistic "municipal science." Demand for urban electrical networks and for the new lighthouses called forth cadres of experts, technicians, and capitalists who operated around the world to construct the circuits that supported the new age of electricity.[47] Other groups of experts, traveling both within imperial administrative networks and outside of them, specialized in port and terminal building, street design, sanitation, food inspection, and social services. Indeed, recent scholars have worked "to make urban history one of the avenues to historicize globalization."[48] The so-called global city, they point out, is not just a phenomenon of today but began to take shape in the late nineteenth century.

Even in the world's least urban continent, Africa, cities played a more important role than their number and population might suggest. The shocks of colonization changed the patterns and institutions of urban life throughout Africa. Cities had long functioned as crossroads, mostly trading posts on inland or coastal waterways. With colonization, however, specific port cities, mostly those linked to Western commercial networks, flourished, and these municipalities, unlike earlier ones, layered white metropolitan models upon already varied and culturally mixed cities. In South Africa's industrial zone of Durban, for example, formal planning began in the early twentieth century and meant replacing "slums"—the products of informal development— with formalized zones that restricted access from "disorderly" Indian and African residential areas. Modern port facilities, Western architecture, including Christian churches, racially separated zoning, regulated and "purified" housing, and uneven installations of sanitary services changed the look and operation of many African cities.[49]

The commercial, imperial, and professional networks that often linked the governance of cities throughout the globe sought to develop a scientific and universalistic approach to urban problems. Germany's zoning laws prompted emulation in many countries; Britain's Garden City Association and America's City Beautiful movement influenced ideas about how urban space might be planned to promote spiritual and physical health among urban dwellers. Urban planning laws in French-administered Morocco influenced France's own planning efforts after World War I. The Union Internationale des Villes, which first met in 1913, emerged from networks of European socialists and internationalists who wished to form a body composed of individual cities. Led by Belgian socialist Emile Vinck, after World War I the Union became a more formalized international association, the International Union of Local Authorities, which expanded its membership into the Americas, Asia, and Africa.

Looking more closely at what Pierre-Yves Saunier called the first wave of "municipalization of the world," it seems clear that there were dense transatlantic and transpacific conversations over urban design and administration. Libraries of municipal planning in Melbourne, Australia, show that city officials there drew ideas not just from British treatises but from sources written in the United States, Mumbai, Dunedin, Toronto, and elsewhere. Daniel Burnham, the famed American architect who formed what became the world's largest architectural firm, oversaw the creation of the "White City" in Chicago, implemented projects in Manila and Baguio City, and saw his 1909 "Plan of Chicago" come to have international influence. Elites in Buenos Aires reconstructed their rapidly growing city in the late nineteenth century and styled it "The Paris of South America." In Meiji Japan in the 1880s, Tokyo also devised a plan modeled on Paris (which was not implemented); German experts helped draft the administrative structure of several Japanese cities, towns, and villages; the progressive mayor of Osaka, Seki Hajime, tried to eclectically adapt urban reforms from many countries; and the mayor of Tokyo invited famed urban expert and historian Charles Beard to advise on rebuilding after the devastating earthquake of 1923 (his recommendations had little effect). The industrial-modernist "internationalist" styles of Le Corbusier in France and Ludwig Mies van der Rohe and Walter Gropius in Germany projected a simplification of form and a rejection of ornamentation. The machine aesthetic of this design movement would influence the look of cities throughout the globe. Even while asserting unique features arising from their own heritages, then, city experts worldwide valued being part of transnational circuits that linked professionals specializing in municipal governance and design.[50]

As with other transnational movements, the "global" and the "local" in cities proved to be mutually constitutive, rather than oppositional, realms. What Michael Smith has called "transnational urbanism" foregrounds cities, with their groups of migrants, refugees, activists, entrepreneurs, and institutions, as localized sites within which transnational realms are created and enacted.[51] Combinations of borrowed forms, of local practices, and of diverse transnational networks influenced city life everywhere, even as they played out differently in each particular location. Exemplifying the theme prevalent throughout this book, municipal transnationalism found expression through differentiated commonalities.

Healing Bodies

Could people really thrive in transnational cities and their hinterlands? The spread of disease made port cities particularly vulnerable and challenged the circulation of goods and people on which they depended. In the last half of the nineteenth century several pandemics swept the globe. Anxieties related to health and the spread of disease mounted.[52]

The connective currents of travel and commerce could, quite suddenly, pose the gravest threats to human well-being. Cholera seemed to follow paths of infection from India, often carried by pilgrims going on Hajj to and from Mecca. Yellow fever outbreaks accelerated with sea travel and reached global proportions in the late 1870s, when they simultaneously claimed thousands of lives in Madrid, Havana, Memphis, and other cities. Bubonic plague carried by ship-borne fleas and rats spread alarmingly, with almost every port city in the world experiencing outbreaks in the two decades before World War I. The influenza pandemic of 1918–1919, called the "Spanish flu" but probably originating in Kansas, may have killed fifty million people worldwide. The virulence and rapidity of such pandemics left scientists scrambling for preventions and cures. Commerce, colonialism, and civilization itself seemed to rest upon halting the global circulation of disease. Pandemics called forth responses from teams of transnational health experts. These professionals increasingly accepted the germ theory of disease and exchanged specimens and theories. Research institutions such as the Pasteur Institute in Paris, the Robert Koch Institute in Berlin, the Lister Institute in London, and the Kitasato Institute in Japan worked on vaccines and antitoxins. By 1930, transnational efforts from a variety of labs had produced vaccines against typhoid, cholera, tuberculosis, smallpox, plague, diphtheria, and tetanus. New public health bureaucracies in many countries carried out vaccination programs and swapped knowledge about how remediation might best work at a grassroots level. Sometimes vaccination programs in colonies had low priority. British policies in Gambia in the first three decades of the twentieth century, for example, included no vaccination efforts even as large expenditures were made on commercial roads and canals and for courts and clubs where European merchants might relax. In many places, however, states and colonial administrators tried to institute programs of compulsory vaccination from the late nineteenth century on, although antivaccination movements formed almost everywhere to contest such exercises of power. Indeed, early vaccination procedures did involve a significant health hazard. Opposition to them at least had the salutary affect of prompting technical improvements, which made vaccinations ever safer and less painful.[53]

A string of international "sanitary conferences" during the late nineteenth century brought together delegates from Europe, the Ottoman Empire, Persia, China, Japan, and the Americas. In 1907 the Office International d'Hygiène Publique was established as a permanent body for global coordination of health policies. Such transnational initiatives helped regularize quarantine procedures, especially applying to port

A line of people waiting to receive vaccinations in Côte d'Ivoire in the 1920s. Epidemic disease, which knew no geographic borders, spurred transnational scientific and medical efforts. Imperial governments, especially concerned with the health of their emissaries and of colonial labor forces, frequently ordered massive vaccination efforts. (Centre Historique des Archives Nationales, Paris, France/Archives Charmet/The Bridgeman Art Library)

cities. They also promoted sanitary projects to improve sewage and water systems in disease-prone areas. After World War I, the League of Nations Health Organization assumed some monitoring and coordinating functions.

Remedies for epidemic disease also often emerged through processes of coproduction between transnational science and local experts, even if medical encounters were uneven. During the US military occupation of Cuba after 1898 and in Panama during the building of the canal, for example, US scientists built on the mosquito theory of Cuban doctor Carlos Finlay to successfully combat yellow fever and other diseases. The successful mosquito eradication measures influenced those who sought to fight disease elsewhere in the world, even as they helped justify US imperialism as necessary to contain disease.

The differences in the meanings of health and disease between China and the West also worked in various ways. Practitioners of traditional medicine in China adapted Western theory to develop their own versions of modern (but non-Western) medicine. Transnational discourses on health that circulated in China layered imperial influences from the West and from Japan alongside the desire of Chinese elites to shed the country's weaknesses by adopting concepts of hygiene that might improve the nation's fitness. Ruth Rogaski has analyzed the embrace by elites in the northern Chinese city of Tianjin of goods and practices that would advance "hygienic modernity" *(weisheng)* to improve cleanliness and hence bodily vigor. Moreover, China both borrowed from and competed with the West. Entrepreneurs in Chinese medicine, for example, waged successful marketing campaigns against Western medical companies to attract buyers in Southeast Asia. And medical knowledge and practice did not simply flow from the West to the East and South. George Soulié de Morant, who served in the French diplomatic corps in China during the first two decades of the twentieth century, became so impressed with the success of Chinese acupuncture during a cholera epidemic that he wrote major works on the technique and, during the 1930s, developed a significant following in France that would expand in the post–World War II period. As in China, instances of "medical pluralism," in which patients exhibited considerable eclecticism in choosing healing practices from an array of local and imported systems, emerged in many areas of the world, even though health-care provision was often inequitably distributed.[54]

The civilizing potential of medicine emerged as a central discourse of imperial justification from the mid-nineteenth century. Epidemic disease hindered imperial stability and infrastructure development, and colonial officials gave it high priority. Colonial rivalries added further urgency. Plant experts in all the imperial powers, for example, competed with each other to smuggle and adapt the Peruvian cinchona in order to produce sufficient quantities of the quinine needed to protect against malaria.

Medical practice, however, could also easily prove to be a site of imperial failure or of resistance to colonial authority. During the early years of French rule in Algeria, for example, imparting modern medical knowledge and administration provided a strong justification for colonialism, both morally and pragmatically. As France began to construct health-care institutions in Algeria, however, the costs and difficulties of building a comprehensive medical system began to eclipse the early optimism. Even if doctors and other personnel operating in the city of Algiers could imagine they were building a structure that would transform the colony's health, their reach into rural areas was spotty and encountered resistance. By the turn of the century, ideologies of racial inferiority had blended into the intractable problems of cost, poor administration, and jurisdictional battles among French colonists, Algerians, and the French army. Plans to train Algerians as doctors and to spread French-style medical care throughout the countryside were largely abandoned, and Algerian medical personnel, who had once supported the French effort, gradually withdrew from the networks of colonial medicine. Complaining about deep injustices in the system, the vision they had once shared with French doctors degenerated into disillusionment and resentment. At the same time, the French effort to spread health gradually devolved into an effort to segregate off the "sickness" in the body of the colony so that it could not escape through the port to contaminate or threaten healthy French cities. Not only did French medical interventions have insignificant or negative effects on the health of Algerians overall, but the French administration labeled Algeria itself as a sick state.[55]

Similarly, during the 1920s, British officials increasingly blamed Sudan's "moral and economic backwardness" on the practice of genital cutting. Spurred by a Western-based transnational movement to abolish the practice, they launched an all-out campaign to introduce "scientific" medicine and especially to change midwifery practices. By the late 1920s a "circumcision crisis" in Kenya and associated debates in the British Parliament led to even stronger directives to end practices that harmed the health of women and children throughout the empire. The interactions among colonial policy, British nurse-midwives sent to reform what were seen as detrimental Arabic cultural practices, local advocates on both sides of the issue, rising nationalism, and differing religious orientations created a complex milieu over several decades, during which genital cutting may have became more, rather than less, culturally entrenched.[56]

Disease thus provided a central cultural trope of this interconnected age, although it framed a variety of meanings. Within transnational circuits, metaphors of disease often became part of a moral discourse that marked tropical bodies as backward and hazardous and justified exogenous interventions, including colonialism. "Tropical medicine," which became a subspecialty of medical knowledge, segmented off the "tropics" as an area of danger and disease, even though the geographic boundaries were anything but clear.[57] At the same time, the sweeps of epidemic disease and famine could also threaten the Western claims of superiority that justified imperial and racial power. Within some communities swept up under colonialism, metaphors of disease could mark outsider-carriers and justify resistance to contact with imperial officials or transnational health workers. Moreover, anticolonial nationalists sometimes embraced public health programs as a way of strengthening local communities and institutions in order to counter colonial or neocolonial power. Ideas about who carried disease and who could stop it thus became parts of larger discussions. The powers of healers, like all other circuits of expertise, involved global circulations and contestations of meaning.[58]

Numerous transnational organizations in this period tackled problems related to global health. For example, the Friends (Quakers), the Catholic Church's Caritas Internationalis, and other religious-based groups led major efforts. Save the Children International concentrated on relief work to help children suffering from war and disaster. Two transnational organizations, the Red Cross and Crescent and the Rockefeller Foundation, deserve special attention because of the influential and long-lasting transnational networks they forged.

The International Committee of the Red Cross (ICRC) began as the inspiration of Swiss businessman Henri Dunant, who witnessed the bloody battle of Solferino in 1859 in northern Italy and became determined to alleviate the suffering of war. The organization adapted the design of the Swiss flag, taking as its emblem a red cross on a white background, and began to spread its services into war-torn areas. In 1877 the ICRC reluctantly agreed that the Ottoman Empire could use a crescent instead of a cross. In 1901 Dunant was awarded the first Nobel Peace Prize. A private institution headquartered in Geneva, the Red Cross and Crescent played a major role as a neutral intermediary during World War I, when it provided medical assistance and advocated improved treatment of prisoners. Through a federated structure, the Red Cross expanded internationally, gradually sprouting local chapters throughout the world.[59]

Clara Barton, who had inspired a volunteer service to soldiers during America's Civil War, helped start an American Red Cross (ARC) chapter in 1887. The ARC served military personnel during America's War of 1898 and became a semiofficial agency in 1905 when it received a charter and subsidies from Congress. Active during World War I and during the interwar era, the ARC expanded its mission beyond wartime emergencies to coordinate international disaster relief and, unlike the ICRC, tried to tackle broader issues related to sanitation reform and prevention of epidemic disease. After the great Japanese earthquake of 1923, President Calvin Coolidge asked that all American donations of food and medicine be channeled through the ARC. Despite some tensions over core mission, the International Red Cross and Crescent and the American Red Cross together provided a strong and ever-expanding global infrastructure for advocacy related to humanitarian and health concerns.[60]

Philanthropic foundations, based on the fortunes of some of American industrial barons, also became heavily involved in global health issues. Oil baron John D. Rockefeller launched a Sanitary Commission in 1909 to combat hookworm in the southern United States. He then expanded the idea by incorporating his new Rockefeller Foundation with the goal of promoting well-being throughout the world. The foundation's International Health Board (IHB), which operated for thirty-eight years after 1913, carried its anti-hookworm campaign to one billion people in fifty-two countries. It also gradually broadened its concerns to include malaria and twenty-two other diseases or health conditions. A special yellow-fever commission, formed in 1915, led work on the eradication of mosquitoes and successfully developed a vaccine.

The work of the foundation frequently emerged from coproductive local relationships. After World War I, the foundation established a European office in Paris and courted European partners for its programs to advance basic science. The foundation built institutes of public health in some two dozen cities to train health-care workers and conduct research. It helped establish women's colleges in China, India, and Japan. In China, where the foundation developed a special interest, its China Medical Board became an independent institution in 1928 and supported the Peking Union Medical College. Using this China model, the foundation formed partnerships through grants to large medical education and research institutions in Beirut, Hong Kong, Singapore, Bangkok, and other locations.

Cadres of locally trained health workers joined the IHB's transnational network. In 1935 the Rockefeller Foundation launched a grassroots initiative to take health care and community development into rural villages in China by relying on midwives and other paramedics to bring basic care to peasants. It also supported the development of local outreach programs for rural health-care delivery at the grassroots level.

In many countries, alliances among the Rockefeller Foundation, local public health reformers, and national state-building elites shaped the programs. In Costa Rica and Brazil, for example, research on and treatment of hookworm disease and yellow fever preceded the foundation's involvement, and Rockefeller grants provided the money for local public health activists who were advocating a more vigorous role for their national governments. Many governments feared the economic consequences of epidemic disease and welcomed efforts to keep ports open and commerce flowing. Foundation money also helped local officials pay for public health educators and professionals focused on hygiene and mosquito eradication.[61]

In the British colony of Ceylon the IHB developed a demonstration project for the eradication of hookworm. Plantation owners first resisted the costly health requirements the IHB tried to enforce, but the IHB then switched course. Broadening its focus to a range of infectious diseases, it promoted educational campaigns operating on the village level, provided training for local herbal doctors, and encouraged provincial governments to create sanitary departments. From the mid-1920s, the IHB teamed up with a new generation of local leaders who advocated a grassroots approach that stressed preventive measures such as vaccinations and maternity services. This switch from curative to preventative medicine dramatically lowered mortality rates.

Any assessment of the role of scientific health professionals and philanthropic foundations depends upon specific context and can hardly be captured in a single interpretive narrative. Professional transnational medicine was, in one sense, allied with capitalist globalization; it disrupted settled ways in the name of modernization. As such, medical professionals might be seen as agents of Western medicine working on behalf of the West's imperial aims. They might also be viewed, however, as participants with local elites in a global circulation of knowledge that both coproduced possible remedies and furthered anticolonial nationalist agendas by extending the power and reach of local officials. Health programs on behalf of grassroots groups and women's empowerment proved to be important, if controversial and sometimes counterproductive, forces in many areas. Like other networks of expertise in this period, health professionals served imperialism, nationalism, local aspirations, and transnational ideals variously and often simultaneously. The currents of their expertise often asserted hierarchies of race and culture, but local impacts varied widely, as recipients of funds sometimes ignored, changed, or adapted methods to their own purposes.

⌣

The nineteenth century exhibited a faith that the transnational and neutral character of science and expertise would foster universal frameworks and propel the progressive convergence of "civilization." Over time this faith came under challenge from various directions. To many, World War I underscored the bankruptcy of the Western fascination with technological change. Chinese reformer and scholar Liang Qichao, who visited the shell-shocked European capitals just after the war, pronounced that the "peaceful" traditions of Eastern civilizations would flourish in the ruins of war-breeding Western techno-materialism. Intellectuals as diverse as Rabindranath Tagore, Muhammad Iqbal, and Liang Shuming developed parallel critiques of Western materialism and called for revivals within their own religious and cultural traditions.[62] Paris hosted a "lost generation" of artists and intellectuals who also hoped to pronounce the death of the West's mechanical approaches to life and the natural world. These dissenters built a transnational aesthetic out of shattering conventions and revolting against formalisms of all kinds. American educator Mary Parker Follett warned that transnational networks of professional elites would breed narrowness. She wrote in *The New State* (1918), "The man who knows the 'best' society of Petrograd, Paris, London, and New York, and that only, is a narrow man because the ideals and standards of the 'best' society in London, Paris, and New York are the same. He knows life across but not down—it is a horizontal civilization instead of a vertical one, with all the lack of depth and height of everything horizontal. This man has always been among the same kind of people, his life has not been enlarged and enriched by the friction of ideas and ideals which comes from the meeting of people of different opportunities and different tastes and different standards." A flat world, she suggested, would be a provincial one.[63]

Bruno Rizzi's *La bureaucratisation du monde,* published in Paris in 1939, and James Burnham's *The Managerial Revolution,* published in New York in 1941, exemplified yet another line of critique. These two works articulated the view that the Soviet Union, Nazi Germany, and the New Deal all manifested a new bureaucratic mentality that had arisen over the past half century. Throughout the world, these two ex-Trotskyists suggested, new groups of people who claimed specialized expertise had come to exert power through governments, empires, and corporate structures. They were neither owners of production nor people of great wealth. They were managers, and they claimed ultimate authority, through the power of specialized knowledge and technical expertise, to know what was best for the public in whose name they presumed to operate. Although Rizzi and Burnham were primarily concerned with how this new class of experts had emerged within national states, their critiques of "bureaucratized" and "managerial" systems also addressed the networks of scientists, technicians, and professionals that had coalesced transnationally since the late nineteenth century.[64]

All such critiques, however, tended to exaggerate the unities within scientific and technical networks. A close look at transnational circulations suggests that circuits of expertise did not simply devise their theories and "facts" from on high and transplant them into various localities throghout the world. Rather, transnational circuit builders interacted with each other from many different geographic and social positions, and in their encounters, specific context interacted with and altered supposedly universalized laws and propositions. Science, technology, and health were neither neutral in the powers they embodied nor consistently one-sided. In a variety of configurations, they were coproduced through encounters, often unequal, between the local and the global. Expertise could both serve and also alter imperial designs; it could work in favor of nationalistic visions but also as a check against them.

If the euphoria associated with late nineteenth-century one-worldism, transnational bonding, and supposedly apolitical networks of science and engineering deflated after the Great War, the crisscrossed transnational networks that had been forged remained in place and even flourished. These "soft" networks constructed within scientific, engineering, and healing communities spanned the globe as surely as did the "hard" ones of cables, telephony, railroads, and ocean liners. The meanings carried in their currents remained complex and often contradictory, but the global reach and importance of transnational epistemic communities continued to grow, generating both broad commonalities and localized variations.

CHAPTER FIVE

Spectacular Flows

The world was shrinking, and ever more people made their way around it—for adventure, education, and even publicity. Li Gui claimed to be the first Chinese official to travel around the world and wrote an account of his 1876 trip, describing for Chinese readers parts of the world he visited: their social customs, industrial organization, and material culture. In the early 1880s King Kalakaua of Hawai'i, determined to investigate immigration and how other rulers governed, became the first ruling monarch to journey around the world and meet with other heads of state. On November 14, 1889, American journalist Elizabeth Cochrane Seaman ("Nellie Bly"), sponsored by Joseph Pulitzer's *New York World* and inspired by Jules Verne's 1873 book *Le tour du monde en quatre-vingts jours (Around the World in Eighty Days),* left New York on a 24,899-mile trip to set a record in speed for circling the globe. Seventy-two days, six hours, eleven minutes, and fourteen seconds later, she arrived back in New York, having traveled through England, France, the Suez Canal, Ceylon, Hong Kong, and Japan. She captured loads of publicity and her coveted world record, which would be broken only a few months later by another American. Pursuing what was now a surefire market for globe-circling adventures and broke because of a bad investment, Mark Twain published an account of his roundabout through the British Empire called *Following the Equator* (1897). Rabindranath Tagore, the Bengali poet, undertook a global oceanic voyage in 1916, going from India to Burma to Japan to North America, and in 1924–1925 traveled from Latin America across the Indian Ocean, the Mediterranean, and the Atlantic. These were only a few of the many late nineteenth- and early twentieth-century globe-trotters whose adventures provided a sense of the vast, yet also small, new world of interconnected currents. In such a world, adventure awaited and encounters with difference expanded imaginations. The new transnational networks, deeply imbedded in commerce and its culture of desire stimulation, altered ideas about the fixity of identity and seemed to offer possibilities of self-fashioning. Borders of all kinds, geographic, racial, and gendered, seemed more permeable and less permanent. Media technology fostered new entertainments that challenged traditions and gave rise to global networks of celebrity and consumerism.

Older histories of this era, organized around a linear teleology, emphasized the spread of the West with its supposedly rational culture of science and reason leading toward an evolutionary future called progress. Recent work in anthropology and history, however, has challenged the narrative structures that framed this view. First, transnational networks, rather than clear geographic centers, map the changes often marked as modernity. Second, scholars as diverse as the historian C. A. Bayly, the anthropologist Arjun Appadurai, and the interdisciplinary Modern Girl collective all see the emerging and networked modern world as characterized by the simultaneous (and related) creation of both uniformity and difference. Bayly's work, for example, "traces the rise of global uniformities" while emphasizing how "connections could also heighten the sense of difference, and even antagonism, between people." Appadurai calls this homogenizing and differentiating process "modernity at large." The Modern Girl project, which analyzed the nearly simultaneous emergence of "modern girls" in every part of the world in the early twentieth century, illustrates what I call differentiated commonalities as it describes the emergence of local variations within uniform global trends.[1] Third, scholars note that modernity did not represent the triumph of the rational as much as the conjuncture of the rational with a new media-driven spectacularity.

The examination of adventurers, celebrities, travel, and consumerism illustrates the networked world of differentiated commonalities and exemplifies how sensationalism—driven by a search for audience and by peoples' yearnings for self-fashioning—merged with the rationalism needed to produce market calculation and machine-driven mass culture.

Adventure

By the nineteenth and early twentieth centuries, the greatest cartographic and cataloging enterprises of the age of exploration were coming to an end. The mapping of the globe, even its remote regions, was mostly complete. But a few blank spaces remained, and the era thus featured some of the most celebrated feats of exploration. The thirst for scientific discovery had once driven geographical exploration. As the scientific justification for new discoveries diminished, however, the emerging popular media lavished increased attention on the "conquests" of the few still-uncharted places.

With the rise of mass-circulation media, adventurers who once emphasized the scientific aspects of their deeds became tempted to join forces with sensation-seeking newspapers to enhance their own fame and profit. Still claiming status as instructors about science and the natural world, many converted themselves into globe-trotting showmen and showwomen. The turn of the century remained a time of daring feats of endurance, as adventurers challenged themselves to reach the remaining unexplored terrain of arctic and high-mountain regions, but it was also a time of sensation seekers and even charlatans, for whom the seductive yearning to become a celebrity often overrode good judgment and truthful representation. "As the world got 'smaller', travelers' tales grew taller," writes Felipe Fernández-Armesto.[2]

The age of industrialization vastly improved the ability of explorers to survive in extreme environments, and increasingly more people became tempted to try. Adventurers had growing access to specialty clothing for tropical and arctic climates, to orienting devices, and to antimalarial remedies. Steam engines, ironclad ships, railroads, and telegraphic communications eased and sped travel to more places. Various kinds of industrial power, now more than sheer physical endurance, made the world smaller and more accessible. Still, the hardships of exploration remained real enough to pack the pages of adventure stories. As surveyor-explorer Kenneth Mason writes about the hardships in the still-remote places, "there were no roads and fewer tracks; there were no maps; the people were suspicious. . . . [Mountaineers] had no mountain equipment, no ice-axes, crampons, pitons, no nylon ropes, windproof clothing or indestructible tents. They learnt about frostbite and snow-blindness the hard and painful way. They carried no oxygen and no Pervitine tablets."[3]

Maurice Isserman and Stewart Weaver's history of Himalayan mountaineering points out one of the central paradoxes of the expeditionary culture that emerged. "It was bound up with visions of imperial destiny that assumed the rule of white Europeans over darker-skinned Asians and drew many of its conventions from the hierarchical order of the English public school and the British Army. At the same time, it harbored individual climbers who were often misfits in their own societies, romantic rebels who found a spiritual purpose and freedom in the mountains." It fostered "colonial arrogance" but also a mix of individualism and "responsibility to others."[4] The media-framed tales of adventure from this period drew from these paradoxes to create iconic sagas of moral, racial, and physical supremacy wrapped within notions of the brotherhood of hardship.

The age of extreme expeditionary culture and the golden age of popular newspapers and journals were a marriage made in heaven. Whereas nineteenth-century explorers usually worked for governments eager to publicize scientific discoveries and to press colonial territorial claims, the new breed often sought stories that could be sold. Well-publicized adventures found their way into theaters, music halls, exhibitions, "yellow journalism" in America, the "penny press" in Britain, and mass-circulation magazines such as *National Geographic.* Almost everywhere in the world the numbers of newspapers and theaters soared. Newspapers printed in China alone, for example, quadrupled from two hundred to eight hundred between 1905 and 1920. The adventure genre would become a staple of photojournalism and of the new film industry. In almost any year of this era, some spectacle-ridden adventure dominated the news everywhere that mass publications reached. Stories with audience appeal circulated feverishly within the emerging information and entertainment networks that connected empires and spanned the globe.[5]

Henry Norton Stanley's expedition best exemplified the union between mass entertainment and adventure. Stanley excelled at grafting imagined "facts" into stories of exploration, even obscuring his own birth as John Rowland in North Wales to claim that he hailed from New Orleans. Sent to Africa in 1869 by James Gordon Bennett Jr., publisher of the *New York Herald,* Stanley was to find and interview Dr. David Livingstone, the British Congregationalist missionary to Africa, explorer, and antislavery activist. Livingstone, whose motto "Christianity, Commerce, and Civilization" was subsequently inscribed into his monument at the base of Victoria Falls in Zimbabwe, had disappeared into the interior of Africa in his obsessive search for the source of the Nile River. Stanley's search for the famous man, chronicled by the newspaper, became a sensation. In November 1871 Stanley landed on the shore of Lake Tanganyika and reportedly met the ailing Livingstone with the soon-to-be-famous words, "Dr. Livingstone, I presume?" Stanley's exclusive stories to the *Herald,* and the adventure's sensational ending (capped by the doctor's death from malaria a year and a half later), boosted the newspaper's circulation and profits.

Stanley became what the twentieth century would call a "celebrity," an emerging cultural phenomenon that sprang from the popular media's new sensational style and global interconnectivity. The Royal Geographic Society, which had sent its own expedition to try to locate Livingstone, derided Stanley's lack of scientific credentials, but London newspapers emulated the *Herald*'s profit-making formula. In 1874 the *Daily Telegraph* of London teamed up with the *Herald* to sponsor another African expedition led by Stanley and to publish his exciting accounts. The *Daily Telegraph* helped spread within the English press the fad of covering sensationalized, often brutal, adventures. The huge popularity of Stanley's writings and the many personae he projected in them also shaped the conventions of adventure writing. The Livingstone-Stanley story became, and remains, one of the most mythologized and familiar tales in the world, and Stanley's fame illustrates the emergence of globally circulated stories that interconnected mission, adventure, colonial violence, and celebrity.[6]

The writings of both the religious Livingstone and the sensationalist Stanley became influential in shaping the views of Africa presented within the global webs of popular publications. A study by Clare Pettitt raises questions about what Livingstone's (and Britain's) relationship with his African servants, Jacob Wainwright, Susi, Chuma, and Wekotani, might further illuminate. She points out that the servants exist in a historical void. They pop up here and there in photographs and scattered accounts but leave no significant trace of how their own perspectives or voices or narratives might have framed the famed Livingstone and his encounters in Africa. The "native" servants are the silent participants in an association in which only one side left the kind of accounts out of which "realities" and then histories are usually made. This era of communications, her study shows, is often not about communication at all but about the projections emanating from those who, through publication, gained access to a future audience. Transnational currents, once again, both bridged but also accentuated differences in power.[7]

National Geographic, of course, became one of the most popular purveyors of adventure and one of the most influential venues through which Americans and others learned to picture and understand the world. In 1903, for example, the magazine featured the explorations of Fanny Bullock Workman, a record-setting woman explorer, and her husband, William Hunter Workman.[8] Their many adventure books, such as *Ice-Bound Heights of the Mustagh,* helped to popularize accounts of mountain climbing in this age when men-women duos were still unusual enough to attract special attention.[9]

Striving for rewards and recognition within the new world of mass publishing came also with hazards. Otto von Ehlers, for example, wrote travelogues that became best-sellers in Germany and beyond. Spurred by success, von Ehlers tried in 1895 to cross New Guinea's central mountain range, coast to coast, but misgauged the time it might take to transverse the 150 miles. The party of forty-three ran out of food, lost their compasses, and suffered from sores made by leeches and from the red maggots that settled in them. After seven weeks, a few remaining native guides shot the Germans in an effort to secure at least their own survival. The adventure had little scientific or even imperial rationale. It showed, however, that a desire to recount a daring exploit to the vast audience that seemed eager to read tales of travail could be deadly.[10] Similarly, Joshua Slocum's *Sailing Alone around the World* (1900) told the exciting tale of Slocum's three-year, forty-six-thousand-mile journey, at age fifty. The first person to make such a trip alone, Slocum enjoyed great popularity from his book. Trying to achieve another celebrity-style feat a decade later, he disappeared at sea.

In the early twentieth century, expeditions to the North and South Poles captured the most frenzied press coverage and popular attention. In 1909 the Americans Frederick A. Cook and Robert E. Peary both claimed to have reached the North Pole (probably neither did), and two rival newspapers, the *New York Herald* and the *New York Times,* magnified the controversy to build sales through sensational stories and charges against the other. After Cook cabled that he had reached the pole, the *New York Herald* splashed the news on its entire front page with the headline "Fighting Famine and Ice, the Courageous Explorer Reaches the Great Goal." Several days later when Peary also cabled success, his sponsor, the *New York Times,* reported that "the world accepts his word without a shadow of hesitation" and quoted Peary as saying that Cook was a fraud who "has simply handed the public a gold brick." With this and other stories, according to historian Beau Riffenburgh, the *Herald*'s publisher, James Gordon Bennett Jr., "established the role of the press in the creation of the modern image of the unknown," emphasizing not facts but exhilarating stories of rivalry, hardship, and perhaps tragedy. The global spread of newspapers and news networks was an essential component in creating the formulas of spectacularity that dominated visions of adventure by the early twentieth century.[11]

The interest in the North Pole controversy culminated in another "race to the pole," this time to Antarctica. Sixteen different expeditions from nine countries headed toward the Antarctic to gain the distinction of being first, but only two ultimately became contenders. Media again played up the stories of the hardships and rivalry. News came in 1912 that Norwegian Roald Amundsen's group had reached the Pole. Then came the gripping story of Robert Falcon Scott, Britain's most famous explorer, whose expedition had struggled to the Pole only to find that Amundsen had attained the goal several weeks earlier. On their arduous return across the glaciers, Scott and others then died from starvation and cold. Apsley Cherry-Garrard, a member of Scott's expedition, wrote one of the most vivid accounts of the travails in *The Worst Journey in the World* (1922). The greatest fame from the race to the Pole, however, came to the experienced Antarctic explorer Sir Ernest Shackleton, who had once been part of Scott's team before the two had a falling out. Shackleton's Imperial Trans-Antarctic Expedition, which embarked early in 1914 aiming to be the first to travel across Antarctica from sea to sea, suffered an almost incredible ordeal when the crew became stranded in the ice and Shackleton endured deadly conditions to rescue them. Shackleton's tale, which he published as *South* (1919), was bone-chilling adventure, and Shackleton became a legend for his remarkable endurance, dedication to his team, and truly sensational story. Amundsen, whose fame also spread, went on to explore the Northwest Passage and the North Pole region, where his plane disappeared in 1928 as he was attempting to rescue a former associate.

After the race to the poles, individuals and nations turned toward the Himalayas as the only "unconquered" place left that held significant challenge. Some called the Himalayan heights the "third pole." In the 1920s the English mountaineer George Mallory joined expeditions that claimed the goal of surveying and subduing hitherto unmapped territory in the Himalayas. Mallory, however, claimed no utilitarian purpose. Displaying his late-Victorian concern with character, he insisted that he climbed only because the mountains were there and posed a personal challenge. He thus exemplified mountaineering as being about self-discipline and self-improvement, values that were widely celebrated in this imperial age. Mallory was no sensation hunter, but his famous climbs of 1921–1924 were nonetheless sensational, and he lost his life attempting to be the first to reach Mount Everest's summit. In the dispirited post–World War I atmosphere, Mallory and other mountaineers captured world attention with their messages stressing the importance of personal fortitude. Throughout the interwar era, expeditions from all over the world made the conquest of Everest a determined goal (not achieved until 1953).[12]

Adventurers pushed not only into remaining uncharted territories but into the skies above. In July 1909, French airman Louis Blériot crossed the English Channel in an airplane in thirty-six and a half minutes, and much of Europe celebrated the achievement. The well-known Viennese author and pacifist Stefan Zweig saw flight as a positive sign.

The feat, he wrote, prompted people to consider "how useless are frontiers when any plane can fly over them with ease, how provincial and artificial are customs-duties, guards and border patrols." Air flight, exclaimed Zweig, promoted "the spirit of these times which visibly seeks unity and world brotherhood!"[13] Some hoped that the very possibility of aerial bombings would deter war, and there were suggestions that the Hague Peace Conference of 1915 (which was not held) should take up the subject.

Although World War I confirmed that air flight could facilitate not just interconnection but killing, the popular fascination with flight nevertheless provided a new arena for adventure headlines. Charles Lindbergh became the greatest celebrity of the late 1920s when his 1927 solo nonstop flight across the Atlantic from Long Island to Paris drew huge crowds and global media attention. Lindbergh's good looks and his feat's celebration of individualism made him a media sensation and contributed to a decade in which adventure flying remained constantly in the news and on the movie screens. The first flight over the South Pole in 1929 brought fresh excitement to this new-style "race to the Pole." And other flying records of all kinds remained to be repeatedly set and then broken. Amelia Earhart, the decorated aviatrix who went missing during her attempt to circumnavigate the globe in 1937, added mystery and tragedy to airborne adventures. All the enormous publicity associated with these early years of flight, of course, drew from the fascination that had captured Zweig and so many others: humans could now glide across geographic borders as though they did not exist; they could reach distant lands in hours rather than weeks. The shrinking of time and space had accelerated very dramatically.[14]

Back on land, or under its surface, the lure of "lost cities" beckoned to other kinds of adventurers and sensation hunters. Ruins of past civilizations from the Mycenaean to the Mayan to the Anasazi spurred searches for more, and it often was not easy to distinguish the line be-

'LUCKY' WINS!

Story on Page 3

"LIKE STEPPING INTO A DEATH CHAMBER—PARIS, LIKE THE GOVERNOR'S PARDON!"

With those words, Capt. Charles (Lucky) Lindbergh climbed into the cockpit of his little but thoroughbred monoplane, The Spirit of St. Louis, and hopped off on a 3,640-mile spin for Paris. Yesterday, 5:21 p. m. N. Y. time, the daring young aviator arrived at his goal in a state of physical collapse, ending the greatest flight in history of aviation. *Story page 3; other pics. page 16.*

FIRST PRESIDENTS GAME WINNERS! SEE PAGE 8

The *New York Daily News* celebrating the completion of aviator Charles Lindbergh's historic nonstop flight from New York to Paris, May 22, 1927. Crowds amassed in Times Square to hear the news of his landing in Paris, and journalists made "Lucky Lindy" into one of the best-known people on the planet. Lindbergh came to symbolize the new globalizing age of flight. (NY Daily News via Getty Images) tween scientist-archeologists and headline-hunting hucksters. In the 1870s, German archeologist Heinrich Schliemann excavated many sites that he claimed showed the historical authenticity of Homer's *Iliad* and Virgil's *Aeneid*. Although garnering great publicity, his finds were and still remain controversial because of the suspicion that he may have planted some of the more spectacular items he then uncovered. The American Hiram Bingham came upon the ruins of Machu Picchu in 1911, and he then excavated, photographed, and publicized them to the world as though he had been the first to "discover" them (which he probably was not). The Incan artifacts he encountered were crated off to Yale University.[15]

American Roy Chapman Andrews typified the showman-scientist. Andrews, a naturalist with the American Museum of Natural History, launched his famous Central Asiatic Expedition into the Gobi Desert in the early 1920s in hopes of finding evidence of earliest human evolution. Exemplifying the America of his era, he sought extensive publicity by traveling in caravans of automobiles through one of the world's most inhospitable terrains. His 1925 expedition required 125 camels and a huge support staff to carry the needed gas, oil, tires, and repair equipment for his six motor vehicles. Finding no significant ancient human remains, he did uncover troves of dinosaur fossils and eggs, many of which he dispatched to New York. His flamboyance and appropriation of fossils raised disputes over ownership with the Chinese government and produced enough complications to end his expeditions. But Andrews published book after book recounting his exploits, and some claim that he became a model for the *Indiana Jones* movies that thrilled a later generation.[16]

The famed American animal collector Frank Buck likewise displayed the flair of a vaudeville agent (which he had been) while promoting his adventures. In the interwar era, his "bring 'em back alive" books, movies, and radio shows dazzled fans worldwide with tales of his encounters with jungle animals and of his travails in transporting them to "civilization." An entire genre of Buck-inspired products—*King Kong* and its many offshoots being the most influential—plotted stories in which rare animals, native "boys," and intrepid Euro-Americans played out predictable scripts in the "jungles" of the world. The drama of such stories came not from a kill or even from a capture but from the physical and financial dangers of trying to keep the beasts alive through the process of transporting them. Frank Buck also promoted his exploits at the New York World's Fair of 1939, where his Jungleland exhibition advertised a display of thirty thousand animals and birds—vastly more than the number featured in even the largest zoo of the era.[17]

As adventurers on, above, and below the earth generated amazing stories about daring the unknown, they fed consumer appetites for even more sensational tales and pictures of distant lands. Avowedly fictional presentations of the discovery and exploration of unmapped or lost worlds boomed, as this new age of connectivity spurred imaginations to go beyond even the often exaggerated exploits of real-life adventurers. French author Jules Verne's tales of adventures under the sea, in the air, and on uncharted islands reached audiences from their first book publications during the 1870s on into the age of mass movies. Japanese writer Oshikawa Shunrō, influenced by Verne, was not translated outside of Japan, but he popularized the adventure genre in Japan just after the turn of the century. German novelist Karl May's tales set in the American West, Asia, and the Middle East sold hundreds of millions of copies in thirty-three languages. In *Lost Horizon* (1933), British author James Hilton wrote of a fictional "Shangri-La" in the forbidding Himalayas. American writer Edgar Rice Burroughs claimed that Stanley's *In Darkest Africa* was by his side as he wrote his extravagantly popular Tarzan fantasies, the first of which came out in 1912. Like Verne's tales, Burroughs's many *Tarzan* books found audiences worldwide and provided staple formulas for the new medium of movies. Meanwhile, a growing global circulation of pulp magazines and their local adaptations, which sprang up on every continent, featured adventure stories and derring-do of all kinds.

Adventures engage readers through drama. There must be physical exploits, of course, but the popularity of the adventure genre arises from the constructed narrative form. Looking at the structure of adventure stories—the hope, the hazard, and then the triumph or tragedy—reveals less about the world than about audience expectations. In short, the transnational encounters embedded in adventure accounts *seemed* to be about the world but often achieved popularity because their dramatic centers and resolutions reinforced familiar verities: the importance of nation, of empire, of manly character. They often seemed to validate notions both of shared humanity and of exceptional races, and they generally obscured the contradictions between the two.

Shows and Entertainments

Adventure stories provided the structures for most popular amusements during this period. This was the heyday of extravagant live shows that traveled the globe while purporting to represent it. During the late nineteenth and early twentieth centuries, so many larger-than-life showmen and showwomen presented the "world" to so many audiences that it is hard to grasp the scale and significance of these spectacles with which people in almost every land became familiar. Even as the disciplinary circuits of sober scientists and engineers spread around the world, these transnational networks based on fantasy and spectacle also burgeoned. Both, in a sense, depended upon each other's achievements.

Looking through the biographical and descriptive material on the great shows of the period, one is quickly struck by the superlative language. Each show is often proclaimed as the most spectacular of its day and as the model for others. It becomes clear that no spatial or chronological ranking makes sense. The art of the spectacle did not "begin" in a particular place or at a single time and then spread in some predictable way. Rather, the currents of entertainment radiated transnationally and often with a kind of simultaneity. Newspapers, migration, travel, and then film created communities of entertainers that spanned the globe, borrowed from each other, and profited from weaving ever more extravagant representations. The major entertainers of the era, discussed below, appear in no order of chronology or importance. As a group, they suggest the pervasiveness of spectacle to this age of rational categorization and also provide background against which to understand the most important transnational entertainment that emerged from the age—the motion picture.

Circuses had become one of the central diversions of the nineteenth century, and just before and after the turn of the century many great circus families attained international fame: George Sanger and Frank Bostock in Britain, Carl Hagenbeck in Germany, the Gautier family in France, Albert Salamonsky in Moscow, Herman Renz in the Netherlands.[18]

The brilliant American promoter Phineas Taylor Barnum used many of the same formulas as these great circuses of Europe. Barnum, however, added scale and also perfected the art of enabling his huge circus entourage to travel widely and rapidly. With Hagenbeck as his designated foreign agent for animal procurement, Barnum found that portrayals of the "world" and its "exotic" creatures provided a circus's most powerful draw, and he took these appeals to their limits and beyond. Barnum's "Great Ethnological Congress of Curious People from All Parts of the World" featured "uncivilized" specimens that he claimed would instruct his viewers about the world. He acquired nine aborigines in Queensland, for example, and they toured with his circus during the 1880s (along with the huge pachyderm, Jumbo). His "Congress" included bearded ladies, armless men, a Chinese giant, a Burmese dwarf, and a family of Sioux Indians.[19]

During the 1870s and 1880s the most prominent showmen in America engaged in a rivalry over elephant displays—first over which could display the greatest numbers, then the greatest in size, then the whitest. In her history of the circus in the United States, Janet Davis speculates about the power of such exotic attractions: "The modern child first glimpsed the exotic Other through circuses and toys, a formative encounter that helped make colonial hierarchies part of the 'natural' world of child's play." This world both blurred and reinforced the lines of gender, race, and class—and especially the lines between animal and human. Well-performing Indian elephants became representatives of India, and "wild" elephants became emblems of Africa. Genuinely white elephants became the most coveted creatures.

Empire building was one of Barnum's standard themes. In his hands, the 1904 Durbar in Delhi became a lavish and popular pageant. His advertisements described the Durbar with the exaggerated codes of Orientalism: "native soldiers riding upon lofty, swaying camels and preceded by the mystic priests of Buddha, leading the sacred zebus and the sacrificial cattle; there is a prince of Siam with his retinue of warriors and shapely oriental dancing girls . . . while the Potentates of the Indian kingdoms pay their tribute to the Imperial power."[20]

The presentations of "abnormality" and difference that lay at the heart of Barnum's spectacles could have many meanings. They could project American middle-class values as normative, but they could also provide tempting glimpses into very different alternative worlds. Being carried off by circus people, after all, could function either as a fearsome cautionary tale or as a tantalizing possibility.

Whatever the exact impact on the sensibilities of individual viewers, however, circus spectacles helped to standardize entertainment formulas. Even as they projected diversity, spontaneity, and surprise, their success rested upon the precision needed for replication of acts and railroad mobility. As circuses traveled from place to place, they spread attention-grabbing sensations and raised expectations for encountering the unusual. They drew viewers away from their own local frameworks and introduced the techniques of regional, national, and even international mass culture.

Regional circuses flourished within this international milieu of circus techniques and performers. In China and Japan, countries whose acrobatic techniques had influenced European circuses in the nineteenth century, troupes of acrobats performed locally and sometimes as traveling parts of European or American circuses. In South Africa after World War I, Boswell Brothers Circus and Menagerie traveled by ox-wagon and train throughout the countryside. The Great Royal Circus of India, dating from 1909, and the Great Bombay Circus, operating primarily in Punjab, attracted regional audiences during the 1920s and 1930s. Argentines and Brazilians in the early twentieth century developed *circoteatro* shows, which combined traveling circus-style acts with musical, melodramatic, and magic-show performances. In all their variety, interconnection, and mutual borrowing, circuses came to be paradigmatic representatives of globalizing networks.

There were many turn-of-the-century extravaganzas that were related both to circuses and to world's fairs. Carl Hagenbeck, the impresario of the animal trade and developer of the much-copied Hamburg Tierpark, for example, merged together the concepts behind zoos, circuses, and exhibitions to establish a global entertainment empire. Although Hagenbeck presented his shows as part of a scientific impulse to document zoological diversity and to "authentically" represent other lands, he enthusiastically embraced the spectacle of the entertainment world. His Tierpark incorporated a dinosaur area with gigantic sculptures. Its ethnographic arena once featured a Wild West show, including forty-two Sioux Indians from the Pine Ridge Reservation in South Dakota that attracted more than a million viewers. Like Barnum's, his traveling circuses circled the globe, presenting the animals, people, and displays that had gained such a following at the Tierpark.

Imre Kiralfy, born in Austria-Hungary, became similarly famous for his extravagant productions. In the United States, Kiralfy and his brothers produced, among other things, a long-running version of Jules Verne's *Around the World in 80 Days,* which featured large female chorus lines and unusual special effects. For the Chicago Columbian Exhibition, Kiralfy staged "America," an extravaganza that grossed almost one million dollars in its seven months. After moving to London, he then built a smaller replica of Chicago's "White City" at Earl's Court and opened an "Empire of India" exhibit in 1895. The height of his career featured a huge Great White City at Shepherd's Bush in London, which hosted yearly exhibitions and the Olympic Games of 1908.[21]

Buffalo Bill Cody's Wild West traveled the world on a scale that was probably unmatched. Like the dime novels and highly mobile circuses from which Cody borrowed ideas and techniques, his Wild West shows generated enormous popularity by reinforcing the familiar formula that linked imperial destiny to the evolutionary progress of civilization. Even his show's musical background, offering such songs as "The Passing of the Red Man," advanced the message. In Cody's pageants the cowboy-hero of the American frontier became a mythic creature of unsurpassed virtue and skill who always vanquished his opponents. He was nature's nobleman: civilized and gentlemanly, yet an enemy of both savagery and of overrefinement. His drama of the triumph of civilization over barbarism seemed to have worldwide appeal.

The Wild West's popularity stemmed also from its skillful promoters and managers. Publicity stunts, larger-than-life images, and simplistic stereotypes all expanded the arts that were being perfected in the nascent advertising industry. Moreover, the mechanized precision of worldwide tours itself became part of the spectacle. Featuring sometimes as many as one thousand people, with all the horses and equipment needed to accompany them, the past represented in the Wild West inevitably met the future of Taylorized efficiency. Specially equipped trains, adapting models from the traveling circus, facilitated the logistics of quickly transporting and setting up the shows in destination after destination. The military campaigns so often celebrated in the dramas became surpassed in the show's own militarized speed and maneuverability.

In 1893 the name of the troupe became "Buffalo Bill's Wild West and Congress of Rough Riders of the World." The change signaled a transnational focus, and the show built a huge global fan base that included kings as well as commoners. Accommodating different audiences and the headlines of the day, Cody's scripts proved flexible in assigning heroes and villains. The Indians who played Cody's defeated nemesis could cue their hair to become Chinese Boxers overwhelmed by the forces of progress; celebratory reenactments of America military victory in the War of 1898 could vanquish assorted Spanish, Filipino, or Cuban foes; Russians could be flattered by epic renditions of their sweep to civilize the steppe. The romance of "The West" helped lure some Germans into dreaming of a frontier of their own in Eastern Europe. At the turn of the twentieth century, Buffalo Bill Cody might have been the most famous American in the world, and his entertainment formula shaped the production of mass culture across the media spectrum, including the new possibilities offered by film.[22]

Motion pictures truly revolutionized the transnational possibilities for show business. Developed more or less concurrently from various kinds of precursors in France, Germany, and the United States, motion picture films meant that images and stories could be projected relatively inexpensively all around the world almost simultaneously. In France the Lumière family created its first projections in 1895, and by 1899 Lumière films were being shown in Istanbul, Damascus, Jerusalem, Cairo, Mumbai, Mexico, Rio de Janeiro, Buenos Aires, Australia, Shanghai, Peking, Tokyo, and Yokohama.[23] Initially films concentrated on documenting and reporting notable events; the technology itself highlighted the spectacle of the object filmed. Most of the earliest films, only a few minutes in length, drew their appeal from collapsing both distance and class status. Popular topics showed images of celebrations that most audiences could never personally have witnessed: *Leaving Jerusalem by Railway* (1896), *The Capture of Rome, September 20, 1870* (1905), *The Coronation of Edward VII* (1902), *The Durbar at Delhi* (1912), *Carnival Scenes at Nice and Cannes* (1909). Before World War I, productions from France and Italy predominated in world markets, but few people thought in terms of national film industries. Production sprouted everywhere in the era of silent film. Distribution channels included a range of venues, from the lavish theaters that opened in every major city to the mobile screens that traveled via carts through even very remote areas of the world.

After World War I, films from America increasingly dominated global production and distribution. In older scholarship, the formulas and techniques that characterized Hollywood films were often cast as "American" and their global spread deemed "Americanization." Hollywood, however, was always a global place that had emerged within early cinema's transnational network. If Hollywood was innovative and popular in diverse localities throughout the globe, it was because filmmakers with transnational backgrounds and connections made it so. American films emerged less from the traditions of elite art (as films had in Europe) than from immigrant filmmakers who sought to develop entertainment for a diverse, multiethnic audience. Such films, especially in the silent era when language proved no barrier, perfectly suited a world market.

Hollywood's global appeal, of course, brought special advantages to investors and manufacturers in the United States. During the interwar era American companies directly owned more than half of the leading movie houses in the world, and American industries manufactured most of the film and production equipment. In 1925, American-produced films constituted approximately 95 percent of the total shown in Britain and Canada, 70 percent of those in France, and 80 percent of those in South America.²⁴ Japan developed a substantial film industry that retained a predominant market share in its own country, but Japanese films did not significantly figure in international distribution networks. During the 1930s especially, many national cinemas declined sharply under competition from Hollywood, depression-era conditions, and the coming of "talkies," which made it difficult for films in small-market languages to flourish.

Still, even when US companies dominated the international movie trade, the transnational currents in film culture remained strong. Some directors developed differentiated commonalities in their moviemaking, as transnational filmmaking came to display what film scholar Miriam Hanson called "vernacular modernism." The film industry boomed in India, for example, where new technologies and styles emerged from coproductive links between local innovations and the globalizing networks of production and distribution. Some thirteen hundred silent films were produced in India from 1912 to 1931. Even after "talkies" came in, the Indian industry flourished. Director Pramathesh Barua, for example, contributed his distinctive touch after study in Paris and London. His movies, wildly popular in India in the 1930s, grafted the narrative traditions, the melodrama, and the visuality of transnational film culture during India's colonial era onto some of India's own precolonial cultural forms. The popular orientation of Barua's films has brought him mixed reviews from later film critics, but he well exemplified filmmaking styles and themes that, as with many popular directors, skillfully mixed the global with the local. In interwar Shanghai, director Sun Yu also sought Chinese forms of modernity that drew from global currents. In Latin America, Argentine and Brazilian filmmakers imported equipment from France in the late nineteenth century; before World War I, Argentina, Uruguay, and Chile had developed a brisk exchange in the production and distribution of films. After the war, even in the face of relentless competition from Hollywood, Argentina produced several dozen movies a year, many featuring tango dancing. Likewise, the pre–World War II Mexican film industry became one of the strongest in the world, influenced by, and also standing apart from, nearby Hollywood.[25]

Hollywood itself became even more internationalized as directors, producers, and film technicians from many countries migrated there when threatened by the rise of fascism in Europe. Although barriers remained high against anyone not from the United States or Europe, "American" movie products of the late 1930s nonetheless emanated from one of the most cosmopolitan settings in the world. *Casablanca* (1942) provides an example: director Michael Curtiz had been born in Budapest, producer Hal Wallis in Chicago, musical creator Max Steiner in Vienna, screenplay writers Julius and Philip Epstein and cinematographer Arthur Edeson in New York City, editor Owen Marks in England, art director Carl Jules Weyl in Stuttgart. The cast featured Humphrey Bogart (New York City), Ingrid Bergman (Stockholm), Paul Henreid (Trieste), Claude Rains (London), Conrad Veidt (Potsdam), Sydney Greenstreet (Kent, England), Peter Lorre (Rózsahegy, Hungary), Madeleine Lebeau (Antony, Seine, France), Dooley Wilson (Tyler, Texas). The film's internationalism in production matched its message.

The global influence of Hollywood's motion pictures joined the spread of mass-produced magazines to set new styles of celebrity-dominated journalism. American physical culturalist and magazine impresario Bernarr Macfadden set the tone. Macfadden's publishing empire, which like Hollywood in the early twentieth century developed strong appeal within America's upwardly mobile immigrant communities, included popular titles such as *Physical Culture, True Story,* and *True Romances.* The largest publisher in the United States for several decades, Macfadden developed a huge global distribution network in the first half of the twentieth century. His publications popu-

A portrait of Dolores del Río, transnational film star. Born María de los Dolores Asúnsolo López Negrete in Durango, Mexico, del Río became a popular part of Hollywood's international social scene and a superstar in the industry's global movie empire during the 1920s and 1930s. Refusing to take part in films that she felt disparaged Mexico or Mexicans, and facing pressure for her leftist politics, she returned to Mexico in the 1940s to star in major Spanish-language films. (Library of Congress)

larized a "look" of modernity that included a reliance on celebrities and confessional formats along with projections of strong bodies, eroticism, and self-fashioning.[26]

The new film and celebrity magazines helped promote global film stars. During the silent era, stars such as Clara Bow (the "it" girl) and Lillian Gish in the United States, and Ruan Lingyu and Hu Die in China helped construct and explore a variety of roles for women. Film culture spread transnationally a feminine look that often combined heavy use of cosmetics and flashy clothing styles, evoking consumerism, with an aura of independence and sexuality. In the same era, Rudolph Valentino, the Italian-American heartthrob, parlayed his ambiguous national and ethnic identification as a "Latin lover" into a sex appeal that brought him global stardom. After the advent of "talkies" in the 1930s and 1940s, many of the most popular film celebrities continued to be figures who embodied transnational appeal in diverse and often personally destructive ways—Anna May Wong, Marlene Dietrich, Rita Hayworth, Carmen Miranda. Very often, the cultural otherness depicted in European, American, and Asian cinema provided ways of suggesting new gender norms and even alternative modernities. The currents of transnational cinema, like popular culture generally, offered a complex interplay of emulation and differentiation.[27]

The medium of film, its celebrants claimed, brought the world together by depicting unfamiliar places. It projected images of New York apartments to people in Patagonia, constructed Chinese rural life for filmgoers in Paris, represented Chicago gangsters to fans in Africa. Especially in Hollywood's world, global diversity could sometimes be mastered quickly and easily. Fox's *Movietone News,* begun in 1919, took viewers "Around the World in Fifteen Minutes in Picture and Sound." Paramount News, begun in 1927, adopted a similar cosmopolitanism-but-be-quick-about-it appeal.

These glimpses of the world, of course, were highly selective and structured in formulaic and misleading ways. Many of the popular documentary films of the first three decades of the twentieth century, for example, claimed an ethnographic authority similar to that supposedly represented in world's fairs and museums. Safari films produced by Nordisk, the first Scandinavian film company, purchased bears and lions from Carl Hagenbeck to stage safaris. Everything about these films was faked, except for the animals, which were shot and killed in front of the camera. For safari and hunt films, body count (of animals) seemed a key factor in popularity. Hagenbeck himself turned toward film. He constructed his own Kino in the Tierpark, shot many films, and killed some of his most troublesome animals after staged hunts. He also allowed other filmmakers to use the dramatic backdrops of his park. Even during and just after World War I, seven different production companies shot films at the Tierpark, which became an all-purpose "foreign" background that could be outfitted to stand in for any exotic terrain in the world.[28]

Robert J. Flaherty's *Nanook of the North: A Story of Life and Love in the Actual Arctic* (1922) is considered the first feature-length documentary film. Flaherty's cameras followed, and sometimes staged, the story of an Inuit man and his family in the Canadian arctic and highlighted their traditional methods of hunting, fishing, and igloo building.[29] A box office success, *Nanook* encouraged other adventurers to try to capture the lives of premodern peoples for the movie screen. Like *Nanook,* the supposedly ethnographic documentaries of the age, however, often exaggerated their presentations by incorporating the formulas that audiences already expected from mass attractions.

The primary purpose of most documentary films, of course, was entertainment, and their formulas borrowed from those pioneered in world's fair midways, zoos, vaudeville, amusement parks, circuses, and adventure novels. Osa and Martin Johnson provide an example. They began their careers in vaudeville and then turned to nature photography and film. With their one million feet of film (their photographs formed one of the initial collections of the Museum of Natural History in New York), eighteen books, and over one hundred articles, they epitomized the way in which various new mass media intertwined to represent the world and to entertain audiences, who seemed to crave spectacles of unfamiliar cultures in a shrinking world. "This was the Africa as no civilized man had seen it," boomed the narrator of their film *Simba* (1928), produced under the auspices of the Museum of Natural

History. *Congorilla* (1932), a voice declared, demonstrated "the age-old story of man emerging from savagery." Osa Johnson, in poses echoed in so many of the photos taken in this age of imperial power, frequently posed with her rifle over the animal kills. In *Simba* she contributed the crucial shot that saved the party from an elephant stampede, killed a charging rhinoceros, brought down a lion that was the object of a village hunt, and then joined the "natives" in celebrating the kill by baking an apple pie. An accomplished shooter of both guns and film, Osa domesticated exotic places and displayed the prowess of white women over both animals and the native males who also participated in the hunts. If Osa and Martin's photos and films fostered greater familiarity with the world, they did so by also reinforcing the highly contrived conventions of racial and cultural hierarchy that permeated the adventure shows of the age.[30]

By purporting to show ethnographic "realities," documentaries constructed cultural differences that could supply humor and even melodrama. One common comedic device involved highlighting the superior knowledge of whites while mocking the inadequacies of "natives." Frank Buck, one of the preeminent procurers of exotic animals for zoos and shows, for example, scored a box office hit in 1932 with his feature-length documentary *Bring 'Em Back Alive,* a film that became the cultural reference for the 1933 hit *King Kong.* One scene features a large hunting party of natives who fearfully flee when they hear a jungle noise. The audience is then treated to a shot of the accompanying white explorer, who unflappably pulls back bushes to reveal a small and harmless honey bear. In such films, the dominant subject was the white hunter-adventurer, the setting included exotic animals and peoples, and the drama came from the testing and ultimately the mastery displayed by the protagonist, an obvious symbol of Western civilization.

The world according to Hollywood's feature films also took shape within such conventions. Although the preponderance of Hollywood

Osa Johnson demonstrating the use of cosmetics to a group of Masai in a carefully posed photograph, 1923. Johnson, alongside her husband Martin, were American vaudevillians, explorers, photographers, and filmmakers who produced influential but highly staged images of Africa. Always on a tight budget, the Johnsons pioneered product-placement advertising in their photographs by depicting odd scenes in which they "introduced" Africans to globally marketed products such as Coca-Cola, Shell Oil, Eveready batteries, Bisquick biscuit mix, Fab detergent, and Colgate toothpaste, along with various brands of cosmetics. (© Bettmann/Corbis)

plots presented images of the United States, those images could become more defined when played off against a "foreign" setting. Producers found that they could easily create rather undifferentiated "foreign" locations by adding a repertoire of various exotic fixings to the same studio lot. As Hagenbeck had discovered when his Tierpark became the standard place to shoot German movies set in foreign locations, one did not need to travel around the world to make movies. Rather, a standard set of "exotic" motifs would do. Film historian Ruth Vesey points out that although Hollywood dressed residents of foreign locations in different costumes, they were generally accorded similar picturesque qualities and set against similar backgrounds. As American-produced films sought export markets, directors had to be sensitive about giving offense to any particular national group. Vesey writes that "since the foreigners' national origins were deliberately obscured, the population of Hollywood's universe came to be broadly comprised of 'Americans' and 'others.'"[31] Film viewers consequently could "travel" without the cultural, physical, or monetary discomfort of actually doing so. The world they experienced through film, however, was a carefully constructed and formulaic product that had evolved out of the mass amusements popularized in the nineteenth century.

Mass Tourism

The adventures represented in novels, the sensationalist press, and film brought visions of a shrinking world to mass audiences throughout the world. They perhaps stimulated wanderlust in many, and they schooled those tempted to stray from their familiar surroundings in the conventions of how to perceive whatever appeared strange. Buoyed by ever cheaper and faster transportation systems, mass travel began its rapid rise, at least for Europeans and Americans. In 1911 the London *Times* reported that one million Britons were visiting the continent yearly. A century before, the number had been fewer than ten thousand.[32] In 1880 about 50,000 US tourists per year traveled to Europe; thirty years later the number had mushroomed to 250,000.[33] Historians of US tourism have emphasized the huge growth in traveling to Europe and to the "Holy Land," but at the turn of the century six steamship lines also served US travelers to Asia.[34] It was within the context of this boom in mass tourism, of course, that the world's fairs flourished as an around-the-world travel destination located closer to home. Mass travel promoted new industries that constructed their own transnational networks. Operators such as the British firm Thomas Cook, which put together some of its first tours for the Crystal Palace Exhibition of 1851, developed the global connections and specialty tours that could ease the hardships of individual travel. Cook and the Berlin-based company Stangen operated almost all over the world. Guidebooks by Baedeker in Germany, John Murray in England, and Michelin in France advised travelers on what was "important" to see in various locations worldwide. Michelin introduced the practice of according stars to favorite eateries and inns. In Germany the Nazi regime also encouraged a carefully controlled tourism designed to offer working people something other than a message of discipline and sacrifice. The "Community Strength Through Joy" agency, created in 1933, sought to build support for the regime and weaken the appeal of the Left by developing a limited but affordable menu of consumer activities and tours. By 1938 Strength Through Joy constituted the largest travel agency in Germany, with buses and twelve cruise ships. It had sent fifty-four million Germans not just on outings to well-known domestic historical and hiking sites but also on excursions to Norway, Greece, Italy, Madeira, and elsewhere.[35]

Inexpensive and easily portable Kodak cameras became signatures of the traveler. The American company Kodak democratized the medium of photography, heavily promoted travel for the middle class, and cleverly used its advertisements to instruct users in how to take engaging and enviable photos. Armed with information on tours, guides, and cameras, armies of new tourists set out on adventures and then brought their experiences and photos back home to church basements, living rooms, and community gatherings.

Women proved critical to the growth of the mass travel industry. In the United States, for example, dozens of American women, often sponsored by newspapers and magazines, wrote about their travels around the globe. The demand for such accounts in women's magazines seemed almost endless. The *Ladies Home Journal,* especially, fed the fascination for romps through the world in its many features of foreign travel and, for young girls, its around-the-world series of paper dolls that wore different national costumes. Moreover, women's travel clubs sprouted in towns all across the United States, providing armchair adventure for those who might not go themselves. For thirty years an American entrepreneur, John Stoddard, successfully marketed his "Travel Series" of lectures and travel accounts to such clubs. As members gathered to discuss different countries and cultures, the women's club culture strengthened the idea that travel was desirable, educational, and generally accessible to the broad middle class. Acts of travel, it seemed, could come from acts of study and imagination as surely as from boarding a ship or rail car.[36]

Film did the most to promote and simulate mass travel. In the new genre of the "travelogue," the Americans Burton Holmes and James A. Fitzpatrick were the kings. Holmes had begun on the lecture circuit, where he coined the word *travelogue* to describe his performances. Like Stoddard, he sold impressive numbers of volumes that interspersed his lectures with photographs. After World War I, however, Holmes took to the screen. Working for Paramount Pictures, he featured titles such as *Burton Holmes' Head Hunters* (1919) and *Torrid Tampico* (1921). Fitzpatrick's *Traveltalks* and other documentaries, which commonly played before feature films in movie palaces worldwide from the mid-1920s through the mid-1950s, perfected the formula for the travel film genre.

Fitzpatrick specialized in introducing his audience, who were presumed to live harried "modern" lives, to the presumed simple pleasures and uncomplicated customs of distant lands. In choosing his world locations, he was keenly aware of fantasies and fascinations with the "primitive." Social evolutionary thought had, of course, placed the primitive at the low end of a progressive continuum, but Fitzpatrick's formulations exalted ideas about how a rural life and closeness to nature could counterbalance the enervating influences of urban civilization. Many of his travelogues ended with the somber "and now we must say a fond farewell" (to some idyllic lifestyle) and return to the thankless pressures of "our" advanced ways. For many moviegoers, Fitzpatrick became the "Voice of the Globe."[37]

Mass travel seemed to promise enlightenment by reaching out to other lands and peoples, but the tours and travel literature often structured experiences designed to confirm Euro-American advancement set against backwardness elsewhere. Not surprisingly, Strength Through Joy's tours began each morning with swastika-draped ceremonies, emphasized racial exclusion, and contrasted the orderliness and cleanliness of German cruise ships with some of the disorderly, poverty-ridden, and darker-skinned ports of call. Travel could establish new bonds among people, but it could just as easily confirm beliefs in racial hierarchy and fuel ethnonationalism.

Consumer Codes and Advertising

The sensational display of adventure, the advent of motion pictures, and the growing appetite for mass travel were all parts of a new ethos of mass consumerism. Spreading within transnational networks, this emerging world of consumerism was not just about buying necessary goods. Rather, "mass consumerism" may be defined as a mass-production and mass-marketing system that imagines an abundance of goods within a culture that emphasizes purchasing, desire, glamour, and flexible, consumption-driven identities. Consumerism, in this usage, is as much a cultural as an economic system. It operates to establish "codes" by which particular mass-marketed items signal specific kinds of associations. The United States, with its large domestic market and adroit advertising industry, emerged as perhaps the most significant global driver of mass consumerism and its codes. The specificities of local cultures, however, also helped coproduce variants of mass consumerism within the expanding transnational networks of commodities, producers, sellers, buyers, and advertisers.

Such transnational flows were inevitably complex and often contradictory. C. A. Bayly has emphasized that colonial rule, by creating networks that introduced Western modes of speech, dress, and sociability, proved critical to the spread of consumerist codes and "modernity." So were global networks of media, which circulated publications, movies, and advertisements. It would be beyond the scope of almost any work to trace out all of the various codes projected within transnational circuits of consumption, much less to speculate on how they might have, over time, shaped the identities of people, regions, nations, empires, classes, genders, sexualities, and ethnicities. As changes in demography, communication, and trade mixed people together as never before and augmented the availability of goods, how would it be possible to represent all of the ways in which consumers might signal affiliations and identifications? Yet the significance of the mass consumer networks that emerged in this era may not be ignored just because their meanings are necessarily elusive and variable.

The consumerist-driven mixing of cultural attributes within transnational space can be described by many terms. *Assimilation* connotes the loss of one culture along with the embrace of another. *Hybridity* connotes the selective adaptation of different cultural elements into some new combination. I prefer to borrow, from linguistics, the term *code-switching,* which seems best to capture what most often occurred in the culture of transnational mass-consumer images.[38] Just as people with fluency in multiple languages may go back and forth, strategically invoking words from different languages at particular times, so consumer code-switching may also connote the going back and forth, strategically producing an assemblage, at any given time, of different cultural and political significations.

Consumer goods coded all kinds of projections and allegiances. Consider, for example, the "modern girls" in Shanghai in the 1920s who assembled their "look" from a *qipao,* high-heeled shoes, and bobbed hair. Or the rebels who fled New York for New Mexico in the 1920s and projected their antimodernist views by mixing western ranch styles with emblems of Mexican indigenous culture. Or the elite Mexican "chica moderna" who mixed European style with folkloric attire and accessories mimicked from indigenous cultures and from Europe's "exotic" representations of them. Or the zigs and zags of men's fashions. Before World War I, many urban men of affairs throughout the world embraced the simplicity and uniformity of Western-style clothes. Rejecting the complex, colorful, and often luxurious robes and coats characteristic of many indigenous styles, the simple top hat and black coat came to signal power and sobriety. Yet, especially after World War I, men in colonies often became more self-conscious about signaling pro- or anticolonial political affiliations by the degree to which they adopted Western business attire and housing styles, and many sought to retain traditional customs in clothing and dwelling. Moreover, political currents, generally controlled by men, often channeled women's fashions in significant ways. Meiji reformers in Japan mandated Western dress in the 1870s, but a nationalist revival later brought the kimono for women back into greater prominence. Soviet authorities scorned the capitalistic overtones of the women's fashion industry, favoring simple garments that facilitated work and were not provocative, but many women dreamed of having access to greater choice and style. Fashion was just one arena in which consumerist identities could be assembled and advanced.[39]

The more open particular societies were to global currents, the more consumer code-switching became a cultural style associated with modernity. Code producers, such as those involved in movies, advertising, governmental fashion policies, or movements of various kinds, helped contour the environment in which different cultural codes might be accepted or rejected. Individuals, however, also played active roles in selecting, mixing, and making meanings from the available codes. Consumerism offered the raw material for a constructed (and reconstructible) projection of self and society that drew upon transnational networks of goods and symbols. As such, it could seem both alluring and subversive.

The power of capital, of course, clearly shaped consumer culture. Commercial advertising, an increasingly transnational set of practices and businesses, became perhaps the most important global purveyor of consumer codes (along with films). From the late nineteenth century, expanding along with trade, advertising sought to foster values and lifestyle aspirations that would boost people's desires to purchase specific products. Advertising agencies became important cultural brokers, working to adapt messages across boundaries and to create what historian Daniel Boorstin called "consumption communities" that transcended geographic space.[40] Although in the twentieth century a substantial critical commentary portrayed advertising-driven mass consumption as a homogenizing influence (and often as an agent of "Americanization" or of "cultural imperialism"), more-contemporary cultural analysis has stressed the interplay between global and local and the possibilities for the often creative juxtapositions that became a mark of modernist pastiche. Advertising strategies have generally responded to pressures for both standardization (the "packaging" of buyers to sell to marketers) and diversification (the flexibility needed to appeal to diverse buyers). As with other transnational phenomena, they exemplify differentiated commonalities, even as they also may embody asymmetries in power.

American advertiser J. Walter Thompson became a leader in forging transnational networks devoted to selling. Founded in 1864 in New York, JWT opened its first branch in 1899 in London and expanded rapidly into dozens of other countries. The American model of advertising departed from the older European approaches that emphasized artistic styles associated with nineteenth-century posters. Centering the appeal of their ads on whatever was likely to make customers respond, US advertisers pioneered techniques developed within the emerging field of psychology. They employed surveys and other types of "scientific" methods to gauge and constantly improve the effectiveness of their persuasive strategies. Partly through advertising—and partly through screen images—constellations of signifying codes became recognizable throughout much of the world. JWT designed ads, used worldwide, for American auto manufacturers that featured sporty, young, unescorted women and appealed to a car's beauty as much as to its performance. It also held the accounts for many cosmetics and soap companies. Especially in the interwar era, such advertising messages constructed and spread a look of modernity that, when often mixed with localized images, aimed to stimulate desire for products, especially among women.[41]

Among urban youth throughout the world in the 1920s, consumerist modernity often seemed to come dressed with cropped hair, cigarette adornments, and fascination with jazz music, movies, cars, and dancing. These codes beckoned toward cultural reorientations, especially changing relations between men and women. They suggested approval of heterosocial relationships, that is, close friendships between men and women who were not related. They signaled the ideal of couple-formation based on individual desire and companionate marriage. In some cases, they hinted at greater acceptance for same-sex attractions. Within patriarchal systems in which male control of female sexuality was paramount, such "modern" styles could represent a threat of social breakdown or a promise of new freedoms, depending on one's perspective.

In the early twentieth century, images of "modern girls" had emerged simultaneously throughout the world as flappers, vamps, *garçonnes, moga, modeng xiaojie, kallege ladki,* schoolgirls, and *neue Frauen.* Everywhere, these were "young women with the wherewithal and desire to

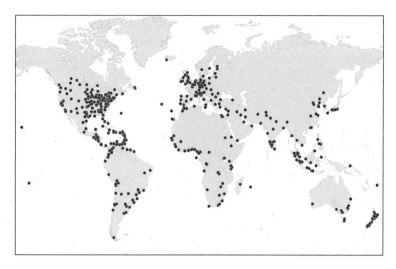

Global operations and distribution centers for the Goodyear Tire and Rubber Company, 1928. The distribution and sales of rubber tires, which accompanied the rapid spread of motorized vehicles, exemplifies the global, but uneven, spread of the automobile/consumer revolution. By the mid-1920s, US-based Goodyear was the largest rubber company in the world.

define themselves in excess of conventional female roles and as transgressive of national, imperial, and racial boundaries." Modern girls seemed especially drawn to automobiles, which signaled independence and mobility. The 1920s became a heyday for women motorists.[42] Moreover, advertisers encouraged the love affair between women and autos. In the United States and in markets around the world, ad campaigns for the American autos that dominated global sales portrayed women as athletic, unsupervised, and fashionable. They showed women driving often simply for recreation. In different languages, they proclaimed the message that "Every Day More and More Women Drive Cars."[43]

As consumer advertising and modern-girl imagery emerged globally, contests over cultural values flared. Cultural wars over the products and entertainments associated with mass consumerism became especially contentious in the 1920s and the depression decade of the 1930s. In countries as diverse as Germany, Mexico, France, Nicaragua, Italy, China, and Japan, custodians of elite culture and groups espousing "traditional" values (especially related to gender) most loudly invoked themes of nationalism and anticonsumerism (or their own consumer-nationalism) against the proliferation of foreign consumer goods and images they regarded as degraded and feminized. The Nazi regime in Germany denounced jazz music, which it depicted as an alien and degenerate art form produced by African-Americans and Jews, and tried to develop a mass culture supposedly rooted in *völkisch* traditions. Popular "swing clubs," however, kept jazz alive, even during the outright bans of the World War II era.[44] On the contentious grounds of mass commercial culture, any particular assemblage of consumer codes could send especially evocative—and provocative—signals.

China, particularly the trading crossroads of urban Shanghai, provides a specific example of the growth of transnational mass consumerism and advertising and of how consumer codes travel. Consumer products, promoted in advertising and film images, washed into urban China during the 1920s and 1930s as American, European, and Japanese entrepreneurs sought to capitalize on the potential of the fabled "China market." At the same time, the ethos of the May Fourth era in China (1917–1921) encouraged both nationalism and an influx of Western writings, as the movement drew from a cosmopolitan spirit that sought to adapt foreign models to national goals.[45] Especially in the treaty ports and particularly in the International Settlement in Shanghai (where approximately thirty thousand foreigners lived among more than eight hundred thousand Chinese), the rapid growth of modern mass media and electrification provided the transnational infrastructure for advertising and consumer awareness. Estimates suggest that by the mid-1930s, nearly two thousand magazines reached over thirty million people in the whole of China; there were seventy-eight broadcast radio stations, and outdoor billboards were increasingly common. In Shanghai specifically, thirty-six newspapers had a combined daily circulation of nearly nine hundred thousand, and there may have been as many as thirty advertising agencies, foreign and local. Eight Hollywood studios established distribution offices in Shanghai, and by 1927 the city boasted 150 domestically owned film production companies. Dozens of gigantic movie palaces proliferated in both the International Settlement and in the Chinese City sections of Shanghai, the world's sixth-largest city. The great Art Deco structure *The Grand* accommodated an audience of two thousand people.[46]

Despite low buying power and occasional nationalist boycotts against foreign goods, the icons of Western and Japanese consumerism grew in familiarity in China. Ads for lipstick, face cream, women's fashions, and a variety of patent medicines found their way into all of these new media outlets. Women's fashions in Shanghai, taking cues from French designs and American movie stars, were popularized in the widely disseminated calendar posters. Dresses narrowed to become more fitted; hems rose; and side splits revealed legs with Western-style shoes. Hair that was bobbed or curled with new permanent-wave machines often complemented these styles.[47] The British-American Tobacco Company advertised its cigarettes on the first neon sign in Shanghai and hired local graphic artists to adapt appeals appropriately to the local setting. Although new Chinese mass consumers generally came from the affluent class, people from across the income spectrum became familiar with the look and tastes associated with mass consumerism—products such as French designer dresses, Singer sewing machines, RCA records, Colgate toothpaste, Palmolive soap, and Max Factor makeup. Shanghai's International Settlement became famous for its neon lights, night life, and entertainments. Jazz music and ballroom dancing provided the sounds and signs of a consumerist culture.

The products and images from America and the West entered China in conjunction with several other major trends: Western colonialism (with its unequal administrative authority as well as a Marxist, anti-imperialist critique of this inequality); Chinese hopes for a modernity consistent with Chinese nationalism; an often chaotic political system faced with trying to accommodate the vast geographical and ethnic diversity within China; and the emergence of an urban sensibility that challenged the intellectual status quo. Within this complex of circumstances, the semiotics of consumerist messages became shifting and ambiguous.

Karl Gerth's study of consumerism and nationalism in early twentieth-century China, *China Made,* discusses the movements that sought to promote the idea that China could become a modern nation by avoiding foreign imports and encouraging the purchase of Chinese-made fashions, foods, and fun. The development of nationalistic consumerist actions and rituals—boycotts of foreign products, exhibitions of Chinese goods, commemorations of national humiliations, and celebrations of Chinese entrepreneurs—came together under the slogan "Chinese people should consume Chinese products!"[48]

Just as consumerism could express nationalism and generate codes against foreign incursion, however, it also contributed to a cosmopolitanism that welcomed external influences. In the interwar era, Shanghai, a city often seen both as a part of but also as different from the rest of China, exemplified a hybrid worldliness. Department store display windows, calendar posters, magazine advertisements, and movie palaces complemented each other in emphasizing visuality, display, and spectatorship. Leo Ou-fan Lee argues that the respectable display of the female body became "part of a new public discourse related to modernity in everyday life."[49] The *Young Companion (Liangyu huabao),* a magazine established in Shanghai in 1925, specialized in photography and featured a "modern" woman on the cover of each issue—at first actual women and later fantasy women. Such publications exemplified the ways in which Chinese cosmopolitans adapted and rescripted cultural forms. Lee describes, for example, how Western formulas for plots in popular cinema and magazine articles were neither rejected nor appropriated outright; they were, instead, often shaped to suggest traditional Chinese narratives and values. Similarly, Chinese female film stars borrowed from Western fashions and poses, but often also conveyed independence less through sexuality than by posing with books as well-educated women. Intellectuals, after all, constituted the most enthusiastic audience for foreign cinema and were most open to the kind of new relationships between men and women that were shown on the movie screens. Although the Chinese "modern girl" of the 1920s and 1930s clearly drew upon the Japanese *moga* style, which had been heavily influenced by Hollywood, she nonetheless projected a complex imagery. For example, the *qipao,* which came to dominate fashions by the late 1920s and 1930s, provided a look that was both modern and Chinese.[50] Wen-hsin Yeh's *Shanghai Splendor,* which elaborates Shanghai's complex modernity, concludes that "not only was it possible to be simultaneously 'modern' and 'Chinese,' it was virtually imperative for a patriotic Chinese to be modern."[51]

People in interwar urban China, of course, were not alone in the complex ways in which they interacted with the spread of consumerist culture. Miriam Silverberg has analyzed how Japanese women in the interwar era used code-switching in consumer practices to articulate identity. Examining the Japanese women's magazine *Shofu no Tomo,* she points out the juxtaposition of Western products and consumer practices with distinctly Japanese aesthetics and contexts. Similarly, the contributors to the "Modern Girl Around the World" project note both the commonalities in the "modern girl" image and also the local differences. Cosmetics and soap advertisements throughout the globe confirm the proliferation of skin-whitening products and their association with sexual attractiveness and modernity; yet individual ads also show significant locally rooted differences in how the ads directed their appeals. In fashion, Parisian houses that set the pace for much of the world's fashion industry attracted an internationally oriented elite clientele, but down-scale adaptations with local twists quickly emerged and catered to larger groups with differentiated tastes.[52]

The images and practices of consumerism thus helped shape the visual environment, particularly of cosmopolitan cities; and by offering code-switching possibilities, consumerism encouraged a style of modernity characterized by pastiche and allowing for differentiated commonalities. Mass consumerism undoubtedly bolstered the power of the world's capital centers, especially those in the United States, an export powerhouse in the 1920s. But it also challenged and played with many seemingly fixed definitions, particularly those related to gender, ethnicity, sexuality, and national culture.

The emergence of an increasingly globalized mass culture may have been one of the most important characteristics of this age. Innovations in media—mass publication, traveling shows, and film— helped create the era's adventurers, entertainers, and mass marketers, whose spreading transnational networks channeled the spectacular forms and formulas that, in turn, looped back to feed the new media. Radiating through the protean and nonspatial geographies of trans-nationalism, the currents that carried mass cultural products mapped, unmapped, and remapped the globe. The sureties of territoriality gave way to movement and to the ever-changing configurations of connectivity.

The new worlds born within the expanding availability of images and codes could be ones of shrunken space and dissolved boundaries, but they could also be worlds that accentuated difference and incommensurability. By drawing together the world's people within representational, often moneymaking, forms of written and visual images, dissimilarities could be both muted and exaggerated. Like all of the global networks of this era, the highly symbolic realms of media worked in no simple or uniform way toward building a global audience or toward accommodating global variation.

The multiplication of consumer codes that different people could accept, reject, adapt, or combine in almost limitless patterns became a hallmark of spectacularized cultural modernity. As transnational circulation of an ever-widening variety of consumer codes spread, the possibilities for interpellation (and reinterpellation) into an increasingly broad array of cultural identifications accelerated. By code-switching to create different assemblages of consumerist goods and activities, individual and national identities could be constructed in a kind of modular fashion. Variously coded attributes could be switched on or off, combined with others, and modified in different degrees. Even as mass consumerism's main productive and profit-making centers remained firmly anchored in the West, its symbols presented an aspirational world of self-fashioning that spanned the globe.

The rise of transnational mass cultural enterprises and codes signaled the broader transformation that was at work during this era— "the move from a nineteenth-century imperial tactic of spatial discovery by occupation to one of territorial ubiquity through technology and representation."[53] The late nineteenth and early twentieth centuries' obsessions with cartography, territorial exploration, nation building, and empire building were parts of a worldview that had framed a civilizing project of global improvement marked by territorial acquisition. The seeming solidity of geographical maps provided an apt symbol of that teleological sensibility. What Charles Maier and others have called the "hyperstates" that embraced communism and fascism tried to use law and repression to control cultural codes they deemed threatening. So did many imperial, and anti-imperial, authorities. By the mid-twentieth century, however, the fleeting and spectacularized images of a transnational, consumerist mass culture increasingly beckoned the future. Coproduced and complex networks stood ready to invade any demarcated territory. Flows of images and other codes held potential for a continual remapping of significations and relationships. The onset of this flickering, unstable, and electronics-shaped modernity came linked, perhaps, to the rise of the United States' particular brand of global dominance in its short "American Century" (famously announced by Henry Luce in 1941), but state power could hardly control the increasingly interactive landscapes of meaning.

⟿

As revolutions in communications and transportation simultaneously expanded and shrank the world in the period 1870–1945, growing numbers of people became involved in global exchanges that histories centering primarily on national states or on markets have often overlooked. This book has highlighted a wide variety of growing transnational social and cultural networks: impulses toward internationalism; social affiliations based on class, ethnicity, gender, and religion; nodes of exhibition and collection such as world fairs, museums, and botanical gardens; connections based on expertise such as engineering, medicine, urban planning, and the new social sciences; and spectacular flows of mass media and consumerism.

The book's central metaphor of "currents," evoking this electrical age, emphasizes crisscrossing flows of power, an interactive though often asymmetrical dynamic, and the simultaneity of both universalizing and differentiating effects. In this age of nationalism and imperialism, transnational currents did not represent some new stage of convergence beyond nation and empire; connected networks both assisted and disrupted concerns over expanding and defending territory. But, at the same time, transnational currents increasingly beckoned beyond territoriality toward a world in which fast-moving technologies of representation, with multiple and shifting codes of meaning, challenged the fixity of space and identity.

Examining this array of global connections highlights distinctive ways in which the technological innovations of "modernity" wedded science and spectacle. From the 1870s, globe-spanning technologies (telegraph cables, railroads and faster ships, radio, cameras, airplanes, and others) extended their reach and brought rapid and dramatic change. Many of technology's innovations created a secular realm of the miraculous. In this new world, suddenly ablaze with electric lights and motion pictures, images dazzled; speed amazed; illumination seemed to promise to sweep away darkness, both physically and metaphorically. Possibilities beckoned—the possibility that technology and expertise could usher in a more harmonious future, the possibility of creating strong bodies and strong nations, the possibility of being "modern," whatever that meant to whoever used the term. More fearful possibilities also circulated—encounters with unfamiliar lands and customs could breed distain and hatred; national and imperial rivalries could erupt into wars with new potential for technological destruction. People in diverse situations throughout the world were positioned differently with respect to the spectacular science and technology of the modern age, but few could escape its fascinations and its rippling effects. The spectacles embedded in the narratives of mechanical and scientific transformation captivated people on every continent and hailed many to embrace some version of the progress that was not just a Western imposition but a global phenomenon generated in differentiated localities ("differentiated commonalities"). At the same time, the technologies and spectacles of modernity might also quite literally *captivate* people by hardening regimes of racial and geographical inequalities. The sirens of modernity could lure with songs of freedom and self-fashioning while obscuring the rocky hierarchies of power.

A focus on transnational realms in this period underscores how homogenization and differentiation, the global and the local, trans- or internationalism and nationalism, reason and spectacle are all sets not of opposites but of complements that operate in creative tension with each other. These seemingly binary poles emerge as coproductive counterparts in transnational space and foreshadow the complexities of the modernity that would continue to characterize the late twentieth century and beyond.

Notes

INTRODUCTION

1 Quoted in Nayan Chanda, *Bound Together: How Traders, Preachers, Adventurers, and Warriors Shaped Globalization* (New Haven, CT: Yale University Press, 2007), 127.

2 C. A. Bayly, *The Birth of the Modern World, 1780–1914: Global Connections and Comparisons* (Oxford: Blackwell, 2004), quotations at 476. Broad scholarship on the role of Europe includes Kenneth Pomeranz, *The Great Divergence: China, Europe, and the Making of the Modern World Economy* (Princeton, NJ: Princeton University Press, 2000); James Belich, *Replenishing the Earth: The Settler Revolution and the Rise of the Anglo-World, 1783–1939* (New York: Oxford University Press, 2009); Jürgen Osterhammel, *Europe, the "West" and the Civilizing Mission* (London: German Historical Institute, 2006); Osterhammel, *Geschichtswissenschaft jenseits des Nationalstaats* (Göttingen: Vandenhoeck & Ruprecht, 2001); Osterhammel, *Die Entzauberung Asiens: Europa und die asiatischen Reiche im 18. Jahrhundert,* 2nd ed. (Munich: C. H. Beck, 2010), 378; Michael Adas, *Machines as the Measure of Men: Science, Technology, and Ideologies of Western Dominance* (Ithaca, NY: Cornell University Press, 1989); Uday Singh Mehta, *Liberalism and Empire: A Study in Nineteenth-Century British Liberal Thought* (Chicago: University of Chicago Press, 1999); Jennifer Pitts, *A Turn to Empire: The Rise of Imperial Liberalism in Britain and France* (Princeton, NJ: Princeton University Press, 2005).

3 For a discussion of the emergence of the concept of "transnational" history, see Kiran Klaus Patel, "Überlegungen zu einer transnationalen Geschichte," in *Weltgeschichte,* ed. Jürgen Osterhammel (Stuttgart: Franz Steiner, 2008), 67–90; and Pierre-Yves Saunier, "Transnational," in *The Palgrave Dictionary of Transnational History from the Mid-nineteenth Century to the Present Day,* ed. Akira Iriye and Pierre-Yves Saunier (New York: Palgrave Macmillan, 2009), 1047–1055. Two examples are Sebastian Conrad and Jürgen Osterhammel, eds., *Das Kaiserreich transnational: Deutschland in der Welt, 1871–1914* (Göttingen: Vandenhoeck und Ruprecht, 2004); and Akira Iriye, *Global Community: The Role of International Organizations in the Making of the Contemporary World* (Berkeley: University of California Press, 2002). Also see Michael Geyer and

Charles Bright, "World History in a Global Age," *American Historical Review* 100 (October 1995): 1034–1060; Sebastian Conrad and Dominic Sachsenmaier, eds., *Competing Visions of World Order: Global Moments and Movements, 1880s–1930s* (New York: Palgrave Macmillan, 2007).

4 Aihwa Ong, *Flexible Citizenship: The Cultural Logics of Transnationality* (Durham, NC: Duke University Press, 1999), is suggestive on this point.

5 Mary Louise Pratt, *Imperial Eyes: Travel Writing and Transculturation,* 2nd ed. (New York: Routledge, 2008); Anna Lowenhaupt Tsing, *Friction: An Ethnography of Global Connection* (Princeton, NJ: Princeton University Press, 2004).

6 The term *differentiated commonalities* is indebted to the idea of "structures of common difference," explored in Alys Eve Weinbaum et al., eds., *The Modern Girl Around the World: Consumption, Modernity, and Globalization* (Durham, NC: Duke University Press, 2008). On global/local, see essays in A. G. Hopkins, ed., *Global History: Interactions between the Universal and the Local* (New York: Palgrave, 2006).

7 Beyond conveying this broad sense of disjuncture, I am not using the word *modernity* as an analytical category with precise meaning. Rather I see the word *modernity* as the representation of a claim that appeared frequently and transnationally over this period and helped animate a wide range of views and disputes over possible futures.

8 James C. Scott, *The Art of Not Being Governed: An Anarchist History of Upland Southeast Asia* (New Haven, CT: Yale University Press, 2009); Frederick Cooper, "What Is the Concept of Globalization Good For? An African Historian's Perspective," *African Affairs* 100 (2001): 189–213.

9 John Tomlinson, *Globalization and Culture* (Chicago: University of Chicago Press, 1999).

1. CURRENTS OF INTERNATIONALISM

1 Albert Marrin, *Sir Norman Angell* (Boston: Twayne, 1979), quotation at 28.

2 *Independent,* February 27, 1913, quoted in J. D. B. Miller, *Norman Angell and the Futility of War: Peace and the Public Mind* (Houndmills, UK: Macmillan, 1986), 9.

3 K. C. Hsiao, *A Modern China and a New World: K'ang Yu-wei, Reformer and Utopian, 1858–1927* (Seattle: University of Washington Press, 1975), 456–460.

4 Helga Haftendorn, Robert O. Keohane, and Celeste A. Wallander, eds., *Imperfect Unions: Security Institutions over Time and Space* (New York: Oxford University Press, 1999), 1–2; Iriye, *Global Community.*

5 As communications networks expanded globally, struggles arose among communications companies, national policies, and advocates of international agreements: Daniel R. Headrick, *The Invisible Weapon: Telecommunications and International Politics, 1851–1945* (New York: Oxford University Press, 1991); Jill Hills, *The Struggle for Control of Global Communication: The Formative Century* (Champaign: University of Illinois Press, 2002); Dwayne R. Winseck and Robert M. Pike, *Communication and Empire: Media, Markets, and Globalization, 1860–1930* (Durham, NC: Duke University Press, 2007); and Jonathan Winkler, *Nexus: Strategic Communications and American Security in World War I* (Cambridge, MA: Harvard University Press, 2008). John Darwin, *The Empire Project: The Rise and Fall of the British World-System, 1830–1870* (Cambridge: Cambridge University Press, 2009), 25, stresses the importance of new communications in propelling Britain's global "empire project" in the late nineteenth century.

6 George A. Codding Jr. and Anthony M. Rutkowski, *The International Telecommunication Union in a Changing World* (Dedham, MA: Artech House, 1982), 3.

7 George A. Codding Jr., *The Universal Postal Union: Coordinator of the International Mails* (New York: NYU Press, 1964); *The Universal Postal Union: Its Creation and Development* (Berne: Universal Postal Union, 1974).

8 David M. Henkin, *The Postal Age: The Emergence of Modern Communications in Nineteenth-Century America* (Chicago: University of Chicago Press, 2006), charts postal connections across the United States.

9 On the standardization of time zones, see Clark Blaise, *Time Lord: Sir Sandford Fleming and the Creation of Standard Time* (New York: Pantheon, 2000).

10 Stephen Kern, *The Culture of Time and Space, 1880–1918* (Cambridge, MA: Harvard University Press, 1983).

11 Nils Brunsson and Bengt Jacobsson, *A World of Standards* (Oxford: Oxford University Press, 2000); Miloš Vec, *Recht und Normierung in der industriellen Revolution: Neue Strukturen der Normsetzung in Völkerrecht, staatlicher Gesetzgebung und gesellschaftlicher Selbstnormierung* (Frankfurt am Main: Klostermann, 2006); the first half of James W. Nixon, *A History of the International Statistical Institute, 1885–1960* (The Hague: International Statistical Institute, 1960); J. Adam Tooze, *Statistics and the German State, 1900–1945: The Making of Modern Economic Knowledge* (Cambridge: Cambridge University Press, 2001).

12 Martin H. Geyer and Johannes Paulmann, eds., *The Mechanics of Internationalism: Culture, Society, and Politics from the 1840s to the First World War* (Oxford: Oxford University Press, 2001).

13 John E. Findling and Kimberly D. Pelle, eds., *Historical Dictionary of the Modern Olympic Movement* (Westport CT: Greenwood Press, 1996); Allen Guttmann, *The Olympics: A History of the Modern Games,* 2nd ed. (Champaign: University of Illinois Press, 2002), 7–84.

14 Maurice Roche, *Mega-events and Modernity: Olympics and Expos in the Growth of Global Culture* (London: Routledge, 2000), 108.

15 Barbara J. Keys, *Globalizing Sport: National Rivalry and International Community in the 1930s* (Cambridge, MA: Harvard University Press, 2006); David Clay Large, *Nazi Games: The Olympics of 1936* (New York: W. W. Norton, 2007).

16 Martti Koskenniemi, *The Gentle Civilizer of Nations: The Rise and Fall of International Law, 1870–1960* (Cambridge: Cambridge University Press, 2002), 11–97.

17 Jürgen Osterhammel, *Europe, the "West" and the Civilizing Mission* (London: German Historical Institute, 2006). On the intersection between colonialism and international law, see Wilhelm G. Grewe, *The Epochs of International Law,* trans. Michael Byers (Berlin: Walter de Gruyter, 2000), 445–524; Antony Anghie, *Imperialism, Sovereignty, and the Making of International Law* (Cambridge: Cambridge University Press, 2005).

18 Arthur Eyffinger, *The 1899 Hague Peace Conference: "The Parliament of Man, the Federation of the World"* (The Hague: Kluwer Academic, 1999), 365.

19 Quoted in Merze Tate, *The Disarmament Illusion: The Movement for a Limitation of Armaments to 1907* (New York: Russell and Russell, 1942), 55.

20 Multilateral conventions signed between 1890 and 1940 are in "Miscellaneous Historical Documents," http://fletcher.tufts.edu/multi/chrono.html#99.

21 Jost Dülffer, *Regeln gegen den Krieg? Die Haager Friedenskonferenzen von 1899 und 1907 in der internationalen Politik* (Frankfurt am Main: Ullstein, 1981).

22 Raymond L. Bridgman, *The First Book of World Law* (Boston: Ginn and Co., 1911).

23 Gary B. Ostrower, *The League of Nations from 1919 to 1929* (Garden City Park, NY: Avery, 1996); Thomas W. Burkman, *Japan and the League of Nations: Empire and World Order, 1914–1938* (Honolulu: University of Hawai'i Press, 2008).

24 Thomas J. Knock, *To End All Wars: Woodrow Wilson and the Quest for a New World Order* (New York: Oxford University Press, 1992).

25 John Milton Cooper Jr., *Woodrow Wilson: A Biography* (New York: Knopf, 2009), 362–534; Derek B. Heater, *National Self-Determination: Woodrow Wilson and His Legacy* (Basingstoke, UK: Macmillan, 1994).

26 JoAnne Pemberton, "New Worlds for Old: The League of Nations in the Age of Electricity," *Review of International Studies* 28 (2002): 311.

27 Several essays in Paul Weindling, ed., *International Health Organisations and Movements, 1918–1939* (Cambridge: Cambridge University Press, 1995).

28 Jasmien Van Daele, "Engineering Social Peace: Networks, Ideas, and the Founding of the International Labour Organization," *International Review of Social History* 50 (2005): 435–466.

29 Susan Pedersen, "The Meaning of the Mandates System: An Argument," *Geschichte und Gesellschaft* 32 (2006): 560–582; Erez Manela, *The Wilsonian Moment: Self-Determination and the International Origins of Anticolonial Nationalism* (Oxford: Oxford University Press, 2007).

30 Norman Angell, *Peace and the Public Mind: Nobel Peace Lecture Delivered at Oslo, June 12, 1935* (Stockholm: P. A. Norstedt, 1935).

31 Mark Mazower, *Hitler's Empire: How the Nazis Ruled Europe* (New York: Penguin Press, 2008); Louise Young, *Japan's Total Empire: Manchuria and the Culture of Wartime Imperialism* (Berkeley: University of California Press, 1998); Prasenjit Duara, *Sovereignty and Authenticity: Manchukuo and the East Asian Modern* (Lanham, MD: Rowman and Littlefield, 2003), 70–71.

32 Akira Iriye, *The Globalizing of America, 1913–1945,* vol. 3 of *The Cambridge History of American Foreign Relations,* ed. Warren I. Cohen (New York: Cambridge University Press, 1995), 116–215.

33 Elizabeth Borgwardt, *A New Deal for the World: America's Vision for Human Rights* (Cambridge, MA: Harvard University Press, 2005); more critical perspectives are reviewed in Sunil S. Amrith and Glenda Sluga, "New Histories of the United Nations," *Journal of World History* 19 (2008): 251–274; and Mark Mazower, *No Enchanted Palace: The End of Empire and the Ideological Origins of the United Nations* (Princeton, NJ: Princeton University Press, 2009), 28–31.

2. SOCIAL NETWORKING AND ENTANGLED ATTACHMENTS

1 On "cultural internationalism," see Akira Iriye, *Cultural Internationalism and World Order* (Baltimore: Johns Hopkins University Press, 1997).

2 Pierre Janton, *Esperanto: Language, Literature, and Community,* ed. Humphrey Tonkin, trans. Humphrey Tonkin, Jane Edwards, and Karen Johnson-Weiner (Albany: State University of New York Press, 1993), xii.

3 Young S. Kim, "Constructing a Global Identity: The Role of Esperanto," in *Constructing World Culture: International Nongovernmental Organizations since 1875,* ed. John Boli and George M. Thomas (Stanford, CA: Stanford University Press, 1999), 127–148, quotation at 147.

4 "The Photographs of John Thompson," at http://www.nls.uk/thomson/index .html.

5 David Okuefuna, *The Dawn of the Color Photograph: Albert Kahn's Archives of the Planet* (Princeton, NJ: Princeton University Press, 2008); Jay M. Winter, *Dreams of Peace and Freedom: Utopian Moments in the Twentieth Century* (New Haven, CT: Yale University Press, 2006), 11–28.

6 Barbara D. Metcalf and Thomas R. Metcalf, *A Concise History of Modern India,* 2nd ed. (Cambridge: Cambridge University Press, 2006), 112–113. See also James R. Ryan, *Picturing Empire: Photography and the Visualization of the British Empire* (Chicago: University of Chicago Press, 1997), 155–175; Christopher Pinney, *Camera Indica: The Social Life of Indian Photographs* (Chicago: University of Chicago Press, 1997), 34–60; John Falconer, "'A Pure Labor of Love': A Publishing History of *The People of India,*" in *Colonialist Photography: Imag(in)ing Race and Place,* ed. Eleanor M. Hight and Gary D. Sampson (London: Routledge, 2002), 51–83.

7 Jürgen Osterhammel, *Die Verwandlung der Welt: Eine Geschichte des 19. Jahrhunderts* (Munich: C. H. Beck, 2009), 79.

8 Many of the essays in Hight and Sampson, *Colonialist Photography,* develop these themes; Rosalind C. Morris, ed., *Photographies East: The Camera and Its Histories in East and Southeast Asia* (Durham, NC: Duke University Press, 2009).

9 Laura Wexler, *Tender Violence: Domestic Visions in an Age of U.S. Imperialism* (Chapel Hill: University of North Carolina Press, 2000); Alexander Missal, *Seaway to the Future: American Social Visions and the Construction of the Panama Canal* (Madison: University of Wisconsin Press, 2008), 95–108.

10 Vicente Rafael, *White Love and Other Events in Filipino History* (Durham, NC: Duke University Press, 2000), quotation at 86; Leonard Bell, "Eyeing Samoa: People, Places, and Spaces in Photographs of the Late Nineteenth and Early Twentieth Centuries," in *Tropical Visions in an Age of Empire,* ed. Felix Driver and Luciana Martins (Chicago: University of Chicago Press, 2005), 156–174; Esther Gabara, *Errant Modernism: The Ethos of Photography in Mexico and Brazil* (Durham, NC: Duke University Press, 2008).

11 David Welch, *The Third Reich: Politics and Propaganda,* 2nd ed. (London: Routledge, 2002).

12 David Brion Davis, *Inhuman Bondage: The Rise and Fall of Slavery in the New World* (Oxford: Oxford University Press, 2006), 323–331; Suzanne Miers, *Slavery in the Twentieth Century: The Evolution of a Global Problem* (Lanham, MD: Rowman and Littlefield, 2003); Adam Hochschild, *Bury the Chains: Prophets and Rebels in the Fight to Free an Empire's Slaves* (Boston: Houghton Mifflin, 2005); Patrick Manning, *The African Diaspora: A History through Culture* (New York: Columbia University Press, 2009), 209–282. William Gervase Clarence-Smith, *Islam and the Abolition of Slavery* (New York: Oxford University Press, 2006), examines the uneven pace of abolition in the Islamic world and how its continued practice in some places was used to help justify colonialism.

13 Harvey Goldberg, *The Life of Jean Jaurés* (Madison: University of Wisconsin Press, 2003).

14 Marcel van der Linden, *Transnational Labour History: Explorations* (Aldershot, UK: Ashgate, 2003), 75–76; Francis Shor, "Masculine Power and Virile Syndicalism: A Gendered Analysis of the IWW in Australia," *Labour History* 63 (1992): 83–99.

15 John Riddell, ed., *To See the Dawn: Baku, 1920—First Congress of the Peoples of the East* (New York: Pathfinder Press, 1993).

16 Robert Service, *Comrades! A History of World Communism* (Cambridge, MA: Harvard University Press, 2007).

17 Patricia Ward D'Itri, *Cross Currents in the International Women's Movement, 1848–1948* (Bowling Green, OH: Bowling Green State University Popular Press, 1999), 101.

18 Rajmohan Gandhi, *Gandhi: The Man, His People, and the Empire* (Berkeley: University of California Press, 2008).

19 Sugata Bose, *A Hundred Horizons: The Indian Ocean in the Age of Global Empire* (Cambridge, MA: Harvard University Press, 2006), 31.

20 Tony Ballantyne and Antoinette Burton, "Empires and the Reach of the Global," in *A World Connecting: 1870–1945,* ed. Emily S. Rosenberg (Cambridge, MA: Belknap Press of Harvard University Press, 2012); Josephine Fowler, *Japanese and Chinese Immigrant Activists: Organizing in American and International Communist Movements, 1919–1933* (New Brunswick, NJ: Rutgers University Press, 2007); Jonathan Derrick, *Africa's 'Agitators': Militant Anti-colonialism in Africa and the West, 1918–1939* (London: Hurst, 2008).

21 Marilyn Lake and Henry Reynolds, *Drawing the Global Colour Line: White Men's Countries and the International Challenge of Racial Equality* (Cambridge: Cambridge University Press, 2008), 246. On Du Bois, see David Levering Lewis,

W. E. B. DuBois: Biography of a Race, 1868–1919 (New York: Henry Holt, 1993); and Lewis, W. E. B. DuBois: The Fight for Equality and the American Century, 1919–1963 (New York: Henry Holt, 2000).

22 Saheed A. Adejumobi, "The Pan-African Congress," in Organizing Black America: An Encyclopedia of African American Associations, ed. Nina Mjagkij (New York: Garland, 2001); Derrick, Africa's 'Agitators.'

23 Colin Grant, Negro with a Hat: The Rise and Fall of Marcus Garvey (New York: Oxford University Press, 2008).

24 Gary Wilder, The French Imperial Nation-State: Negritude and Colonial Humanism between the Two World Wars (Chicago: University of Chicago Press 2005), 252.

25 Paul Gilroy, The Black Atlantic: Modernity and Double Consciousness (Cambridge, MA: Harvard University Press, 1993).

26 James T. Campbell, Middle Passages: African American Journeys to Africa, 1787–2005 (New York: Penguin Press, 2006); Kevin Kelly Gaines, American Africans in Ghana: Black Expatriates and the Civil Rights Era (Chapel Hill: University of North Carolina Press, 2006); Winston James, Holding Aloft the Banner of Ethiopia: Caribbean Radicalism in Early Twentieth-Century America (New York: Verso, 1998).

27 Prasenjit Duara, Sovereignty and Authenticity: Manchukuo and the East Asian Modern (Lanham, MD: Rowman and Littlefield, 2003).

28 The expression "international nationalism" is used by Michael Brenner in Zionism: A Brief History, trans. Shelley Frisch (Princeton, NJ: Markus Wiener, 2003), 255–318. A more controversial history of the Jews is Shlomo Sand, The Invention of the Jewish People, trans. Yael Lotan (New York: Verso, 2009).

29 C. A. Bayly, The Birth of the Modern World, 1780–1914: Global Connections and Comparisons (Oxford: Blackwell, 2004), quotation at 362.

30 Diarmaid MacCulloch, Christianity: The First Three Thousand Years (New York: Viking, 2010), 915.

31 Harold Fischer-Tiné, "Global Civil Society and the Forces of Empire: The Salvation Army, British Imperialism, and the 'Prehistory' of NGOs," in Competing Visions of World Order: Global Moments and Movements, 1880s–1930s, ed. Sebastian Conrad and Dominic Sachsenmaier (London: Palgrave Macmillan, 2007), 30–31.

32 Sherwood Eddy, A Pilgrimage of Ideas; or, the Reeducation of Sherwood Eddy (New York: Farrar and Rinehart, 1934), quotation at 59; Ian R. Tyrrell, Reform-

ing the World: The Creation of America's Moral Empire (Princeton, NJ: Princeton University Press, 2010), 49–89.

33 Merle Curti, *American Philanthropy Abroad: A History* (New Brunswick, NJ: Rutgers University Press, 1963), 134–174.

34 Dana L. Robert, *Christian Mission: How Christianity Became a World Religion* (Malden, MA: Wiley-Blackwell, 2009), 62–63; MacCulloch, *Christianity,* 879–882.

35 Adam Mohr, "Capitalism, Chaos, and Christian Healing: Faith Tabernacle Congregation in Southern Colonial Ghana, 1918–26," *Journal of African History* 52 (2011): 63–83.

36 Robert, *Christian Mission,* 56–64; J. P. Daughton, *An Empire Divided: Religion, Republicanism, and the Making of French Colonialism, 1880–1914* (New York: Oxford University Press, 2006).

37 Robert Bickers, *Britain in China: Community, Culture, and Colonialism, 1900–1949* (Manchester: Manchester University Press, 1999), 92–94.

38 For the complicated relationship between British missionary activity and empire, see Andrew N. Porter, *Religion versus Empire? British Protestant Missionaries and Overseas Expansion, 1700–1914* (Manchester: Manchester University Press, 2004); and Richard Price, *Making Empire: Colonial Encounters and the Creation of Imperial Rule in Nineteenth-Century Africa* (New York: Cambridge University Press, 2008).

39 Robert, *Christian Mission,* 159–171.

40 Sean Hanretta, *Islam and Social Change in French West Africa: History of an Emancipatory Community* (New York: Cambridge University Press, 2009); Donald R. Wright, *The World and a Very Small Place in Africa* (Armonk, NY: M. E. Sharpe, 1997), 197–200.

41 Ira M. Lapidus, *A History of Islamic Societies,* rev. ed. (New York: Cambridge University Press, 2002); see also David Gilmartin, "A Networked Civilization?" in *Muslim Networks from Hajj to Hip Hop,* ed. Miriam Cooke and Bruce B. Lawrence (Chapel Hill: University of North Carolina Press, 2005), 51–68.

42 Quotation from Bose, *A Hundred Horizons,* 195.

43 Ghislaine Lydon, *On Trans-Saharan Trails: Islamic Law, Trade Networks, and Cross-Cultural Exchange in Nineteenth-Century Western Africa* (Cambridge: Cambridge University Press, 2009). The interface between Islam and Christianity is illuminated in Benjamin F. Soares, ed., *Muslim-Christian Encounters in Africa* (Leiden: Brill, 2006); and Roman Loimeier and Rüdiger Seesemann, *The*

Global Worlds of the Swahili: Interfaces of Islam, Identity and Space in 19th- and 20th-Century East Africa (Berlin: LIT, 2006).

44 Robert R. Bianchi, *Guests of God: Pilgrimage and Politics in the Islamic World* (New York: Oxford University Press, 2004), 42–46.

45 Bose, *A Hundred Horizons,* 232; Ayesha Jalal, *Self and Sovereignty: Individual and Community in South Asian Islam since 1850* (London: Routledge, 2000), 188–189.

46 P. R. Bhuyan, *Swami Vivekananda: Messiah of Resurgent India* (New Delhi: Atlantic, 2003), 22; Dorothea Lüddeckens, *Das Weltparlament der Religionen von 1893: Strukturen interreligiöser Begegnung im 19. Jahrhundert* (Berlin: Walter de Gruyter, 2002).

47 Gauri Viswanathan, *Outside the Fold: Conversion, Modernity, and Belief* (Princeton, NJ: Princeton University Press, 1998), 177–209.

48 Jacob K. Olupona and Terry Rey, eds., *Òrìsà Devotion as World Religion: The Globalization of Yorùbá Religious Culture* (Madison: University of Wisconsin Press, 2008).

49 Richard J. Evans, *The Feminists: Women's Emancipation Movements in Europe, America and Australasia, 1840–1920* (London: Croom Helm, 1977); Leila Rupp, *Worlds of Women: The Making of an International Women's Movement* (Princeton, NJ: Princeton University Press, 1997); and Karen M. Offen, *European Feminisms, 1700–1950: A Political History* (Stanford, CA: Stanford University Press, 2000), suggest the diversity of goals.

50 Nitza Berkovitch, *From Motherhood to Citizenship: Women's Rights and International Organizations* (Baltimore: Johns Hopkins University Press, 1999), surveys major issues for advocacy.

51 Albert Hourani, *A History of the Arab Peoples* (Cambridge, MA: Harvard University Press, 1991), 345.

52 Ian R. Tyrrell, *Woman's World/Woman's Empire: The Woman's Christian Temperance Union in International Perspective, 1880–1930* (Chapel Hill: University of North Carolina Press, 1991). See more generally Mark Lawrence Schrad, *The Political Power of Bad Ideas: Networks, Institutions, and the Global Prohibition Wave* (New York: Oxford University Press, 2010).

53 D'Itri, *Cross Currents,* 163.

54 Padma Anagol, *Emergence of Feminism in India, 1850–1920* (Aldershot, UK: Ashgate, 2005); Gauri Viswanathan, *Outside the Fold: Conversion, Modernity, and Belief* (Princeton, NJ: Princeton University Press, 1998), 118–152.

55 Quoted from Catt's journal in D'Itri, *Cross Currents,* 104.

56 Rupp, *Worlds of Women*, 60–62.

57 Provocative works include Ann Laura Stoler, *Carnal Knowledge and Imperial Power: Race and the Intimate in Colonial Rule*, 2nd ed. (Berkeley: University of California Press, 2 ed., 2010); Ulrike Strasser and Heidi Tinsman, "It's a Man's World? World History Meets the History of Masculinity, in Latin American Studies, for Instance," *Journal of World History* 21 (2010): 75–96; and Leela Gandhi, *Affective Communities: Anticolonial Thought, Fin-de-Siècle Radicalism, and the Politics of Friendship* (Durham, NC: Duke University Press, 2006).

58 For example, the first attempt to sketch the outlines of a global history of scouting organizations may be found in Nelson R. Block and Tammy R. Proctor, eds., *Scouting Frontiers: Youth and the Scout Movement's First Century* (Newcastle upon Tyne, UK: Cambridge Scholars, 2009).

3. EXHIBITIONARY NODES

1 Thomas Richards, *The Imperial Archive: Knowledge and the Fantasy of Empire* (London: Verso, 1993), 1–9, quotation at 4. See also Tony Bennett, *The Birth of the Museum: History, Theory, Politics* (London: Routledge, 1995).

2 See John E. Findling and Kimberly D. Pelle, eds., *Encyclopedia of World's Fairs and Expositions,* rev. 2nd ed. (Jefferson, NC: McFarland, 2008).

3 Hermione Hobhouse, *Crystal Palace and the Great Exhibition: Art, Science, Productive Industry* (London: Athlone Press, 2004); Peter Henry Hoffenberg, *An Empire on Display: English, Indian and Australian Exhibitions from the Crystal Palace to the Great War* (Berkeley: University of California Press, 2001).

4 Lara Kriegel, *Grand Designs: Labor, Empire, and the Museum in Victorian Culture* (Durham, NC: Duke University Press, 2007), 16.

5 Paul Young, "Mission Impossible: Globalization and the Great Exhibition," in *Britain, the Empire, and the World at the Great Exhibition of 1851,* ed. Jeffrey A. Auerbach and Peter H. Hoffenberg (Aldershot, UK: Ashgate, 2008), quotation at 11.

6 Jeffrey A. Auerbach, *The Great Exhibition of 1851: A Nation on Display* (New Haven, CT: Yale University Press, 1999).

7 Zeynep Çelik, *Displaying the Orient: Architecture and Islam at Nineteenth-Century World's Fairs* (Berkeley: University of California Press, 1992), quotation at 152.

8 Quoted in Paul Greenhalgh, *Ephemeral Vistas: The Expositions Universelles, Great Exhibitions, and World's Fairs, 1851–1939* (Manchester: Manchester University Press, 1988), 88.

9   Annegret Fauser, *Musical Encounters at the 1889 Paris World's Fair* (Rochester, NY: University of Rochester Press, 2005), 183–206.

10 Quoted in Charles Desnoyers, "'Toward One Enlightened and Progressive Civilization': Discourses of Expansion and Nineteenth Century Chinese Missions Abroad," *Journal of World History* 8 (1997): 135–156, quotation at 152.

11 Quotations from http://libwww.library.phila.gov/CenCol/exh-testimony.htm.

12 Camilla Fojas, "American Cosmopolis: The World's Columbian Exposition and Chicago across the Americas," *Comparative Literature Studies* 42 (2005): 264–287.

13 John E. Findling, *Chicago's Great World's Fairs* (Manchester: Manchester University Press, 1994), 27.

14 Christopher Robert Reed, *All the World Is Here! The Black Presence at White City* (Bloomington: Indiana University Press, 2000).

15 Lee D. Baker, *From Savage to Negro: Anthropology and the Construction of Race, 1896–1954* (Berkeley: University of California Press, 1998), 26.

16 Daniel T. Rodgers, *Atlantic Crossings: Social Politics in a Progressive Age* (Cambridge, MA: Belknap Press of Harvard University Press, 1998), 20.

17 Richard D. Mandell, *Paris 1900: The Great World's Fair* (Toronto: University of Toronto Press, 1967); Diana P. Fischer, et al., eds., *Paris 1900: The "American School" at the Universal Exposition* (New Brunswick, NJ: Rutgers University Press, 1999); Patricia Morton, *Hybrid Modernities: Architecture and Representation at the 1931 Colonial Exposition, Paris* (Cambridge, MA: MIT Press, 2000).

18 Çelik, *Displaying the Orient,* 49.

19 Quoted in Greenhalgh, *Ephemeral Vistas,* 83.

20 Robert W. Rydell, *All the World's a Fair: Visions of Empire at American International Expositions, 1876–1916* (Chicago: University of Chicago Press, 1984).

21 Morton, *Hybrid Modernities.*

22 David Levering Lewis and Deborah Willis, *A Small Nation of People: W. E. B. DuBois and African-American Portraits of Progress* (New York: Amistad, 2003).

23 Findling, *Chicago's Great World's Fairs,* 124–126; Robert W. Rydell, *World of Fairs: The Century-of-Progress Expositions* (Chicago: University of Chicago Press, 1993); Cheryl R. Ganz, *The 1933 Chicago World's Fair: A Century of Progress* (Champaign: University of Illinois Press, 2008).

24 Jay M. Winter, *Dreams of Peace and Freedom: Utopian Moments in the Twentieth Century* (New Haven, CT: Yale University Press, 2006), 86.

25 Bennett, *Birth of the Museum.*

26 H. Glenn Penny, *Objects of Culture: Ethnology and Ethnographic Museums in Imperial Germany* (Chapel Hill: University of North Carolina Press, 2002); Rainer F. Buschmann, *Anthropology's Global Histories: The Ethnographic Frontier in German New Guinea, 1870–1935* (Honolulu: University of Hawai'i Press, 2009).

27 Carla Yanni, *Nature's Museums: Victorian Science and the Architecture of Display* (London: Athlone Press, 1999), 144–146.

28 Maria Margaret Lopes and Irina Podgorny, "The Shaping of Latin American Museums of Natural History, 1850–1990," in *Nature and Empire: Science and the Colonial Enterprise,* ed. Roy MacLeod (Chicago: University of Chicago Press, 2000), 108–118.

29 Robert E. Kohler, *All Creatures: Naturalists, Collectors, and Biodiversity, 1850–1950* (Princeton, NJ: Princeton University Press, 2006), 111, 117; Lopes and Podgorny, "Latin American Museums," 116.

30 Bennett, *Birth of the Museum.*

31 Kenn Harper, *Give Me My Father's Body: The Life of Minik, the New York Eskimo* (New York: Washington Square Press, 2001). For background, see Michael F. Robinson, *The Coldest Crucible: Arctic Exploration and American Culture* (Chicago: University of Chicago Press, 2006).

32 Young-tsu Wong, *A Paradise Lost: The Imperial Garden Yuanming Yuan* (Honolulu: University of Hawai'i Press, 2001), quotation at 160; James L. Hevia, *English Lessons: The Pedagogy of Imperialism in Nineteenth-Century China* (Durham, NC: Duke University Press, 2003).

33 Michael A. Osborne, "Acclimatizing the World," in MacLeod, *Nature and Empire,* 135–151.

34 Darin Kinsey, "'Seeding the Water as the Earth': The Epicenter and Peripheries of a Western Aquacultural Revolution," *Environmental History* 11 (July 2006): 527–566, quotation at 550.

35 C. Wayne Smith and J. Tom Cothren, eds., *Cotton: Origin, History, Technology, and Production* (New York: John Wiley, 1999), 159; Thomas Kearney, "Louis Trabut: Botanist and Plant Breeder," *Journal of Heredity* 13 (1922): 153–160.

36 Richard H. Drayton, *Nature's Government: Science, Imperial Britain, and the "Improvement" of the World* (New Haven, CT: Yale University Press, 2000); Ray Desmond, *The History of the Royal Botanic Gardens Kew* (London: Royal Botanic Gardens, Kew, 2007).

37 Lucile H. Brockway, *Science and Colonial Expansion: The Role of the British Royal Botanic Gardens* (New York: Academic Press, 1979), 101.

38 Christophe Bonneuil, "The Manufacture of Species: Kew Gardens, The Empire, and the Standardisation of Taxonomic Practices in Late Nineteenth-Century Botany," in *Instruments, Travel, and Science: Itineraries of Precision from the Seventeenth to the Twentieth Century,* ed. Marie-Noëlle Bourguet, Christian Licoppe, and H. Otto Sibum (London: Routledge, 2002), 189–215.

39 Brockway, *Science and Colonial Expansion,* 102, 124.

40 Fa-ti Fan, *British Naturalists in Qing China: Science, Empire, and Cultural Encounter* (Cambridge, MA: Harvard University Press, 2004), 110–154, examines the textual and interpersonal practices involved in the cross-cultural exchange of information about plants and animals.

41 Ernst Mayr, "In Memorium: Jean (Theodore) Delacour," *The Auk* 103 (1986): 603–605.

42 Elizabeth Hanson, *Animal Attractions: Nature on Display in American Zoos* (Princeton, NJ: Princeton University Press, 2002), 14; Eric Baratay and Elisabeth Hardouin-Fugier, *Zoo: A History of Zoological Gardens in the West,* trans. Oliver Welsh (London: Reaktion Books, 2002); Vernon N. Kisling Jr., ed., *Zoo and Aquarium History: Ancient Animal Collections to Zoological Gardens* (Boca Raton, FL: CRC Press, 2001).

43 Baratay and Hardouin-Fugier, *Zoo,* 135–136.

44 Hanson, *Animal Attractions,* 1–40. Quote from Robert J. Hoage and William A. Deiss, eds., *New Worlds, New Animals: From Menagerie to Zoological Park in the Nineteenth Century* (Baltimore: Johns Hopkins University Press, 1996), x; see Michael A. Osborne, "Zoos in the Family: The Geoffroy Saint-Hilaire Clan and the Three Zoos of Paris," in Hoage and Deiss, *New Worlds, New Animals,* 33–42.

45 Nigel Rothfels, *Savages and Beasts: The Birth of the Modern Zoo* (Baltimore: Johns Hopkins University Press, 2002).

46 Hanson, *Animal Attractions,* 79.

47 Quotation in ibid., 112.

48 Ibid., 117–118.

49 Oliver H. Orr Jr., *Saving American Birds: T. Gilbert Pearson and the Founding of the Audubon Movement* (Gainesville: University of Florida Press, 1992); Hilda Kean, *Animal Rights: Political and Social Change in Britain since 1800* (London: Reaktion, 1998); Mark Cioc, *The Game of Conservation: International Treaties to Protect the World's Migratory Animals* (Athens: Ohio University Press, 2009), 14–57.

50 John M. MacKenzie, *The Empire of Nature: Hunting, Conservation, and British Imperialism* (Manchester: Manchester University Press, 1988); Alexandra Minna Stern, *Eugenic Nation: Faults and Frontiers of Better Breeding in Modern America* (Berkeley: University of California Press, 2005); Thomas Lekan, *Imagining the Nation: Landscape Preservation and German Identity, 1885–1945* (Cambridge, MA: Harvard University Press, 2004), 262; Jane Carruthers, "Creating a National Park, 1910–1925," *Journal of Southern Africa Studies* 15 (January 1989): 188–216. For a broad perspective on environmental history see J. R. McNeill, *Something New under the Sun: An Environmental History of the Twentieth Century World* (New York: W. W. Norton, 2001).

4. CIRCUITS OF EXPERIENCE

1 On Japan, see William G. Beasley, *Japan Encounters the Barbarian: Japanese Travellers in America and Europe* (New Haven, CT: Yale University Press, 1995), 157–177; on China, Benjamin A. Elman, *A Cultural History of Modern Science in China* (Cambridge, MA: Harvard University Press, 2006), 132–157. Elman points out, however, that many of these missionary-inspired works hardly mentioned Darwin or evolutionary thought, so the Western science they brought to China had distinctive omissions.

2 The phrase "shared developmentalist project" comes from Kenneth Pomeranz, introduction to *The Environment and World History,* ed. Edmund Burke III and Kenneth Pomeranz (Berkeley: University of California Press, 2009).

3 Peter Wagner, "Introduction to Part I," in *Transnational Intellectual Networks: Forms of Academic Knowledge and the Search for Cultural Identities,* ed. Christophe Charle, Jürgen Schriewer, and Peter Wagner (Frankfurt: Campus, 2004), quotation at 17.

4 Michael Adas, *Machines as the Measure of Men: Science, Technology, and Ideologies of Western Dominance* (Ithaca, NY: Cornell University Press, 1989), 156–162, 339, makes the point that the use of technology, even more than racial ideology, constructed the social categories that encompassed "advanced" and "backward" peoples. See also Daniel R. Headrick, *The Tools of Empire: Technology and European Imperialism in the Nineteenth Century* (New York: Oxford University Press, 1981); Headrick, *The Tentacles of Progress: Technology Transfer in the Age of Imperialism, 1850–1940* (New York: Oxford University Press, 1988); and Headrick, *Power over Peoples: Technology, Environments, and Western Imperialism, 1400 to the Present* (Princeton, NJ: Princeton University Press, 2010).

5 S. Irfan Habib and Dhruv Raina, eds., *Social History of Science in Colonial India* (New Delhi: Oxford University Press, 2007), introduction.

6 For the emphasis on circulation and coproduction, see Kapil Raj, *Relocating Modern Science: Circulation and the Construction of Knowledge in South Asia and Europe, 1650–1900* (New York: Palgrave, 2007); and see David Turnbull, "Travelling Knowledge: Narratives, Assemblage and Encounters," in *Instruments, Travel, and Science: Itineraries of Precision from the Seventeenth to the Twentieth Century,* ed. Marie-Noëlle Bourguet, Christian Licoppe, and H. Otto Sibum (London: Routledge, 2002), 273–294, along with other essays in that volume.

7 Michael Shermer, *In Darwin's Shadow: The Life and Science of Alfred Russel Wallace* (New York: Oxford University Press, 2002), 258–261.

8 John Noble Wilford, *The Mapmakers: The Story of the Great Pioneers in Cartography from Antiquity to the Space Age* (New York: Knopf, 1981), pt. 2; Raj, *Relocating Modern Science,* 181–222; John Keay, *The Great Arc: The Dramatic Tale of How India Was Mapped and Everest Was Named* (London: HarperCollins, 2000).

9 Donald Worster, *A River Running West: The Life of John Wesley Powell* (New York: Oxford University Press, 2001); Paul N. Edison, "Conquest Unrequited: French Expeditionary Science in Mexico, 1864–1867," *French Historical Studies* 26 (2003): 459–495; Francis Sejersted, *The Age of Social Democracy: Norway and Sweden in the Twentieth Century,* trans. Richard Daly (Princeton, NJ: Princeton University Press, 2011), quotation at 17.

10 Ian J. Barrow, *Making History, Drawing Territory: British Mapping in India, c. 1756–1905* (New Delhi: Oxford University Press, 2003). For background, see Matthew H. Edney, *Mapping an Empire: The Geographical Construction of British India, 1765–1843* (Chicago: University of Chicago Press, 1997).

11 Vicente Rafael, *White Love and Other Events in Filipino History* (Durham, NC: Duke University Press, 2000).

12 Suzanne L. Marchand, *Down from Olympus: Archaeology and Philhellenism in Germany, 1750–1970* (Princeton, NJ: Princeton University Press, 1996); Stephen L. Dyson, *In Pursuit of Ancient Pasts: A History of Classical Archaeology in the Nineteenth and Twentieth Centuries* (New Haven, CT: Yale University Press, 2006), which stresses the role in nationalism and museum building in Europe; Michael D. Coe, *Breaking the Maya Code* (London: Thames and Hudson, 1992); Neil Asher Silberman, *Digging for God and Country: Exploration, Archeology, and the Secret Struggle for the Holy Land, 1799–1917* (New York:

Alfred A. Knopf, 1982), 147–170; and David A. Traill, *Schliemann of Troy: Treasure and Deceit* (New York: St. Martin's Press, 1995).

13   Clark Blaise, *Time Lord: Sir Sandford Fleming and the Creation of Standard Time* (New York: Pantheon, 2000), 67.

14   Julie Greene, *The Canal Builders: Making America's Empire at the Panama Canal* (New York: Penguin Press, 2009).

15   Zaheer Baber, "Science, Technology, and Colonial Power," and Russell Dionne and Roy MacLeod, "Science and Policy in British India, 1858–1914: Perspectives on a Persisting Belief," both in Habib and Raina, *Science in Colonial India,* 102–158, 159–195. On British colonialism, expertise, and agrarian development in Africa, see Joseph Morgan Hodge, *Triumph of the Expert: Agrarian Doctrines of Development and the Legacies of British Colonialism* (Athens: Ohio University Press, 2007).

16   Edmund Burke III, "The Transformation of the Middle Eastern Environment, 1500 B.C.E.–2000 C.E.," in Burke and Pomeranz, *Environment and World History,* 99.

17   Elman, *Modern Science in China,* 158–181; William C. Kirby, *Germany and Republican China* (Stanford, CA: Stanford University Press, 1984).

18   Essays in Ardath W. Burks, ed., *The Modernizers: Overseas Students, Foreign Employees and Meiji Japan* (Boulder, CO: Westview Press, 1985).

19   Quoted in Beasley, *Japan Encounters the Barbarian,* 223.

20   Mark Cioc, *The Rhine: An Eco-Biography, 1815–2000* (Seattle: University of Washington Press, 2002); David Blackbourn, *The Conquest of Nature: Water, Landscape, and the Making of Modern Germany* (New York: W. W. Norton, 2006), 189–303; Kenneth Pomeranz, "China's Environment, 1500–2000," in Burke and Pomeranz, *Environment and World History,* 135; William Kirby, "Engineering China: Birth of the Developmental States, 1928–1937," in *Becoming Chinese: Passages to Modernity and Beyond,* ed. Wen-hsin Yeh (Berkeley: University of California Press, 2000).

21   David Ekbladh, "'Mr. TVA': Grass-Roots Development, David Lilienthal, and the Rise and Fall of the Tennessee Valley Authority as a Symbol for U.S. Overseas Development, 1933–1973," *Diplomatic History* 26 (2007): 335–374.

22   Quoted in S. Irfan Habib and Dhruv Raina, "Copernicus, Columbus, Colonialism, and the Role of Science in Nineteenth-Century India," in Habib and Raina, *Science in Colonial India,* 246. See also Gyan Prakash, *Another Reason: Science and the Imagination of Modern India* (Princeton, NJ: Princeton University Press, 1999).

23 Quoted in Shiv Visvanathan, *Organizing for Science: The Making of an Industrial Research Laboratory* (New Delhi: Oxford University Press, 1985), 108; Zaheer Baber, *The Science of Empire: Scientific Knowledge, Civilization, and Colonial Rule in India* (Albany: State University of New York Press, 1996), 184–245.

24 Ashis Nandy, *Alternative Sciences: Creativity and Authenticity in Two Indian Scientists* (New Delhi: Oxford University Press, 1980).

25 Baber, *The Science of Empire*, 129; Randall E. Stross, *The Stubborn Earth: American Agriculturalists on Chinese Soil, 1898–1937* (Berkeley: University of California Press, 1986).

26 Grace Carswell, *Cultivating Success in Uganda: Kigezi Farmers and Colonial Policies* (Athens: Ohio University Press, 2007).

27 Leslie Potter, "Forests versus Agriculture: Colonial Forest Services, Colonial Ideas, and Regulation of Land-Use Change in Southeast Asia," in *The Political Ecology of Tropical Forests in Southeast Asia: Historical Perspectives,* ed. Ken-ichi Abe, Wil de Jong, and Tuck-Po Lye (Melbourne: Trans Pacific Press, 2003); Richard P. Tucker and J. F. Richards, eds., *Global Deforestation and the Nineteenth-Century World Economy* (Durham, NC: Duke University Press, 1983); Richard P. Tucker, *Insatiable Appetite: The United States and the Ecological Degradation of the Tropical World* (Berkeley: University of California Press, 2000); Michael Williams, *Deforesting the Earth: From Prehistory to Global Crisis: An Abridgement* (Chicago: University of Chicago Press, 2006), 242–419; Thaddeus R. Sunseri, *Wielding the Ax: State Forestry and Social Conflict in Tanzania, 1820–2000* (Athens: Ohio University Press, 2009).

28 Ian R. Tyrrell, *True Gardens of the Gods: Californian-Australian Environmental Reform, 1860–1930* (Berkeley: University of California Press, 1999), 17–35.

29 Shermer, *In Darwin's Shadow.*

30 Daniel T. Rodgers, *Atlantic Crossings* (Cambridge, MA: Harvard University Press, 1998). See also Theodore M. Porter and Dorothy Ross, eds., *The Modern Social Sciences,* vol. 7 of *The Cambridge History of Science* (Cambridge: Cambridge University Press, 2003); Charle, Schriewer, and Wagner, *Transnational Intellectual Networks.*

31 James B. Gilbert, *Designing the Industrial State: The Intellectual Pursuit of Collectivism in America, 1880–1940* (New York: Quadrangle, 1972), 45.

32 Frank Andre Guridy, *Forging Diaspora: Afro-Cubans and African Americans in a World of Empire and Jim Crow* (Chapel Hill, NC: University of North Carolina Press, 2010), 17–60; Andrew Zimmerman, *Alabama in Africa: Booker T. Washington, the German Empire, and the Globalization of the New South*

(Princeton, NJ: Princeton University Press, 2010); Sebastian Conrad, *Globalisation and the Nation in Imperial Germany,* trans. Sorcha O'Hagan (Cambridge: Cambridge University Press, 2010), 101.

33 Richard Price, *Making Empire: Colonial Encounters and the Creation of Imperial Rule in Nineteenth-Century Africa* (New York: Cambridge University Press, 2008), 179, on Holden; Joel Pfister, *Individuality Incorporated: Indians and the Multicultural Modern* (Durham, NC: Duke University Press, 2004), 31–97, on Pratt.

34 *New York Times,* June 24, 1910.

35 Warwick P. Anderson, *The Cultivation of Whiteness: Science, Health and Racial Destiny in Australia* (New York: Basic Books, 2003); Radhika Mohanram, *Imperial White: Race, Diaspora, and the British Empire* (Minneapolis: University of Minnesota Press, 2007). More broadly, see Alys Eve Weinbaum, *Wayward Reproductions: Genealogies of Race and Nation in Transatlantic Modern Thought* (Durham, NC: Duke University Press, 2004), and Kate Baldwin, *Beyond the Color Line and the Iron Curtain: Reading Encounters between Black and Red* (Durham, NC: Duke University Press, 2002).

36 Thomas E. Skidmore, *Black into White: Race and Nationality in Brazilian Thought* (Oxford: Oxford University Press, 1974), provides an extensive interpretation of this theme.

37 Alexandra Minna Stern, *Eugenic Nation: Faults and Frontiers of Better Breeding in Modern America* (Berkeley: University of California Press, 2005), and Edwin Black, *War against the Weak: Eugenics and America's Campaign to Create a Master Race* (New York: Four Walls Eight Windows Press, 2003), on the United States; Sejersted, *The Age of Social Democracy,* on Sweden; Chloe Campbell, *Race and Empire: Eugenics in Colonial Kenya* (Manchester: Manchester University Press, 2007), on Kenya.

38 George W. Stocking, *Victorian Anthropology* (New York: Free Press, 1987); Baker, Lee D. Baker, *From Savage to Negro: Anthropology and the Construction of Race, 1896–1954* (Berkeley: University of California Press, 1998); and H. Glenn Penny and Matti Bunzl, eds., *Worldly Provincialism: German Anthropology in the Age of Empire* (Ann Arbor: University of Michigan Press, 2003).

39 The large and varied scholarship may be sampled in Andrew D. Evans, *Anthropology at War: World War I and the Science of Race in Germany* (Chicago: University of Chicago Press, 2010); Paul Weindling, *Epidemics and Genocide in Eastern Europe, 1890–1945* (New York: Oxford University Press, 2000); Jürgen Zimmerer and Joachim Zeller, eds., *Genocide in German South-West Africa:*

The Colonial War of 1904–1908 and Its Aftermath, trans. E. J. Neather (Monmouth, Wales: Merlin Press, 2007); Sandra Mass, *Weisse Helden, schwarza Krieger: Zur Geschichte kolonialer Männlichkeit in Deutschland, 1918–1964* (Cologne: Böhlau Verlag, 2006); essays in *Das Kaiserreich transnational: Deutschland in der Welt, 1871–1914,* ed. Sebastian Conrad and Jürgen Osterhammel (Göttingen: Vandenhoeck und Ruprecht, 2004); Robert Proctor, *Racial Hygiene: Medicine under the Nazis* (Cambridge, MA: Harvard University Press, 1988); Götz Aly, Peter Chroust, and Christian Pross, eds., *Cleansing the Fatherland: Nazi Medicine and Racial Hygiene,* trans. Belinda Cooper (Baltimore: Johns Hopkins University Press, 1994).

40 Mark B. Adams, ed., *The Wellborn Science: Eugenics in Germany, France, Brazil, and Russia* (New York: Oxford University Press, 1990); Daniel J. Kevles, *In the Name of Eugenics: Genetics and the Uses of Human Heredity* (New York: Knopf, 1985); Matthew J. Connelly, *Fatal Misconception: The Struggle to Control World Population* (Cambridge, MA: Harvard University Press, 2008).

41 Marilyn Lake and Henry Reynolds, *Drawing the Global Colour Line: White Men's Countries and the International Challenge of Racial Equality* (Cambridge: Cambridge University Press, 2008), 251–261.

42 Alfred L. Kroeber, "Eighteen Professions," *American Anthropologist* 17 (1915): 285.

43 Jeffrey D. Needell, "Identity, Race, Gender, and Modernity in the Origins of Gilberto Freyre's Oeuvre," *American Historical Review* 100 (1995): 51–77.

44 J. R. McNeill, *Something New under the Sun: An Environmental History of the Twentieth-Century World* (New York: W. W. Norton, 2000), 58.

45 Thomas G. Andrews, *Killing for Coal: America's Deadliest Labor War* (Cambridge, MA: Harvard University Press, 2008), 70.

46 Thomas Parke Hughes, *Networks of Power: Electrification in Western Society, 1880–1930* (Baltimore: Johns Hopkins University Press, 1983), 1; William J. Hausman, Peter Hertner, and Mira Wilkins, eds., *Global Electrification: Multinational Enterprise and International Finance in the History of Light and Power, 1878–2007* (New York: Cambridge University Press, 2008).

47 Hausman, Hertner, and Wilkins, *Global Electrification.*

48 Pierre-Yves Saunier and Shane Ewen, eds., *Another Global City: Historical Explorations into the Transnational Municipal Moments, 1850–2000* (New York: Palgrave Macmillan, 2008), 8.

49 Catherine Coquery-Vidrovitch, *The History of African Cities South of the Sahara: From Origins to Colonization,* trans. Mary Baker (Princeton, NJ: Markus

Wiener, 2005), 209–318; Patrick Manning, *Migration in World History* (New York: Routledge, 2005), 157–180; Bill Freund, *The African City: A History* (New York: Cambridge University Press, 2007); Dianne Scott, "Creative Destruction: Early Modernist Planning in the South Durban Industrial Zone, South Africa," *Journal of Southern African Studies* 29 (2003): 235–259.

50 Renaud Payre and Pierre-Yves Saunier, "A City in the World of Cities: Lyon, France; Municipal Associations as Political Resources in the Twentieth Century," Andrew Brown-May, "In the Precincts of the Global City: The Transnational Network of Municipal Affairs in Melbourne, Australia, at the End of the Nineteenth Century," and Jeffrey Hanes, "Pacific Crossings? Urban Progressivism in Modern Japan," all in Saunier and Ewen, *Another Global City*, 69–84, 19–34, 51–68; Stephen V. Ward, *Planning the Twentieth Century City: The Advanced Capitalist World* (Chichester, UK: Wiley, 2002).

51 Michael P. Smith, *Transnational Urbanism: Locating Globalization* (London: Blackwell, 2001).

52 Myron Echenberg, *Plague Ports: The Global Urban Impact of Bubonic Plague, 1894–1901* (New York: NYU Press, 2007).

53 Context is provided by Mark Harrison, *Disease and the Modern World: 1500 to the Present Day* (Cambridge: Polity Press, 2004), 93–96; Sheldon J. Watts, *Epidemics and History: Disease, Power, and Imperialism* (New Haven, CT: Yale University Press, 1999); and Nancy Tomes, *The Gospel of Germs: Men, Women, and Microbe in American Life* (Cambridge, MA: Harvard University Press, 1998). On Gambia, see Donald R. Wright, *The World and a Very Small Place in Africa* (Armonk, NY: M. E. Sharpe, 1997), 194–195.

54 Mariola Espinosa, *Epidemic Invasions: Yellow Fever and the Limits of Cuban Independence, 1878–1930* (Chicago: University of Chicago Press, 2009); Sherman Cochran, *Chinese Medicine Men: Consumer Culture in China and Southeast Asia* (Cambridge, MA: Harvard University Press, 2006); Ruth Rogaski, *Hygienic Modernity: Meanings of Health and Disease in Treaty-Port China* (Berkeley: University of California Press, 2004); Anne Digby, *Diversity and Division in Medicine: Health Care in South Africa from the 1800s* (Oxford: Peter Lang, 2006).

55 William Gallois, *The Administration of Sickness: Medicine and Ethics in Nineteenth-Century Algeria* (Basingstoke, UK: Palgrave Macmillan, 2008), 4–6.

56 Janice Boddy, *Civilizing Women: British Crusades in Colonial Sudan* (Princeton, NJ: Princeton University Press, 2007).

57 Rod Edmond, "Returning Fears: Tropical Disease and the Metropolis," and other essays in *Tropical Visions in an Age of Empire,* ed. Felix Driver and Luciana Martins (Chicago: University of Chicago Press, 2005).

58 David Arnold, *Colonizing the Body: State Medicine and Epidemic Disease in Nineteenth-Century India* (Berkeley: University of California Press, 1993), suggests the complicated interactions.

59 David P. Forsythe, *The Humanitarians: The International Committee of the Red Cross* (New York: Cambridge University Press, 2005); Caroline Moorehead, *Dunant's Dream: War, Switzerland and the History of the Red Cross* (London: HarperCollins, 1998).

60 Merle Curti, *American Philanthropy Abroad: A History* (New Brunswick, NJ: Rutgers University Press, 1963), 339–360.

61 Steven P. Palmer, *Launching Global Health: The Caribbean Odyssey of the Rockefeller Foundation* (Ann Arbor: University of Michigan Press, 2010); Steven C. Williams, "Nationalism and Public Health: The Convergence of Rockefeller Foundation Technique and Brazilian Federal Authority during the Time of Yellow Fever, 1925–1930," in *Missionaries of Science: The Rockefeller Foundation and Latin America,* ed. Marcos Cueto (Bloomington: Indiana University Press, 1994), 23–51; Ann Zulawski, *Unequal Cures: Public Health and Political Change in Bolivia, 1900–1950* (Durham, NC: Duke University Press, 2007), 86–117.

62 Elman, *Modern Science in China,* 225; Adam K. Webb, "The Countermodern Moment: A World-Historical Perspective on the Thought of Rabindranath Tagore, Muhammad Iqbal, and Liang Shuming," *Journal of World History* 19 (2008): 189–212. On the World War I break, see Michael Adas, "Contested Hegemony: The Great War and the Afro-Asian Assault on the Civilizing Mission Ideology," *Journal of World History* 15 (2004): 31–63.

63 Mary Parker Follett, *The New State* (1918), 196, http://sunsite.utk.edu/FINS/Mary_Parker_Follett/Fins-MPF-01.html. Thanks to Daniel Immerwahr for calling this quotation to my attention.

64 On Burnham, see Gilbert, *Designing the Industrial State;* and Daniel Kelly, *James Burnham and the Struggle for the World: A Life* (Wilmington, DE: Isi Books, 2002).

5. SPECTACULAR FLOWS

1 C. A. Bayly, *The Birth of the Modern World, 1780–1914: Global Connections and Comparisons* (Oxford: Blackwell, 2004), 1–2; Arjun Appadurai, *Modernity at*

Large: *Cultural Dimensions of Globalization* (Minneapolis: University of Minnesota Press, 1996); Alys Eve Weinbaum et al., eds., *The Modern Girl around the World: Consumption, Modernity, and Globalization* (Durham, NC: Duke University Press, 2008).

2 Felipe Fernández-Armesto, *Pathfinders: A Global History of Exploration* (New York: W. W. Norton, 2006), 385.

3 Kenneth Mason, *Abode of Snow: A History of Himalayan Exploration and Mountaineering from Earliest Times to the Ascent of Everest* (1955; repr., London: Diadem Books, 1987), xvi.

4 Maurice Isserman and Stewart Weaver, *Fallen Giants: A History of Himalayan Mountaineering from the Age of Empire to the Age of Extremes* (New Haven, CT: Yale, 2008), xi.

5 Beau Riffenburgh, *The Myth of the Explorer: The Press, Sensationalism, and Geographical Discovery* (New York: Oxford University Press, 1994); Dwayne R. Winseck and Robert M. Pike, *Communication and Empire: Media, Markets, and Globalization, 1860–1930* (Durham, NC: Duke University Press, 2007), 294.

6 James L. Newman, *Imperial Footprints: Henry Morton Stanley's African Journeys* (Dulles, VA: Potomac, 2006). Tim Jeal, *Stanley: The Impossible Life of Africa's Greatest Explorer* (New Haven, CT: Yale University Press, 2007), claims that Stanley greatly exaggerated his accounts of brutality and killing.

7 Claire Pettitt, *Dr. Livingstone, I Presume? Missionaries, Journalists, Explorers and Empire* (London: Profile Books, 2007).

8 *National Geographic Magazine*, 13 (1903): 405–406.

9 Fanny Bullock Workman and William Hunter Workman, *Ice-Bound Heights of the Mustagh: An Account of Two Seasons of Pioneer Exploration in the Baltistan Himalaya* (New York: Scribner's, 1908).

10 Fernández-Armesto, *Pathfinders,* 362.

11 Beau Riffenburgh, *The Myth of the Explorer: The Press, Sensationalism, and Geographical Discovery* (New York: Oxford University Press, 1994), 196. Osterhammel, *Die Verwandlung der Welt,* 63–76, surveys the worldwide spread of newspapers, popular journalism, and international news services before World War I.

12 Isserman and Weaver, *Fallen Giants,* 83–222.

13 Quoted from Stefan Zweig, *The World of Yesterday,* 196, in Stephen Kern, *The Culture of Time and Space, 1880–1918* (Cambridge, MA: Harvard University Press, 1983), 244.

14 Rosalie Schwartz, *Flying Down to Rio: Hollywood, Tourists, and Yankee Clippers* (College Station: Texas A&M University Press, 2004); Jennifer Van Vleck, *No Distant Places* (Cambridge, MA: Harvard University Press, forthcoming).

15 Daniel Boorstin, *The Discoverers: A History of Man's Search to Know His World and Himself* (New York: Random House, 1983); David A. Traill, *Schliemann of Troy: Treasure and Deceit* (New York: St. Martin's Press, 1995).

16 Charles Gallenkamp, *Dragon Hunter: Roy Chapman Andrews and the Central Asiatic Expeditions* (New York: Viking, 2001).

17 Elizabeth Hanson, *Animal Attractions: Nature on Display in American Zoos* (Princeton, NJ: Princeton University Press, 2002), 36.

18 John S. Clarke, *Circus Parade* (1936; Yorkshire, UK: Jeremy Mills, 2008), 1–30.

19 Janet Davis, *The Circus Age: Culture and Society under the American Big Top* (Chapel Hill: University of North Carolina Press, 2002), 34; Richard W. Flint, "American Showmen and European Dealers: Commerce in Wild Animals in Nineteenth-Century America," in *New Worlds, New Animals: From Menagerie to Zoological Park in the Nineteenth Century,* ed. Robert J. Hoage and William A. Deiss (Baltimore: Johns Hopkins University Press, 1996), 97–108.

20 Davis, *The Circus Age,* 218.

21 Paul Greenhalgh, *Ephemeral Vistas: The Expositions Universelles, Great Exhibitions, and World's Fairs, 1851–1939* (Manchester: Manchester University Press, 1988).

22 Robert W. Rydell and Rob Kroes, *Buffalo Bill in Bologna: The Americanization of the World, 1869–1922* (Chicago: University of Chicago Press, 2005).

23 Osterhammel, *Die Verwandlung der Welt,* 80–81.

24 Emily S. Rosenberg, *Spreading the American Dream: Economic and Cultural Expansion, 1890–1945* (New York: Hill and Wang, 1982); Kristin Thompson, *Exporting Entertainment: America in the World Film Market, 1907–1934* (London: BFI, 1985).

25 Rachel Dwyer and Divia Patel, *Cinema India: The Visual Culture of Hindi Film* (New Brunswick, NJ: Rutgers University Press, 2002); Zhang Zhen, *An Amorous History of the Silver Screen: Shanghai Cinema, 1896–1937* (Chicago: University of Chicago Press, 2005), 296; Priti Ramamurthy, "All-Consuming Nationalism: The Indian Modern Girl in the 1920s and 1930s," in Weinbaum et al., *Modern Girl,* 147–173.

26 The author thanks Shanon Fitzpatrick for sharing her ongoing research on this topic.

27 Catherine Russell, "New Women of the Silent Screen: China, Japan, Hollywood," in *Camera Obscura: Feminism, Culture, and Media Studies Special Issue* (Durham, NC: Duke University Press, 2005), 4.

28 Eric Ames, *Carl Hagenbeck's Empire of Entertainments* (Seattle: University of Washington Press, 2008), 198–229.

29 Melanie McGrath, *The Long Exile: A Tale of Inuit Betrayal and Survival in the High Arctic* (New York: Knopf, 2007).

30 Pascal James Imperato and Eleanor M. Imperato, *They Married Adventure: The Wandering Lives of Martin and Osa Johnson* (New Brunswick, NJ: Rutgers University Press, 1992).

31 Ruth Vasey, *The World according to Hollywood* (Madison: University of Wisconsin Press, 1997).

32 Richard Mullen and James Munson, *"The Smell of the Continent": The British Discover Europe* (London: Macmillan, 2009); Frank Costigliola, *Awkward Dominion: American Political, Economic and Cultural Relations with Europe, 1919–1933* (Ithaca, NY: Cornell University Press, 1984).

33 Kristin Hoganson, *Consumers' Imperium: The Global Production of American Domesticity, 1865–1920* (Chapel Hill: University of North Carolina Press, 2007), 171.

34 Ian R. Tyrrell, *Transnational Nation: United States History in Global Perspective since 1789* (New York: Palgrave, 2007), 97.

35 Shelley Baronowski and Ellen Furlough, eds., *Being Elsewhere: Tourism, Consumer Culture, and Identity in Modern Europe and North America* (Ann Arbor: University of Michigan Press, 2001).

36 Hoganson, *Consumers' Imperium,* 153–196.

37 Emily S. Rosenberg, *Financial Missionaries to the World: The Politics and Culture of Dollar Diplomacy* (Durham, NC: Duke University Press, 2000).

38 Miriam Silverberg, *Erotic Grotesque Nonsense: The Mass Culture of Japanese Modern Times* (Berkeley: University of California Press, 2006), employs this concept.

39 Joanne Hershfield, *Imagining la Chica Moderna: Women, Nation, and Visual Culture in Mexico, 1917–1936* (Durham, NC: Duke University Press, 2008), 126–155; and many essays in Weinbaum et al., *Modern Girl.*

40 On consumption communities, see Daniel Boorstin, *The Americans: The Democratic Experience* (New York: Random House, 1973). On the history of consumption generally see Peter N. Stearns, *Consumerism in World History: The Global Transformation of Desire* (London: Routledge, 2001); Jan de Vries, *The*

Industrious Revolution: Consumer Behavior and the Household Economy, 1650 to the Present (Cambridge: Cambridge University Press, 2008); and Sheldon Garin, *Beyond Our Means: Why America Spends while the World Saves* (Princeton: Princeton University Press, 2012).

41 Victoria de Grazia, *Irresistible Empire: America's Advance through Twentieth-Century Europe* (Cambridge, MA: Harvard University Press, 2005).

42 Georgine Clarsen, *Eat My Dust: Early Women Motorists* (Baltimore: Johns Hopkins University Press, 2008).

43 For international automobile ads, see N. W. Ayer Collection No. 59, Ford Motor Company, series 3, boxes 220–225, National Museum of American History Archives, Washington, DC.

44 Weinbaum et al., *Modern Girl;* Francesca Orsini, ed., *Love in South Asia: A Cultural History* (Cambridge: Cambridge University Press, 2006); Rachel Dwyer and Christopher Pinney, eds., *Pleasure and the Nation: The History, Politics and Consumption of Public Culture in India* (New Delhi: Oxford University Press, 2001); Michel Gobat, *Confronting the American Dream: Nicaragua under U.S. Imperial Rule* (Durham, NC: Duke University Press, 2005), 175–202; Julio Moreno, *Yankee Don't Go Home: Mexican Nationalism, American Business Culture, and the Shaping of Modern Mexico, 1920–1950* (Chapel Hill: University of North Carolina Press, 2003), 137–151; Jeffrey H. Jackson, *Making Jazz French: Music and Modern Life in Interwar Paris* (Durham, NC: Duke University Press, 2003); Mary Nolan, *Visions of Modernity: American Business and the Modernization of Germany* (New York: Oxford University Press, 1994); Michael H. Kater, *Different Drummers: Jazz in the Culture of Nazi Germany* (New York: Oxford University Press, 1992).

45 Jonathan D. Spence, *The Search for Modern China* (New York: W. W. Norton, 1990), 311–333, for context.

46 Jian Wang, *Foreign Advertising in China: Becoming Global, Becoming Local* (Ames: Iowa State University Press, 2000), 25–32; Beverley Jackson, *Shanghai Girl Gets All Dressed Up* (Berkeley: Ten Speed Press, 2005), 38, 104–105; Lynn Pan, *Shanghai Style: Art and Design between the Wars* (San Francisco: Long River Press, 2008), explores the diverse sources of Shanghai modernist style.

47 Antonia Finnane, *Changing Clothes in China: Fashion, History, Nation* (New York: Columbia University Press, 2008), 101–175; Jackson, *Shanghai Girl,* 45–67, 81–90; Sherman Cochrane, ed., *Inventing Nanjing Road: Commercial Culture in Shanghai, 1900–1945* (Ithaca, NY: Cornell University Press, 1999).

48 Karl Gerth, *China Made: Consumer Culture and the Creation of the Nation* (Cambridge, MA: Harvard University Press, 2003).

49 Leo Ou-fan Lee, *Shanghai Modern: The Flowering of a New Urban Culture in China, 1930–1945* (Cambridge, MA: Harvard University Press, 1999), 64–74, quotation at 74; Finnane, *Changing Clothes in China*, 125–137.

50 Jackson, *Shanghai Girl*, 111–112. Ou-fan Lee, *Shanghai Modern*, 82–119, 199–231, explains the interpretive controversies over the influence of Hollywood cinema on Chinese film and portrayals of "modern girls." See also Yingjin Zhang, ed., *Cinema and Urban Culture in Shanghai, 1922–1943* (Palo Alto, CA: Stanford University Press, 1999). On the *qipao*, see Finnane, *Changing Clothes in China*, 139–175.

51 Wen-hsin Yeh, *Shanghai Splendor: Economic Sentiments and the Making of Modern China, 1843–1949* (Berkeley: University of California Press, 2007), 101.

52 Weinbaum et al., *Modern Girl;* Silverberg, *Erotic Grotesque Nonsense;* Finnane, *Changing Clothes in China*, 167; Hershfield, *Imagining la Chica Moderna*.

53 Helena Michie and Ronald R. Thomas, "Introduction," and Jon Hegglund, "Empire's Second Take: Projecting America in Stanley and Livingstone," both in *Nineteenth-Century Geographies: The Transformation of Space from the Victorian Age to the American Century*, ed. Helena Michie and Ronald R. Thomas (New Brunswick, NJ: Rutgers University Press, 2003), 17, 265–278.

Selected Bibliography

Abu-Lughod, Lila, ed. *Remaking Women: Feminism and Modernity in the Middle East.* Princeton, NJ: Princeton University Press, 1998.

Adams, Mark B., ed. *The Wellborn Science: Eugenics in Germany, France, Brazil, and Russia.* New York: Oxford University Press, 1990.

Adas, Michael. *Machines as the Measure of Men: Science, Technology, and Ideologies of Western Dominance.* Ithaca, NY: Cornell University Press, 1989.

Adi, Hakim, and Marika Sherwood. *Pan-African History: Political Figures from Africa and the Diaspora since 1787.* London: Routledge, 2003.

Anagol, Padma. *The Emergence of Feminism in India, 1850–1920.* Aldershot, UK: Ashgate, 2005.

Anderson, Warwick. *The Cultivation of Whiteness: Science, Health and Racial Destiny in Australia.* New York: Basic Books, 2003.

Anghie, Antony. *Imperialism, Sovereignty, and the Making of International Law.* Cambridge: Cambridge University Press, 2005.

Appadurai, Arjun. *Modernity at Large: Cultural Dimensions of Globalization.* Minneapolis: University of Minnesota Press, 1996.

Arnold, David. *Colonizing the Body: State Medicine and Epidemic Disease in Nineteenth-Century India.* Berkeley: University of California Press, 1993.

Auerbach, Jeffrey A. *The Great Exhibition of 1851: A Nation on Display.* New Haven, CT: Yale University Press, 1999.

Baber, Zaheer. *The Science of Empire: Scientific Knowledge, Civilization, and Colonial Rule in India.* Albany: State University of New York Press, 1996.

Baratay, Éric, and Élisabeth Hardouin-Fugier. *Zoo: A History of Zoological Gardens in the West.* Translated by Oliver Welch. London: Reaktion Books, 2002.

Barrow, Ian J. *Making History, Drawing Territory: British Mapping in India, c. 1756–1905.* New Delhi: Oxford University Press, 2003.

Bayly, C. A. *The Birth of the Modern World, 1780–1914: Global Connections and Comparisons.* Oxford: Blackwell, 2004.

Beasley, William G. *Japan Encounters the Barbarian: Japanese Travellers in America and Europe.* New Haven, CT: Yale University Press, 1995.

Beinart, William, and Lotte Hughes. *Environment and Empire.* New York: Oxford University Press, 2007.

Bennett, Tony. *The Birth of the Museum: History, Theory, Politics.* London: Routledge, 1995.

Berkovitch, Nitza. *From Motherhood to Citizenship: Women's Rights and International Organizations.* Baltimore: Johns Hopkins University Press, 1999.

Bhabha, Homi K. *The Location of Culture.* London: Routledge, 1994.

Blackbourn, David. *The Conquest of Nature: Water, Landscape, and the Making of Modern Germany.* New York: W. W. Norton, 2006.

Blaise, Clark. *Time Lord: Sir Sandford Fleming and the Creation of Standard Time.* New York: Pantheon, 2000.

Block, Nelson R., and Tammy R. Proctor, eds. *Scouting Frontiers: Youth and the Scout Movement's First Century.* Newcastle upon Tyne: Cambridge Scholars, 2009.

Boli, John, and George M. Thomas, eds. *Constructing World Culture: International Nongovernmental Organizations since 1875.* Stanford, CA: Stanford University Press, 1999.

Bose, Sugata. *A Hundred Horizons: The Indian Ocean in the Age of Global Empire.* Cambridge, MA: Harvard University Press, 2006.

Bottenburg, Maarten van. *Global Games.* Translated by Beverley Jackson. Urbana: University of Illinois Press, 2001.

Brunsson, Nils, and Bengt Jacobsson. *A World of Standards.* Oxford: Oxford University Press, 2000.

Burke, Edmund, III, and Kenneth Pomeranz, eds. *The Environment and World History.* Berkeley: University of California Press, 2009.

Camiscioli, Elisa. *Reproducing the French Race: Immigration, Intimacy, and Embodiment in the Early Twentieth Century.* Durham, NC: Duke University Press, 2009.

Campbell, James T. *Middle Passages: African American Journeys to Africa, 1787–2005.* New York: Penguin, 2006.

Çelik, Zeynep. *Displaying the Orient: Architecture of Islam at Nineteenth-Century World's Fairs.* Berkeley: University of California Press, 1992.

Charle, Christophe, Jürgen Schriewer, and Peter Wagner, eds. *Transnational Intellectual Networks: Forms of Academic Knowledge and the Search for Cultural Identities.* Frankfurt: Campus, 2004.

Cioc, Mark. *The Game of Conservation: International Treaties to Protect the World's Migratory Animals.* Athens: Ohio University Press, 2009.

Clarsen, Georgine. *Eat My Dust: Early Women Motorists.* Baltimore: Johns Hopkins University Press, 2008.

Cochran, Sherman. *Chinese Medicine Men: Consumer Culture in China and Southeast Asia.* Cambridge, MA: Harvard University Press, 2006.

Codding, George A., Jr. *The International Telecommunication Union: An Experiment in International Cooperation.* Leiden: E. J. Brill, 1952.

———. *The Universal Postal Union: Coordinator of the International Mails.* New York: New York University Press, 1964.

Connelly, Matthew J. *Fatal Misconception: The Struggle to Control World Population.* Cambridge, MA: Belknap Press of Harvard University Press, 2008.

Conrad, Sebastian. *Globalisation and the Nation in Imperial Germany.* Translated by Sorcha O'Hagan. Cambridge: Cambridge University Press, 2010.

Conrad, Sebastian, and Jürgen Osterhammel, eds. *Das Kaiserreich transnational: Deutschland in der Welt, 1871–1914.* Göttingen: Vandenhoeck und Ruprecht, 2004.

Conrad, Sebastian, and Dominic Sachsenmaier, eds. *Competing Visions of World Order: Global Moments and Movements, 1880s–1930s.* London: Palgrave Macmillan, 2007.

Cooper, Frederick. "What Is the Concept of Globalization Good For? An African Historian's Perspective." *African Affairs* 100 (2001): 189–213.

Cooper, John Milton, Jr. *Woodrow Wilson: A Biography.* New York: Alfred A. Knopf, 2009.

Crosby, Alfred W. *Ecological Imperialism: The Biological Expansion of Europe, 900–1900.* Cambridge: Cambridge University Press, 1986.

Curti, Merle. *American Philanthropy Abroad: A History.* New Brunswick, NJ: Rutgers University Press, 1963.

Darby, Paul. *Africa, Football, and FIFA: Politics, Colonialism, and Resistance.* London: Routledge, 2002.

Darwin, John. *The Empire Project: The Rise and Fall of the British World-System, 1830–1870.* Cambridge: Cambridge University Press, 2009.

Daughton, J. P. *An Empire Divided: Religion, Republicanism, and the Making of French Colonialism, 1880–1914.* New York: Oxford University Press, 2006.

Davis, Mike. *Late Victorian Holocausts: El Niño Famines and the Making of the Third World.* New York: Verso, 2001.

De Grazia, Victoria. *Irresistible Empire: America's Advance through Twentieth-Century Europe.* Cambridge, MA: Belknap Press of Harvard University Press, 2005.

Dennis, Richard. *Cities in Modernity: Representations and Productions of Metropolitan Space, 1840–1930.* New York: Cambridge University Press, 2008.

Desmond, Ray. *The History of the Royal Botanic Gardens Kew*. London: Harvill Press, 1995.

De Vries, Jan. *The Industrious Revolution: Consumer Behavior and the Household Economy, 1650 to the Present*. Cambridge: Cambridge University Press, 2008.

Digby, Anne. *Diversity and Division in Medicine: Health Care in South Africa from the 1800s*. Oxford: Lang, 2006.

Drayton, Richard H. *Nature's Government: Science, Imperial Britain, and the "Improvement" of the World*. New Haven, CT: Yale University Press, 2000.

Duara, Prasenjit. *Sovereignty and Authenticity: Manchukuo and the East Asian Modern*. Lanham, MD: Rowman and Littlefield, 2003.

Dülffer, Jost. *Regeln gegen den Krieg? Die Haager Friedenskonferenzen von 1899 und 1907 in der internationalen Politik*. Frankfurt: Ullstein, 1981.

Ďurovičová, Nataša, and Kathleen Newman, eds. *World Cinemas, Transnational Perspectives*. New York: Routledge, 2010.

Dyson, Stephen L. *In Pursuit of Ancient Pasts: A History of Classical Archaeology in the Nineteenth and Twentieth Centuries*. New Haven, CT: Yale University Press, 2006.

Echenberg, Myron. *Plague Ports: The Global Urban Impact of Bubonic Plague, 1894–1901*. New York: New York University Press, 2007.

Ekbladh, David. *The Great American Mission: Modernization and the Construction of an American World Order*. Princeton, NJ: Princeton University Press, 2010.

Elman, Benjamin A. *A Cultural History of Modern Science in China*. Cambridge, MA: Harvard University Press, 2006.

Evans, Andrew D. *Anthropology at War: World War I and the Science of Race in Germany*. Chicago: University of Chicago Press, 2010.

Eyffinger, Arthur. *The 1899 Hague Peace Conference: "The Parliament of Man, the Federation of the World."* The Hague: Kluwer Academic, 1999.

Fan, Fa-ti. *British Naturalists in Qing China: Science, Empire, and Cultural Encounter*. Cambridge, MA: Harvard University Press, 2004.

Fernández-Armesto, Felipe. *Pathfinders: A Global History of Exploration*. New York: W. W. Norton, 2006.

Findling, John E., and Kimberly D. Pelle, eds. *Historical Dictionary of the Modern Olympic Movement*. Westport, CT: Greenwood Press, 1996.

Finnane, Antonia. *Changing Clothes in China: Fashion, History, Nation*. New York: Columbia University Press, 2008.

Forster, John, and Nigel K. Ll. Pope. *The Political Economy of Global Sporting Organisations*. London: Routledge, 2004.

Forsythe, David P. *The Humanitarians: The International Committee of the Red Cross.* New York: Cambridge University Press, 2005.

Foucault, Michel. *The Order of Things: An Archaeology of the Human Sciences.* New York: Pantheon, 1971.

Gandhi, Leela. *Affective Communities: Anticolonial Thought, Fin-de-Siècle Radicalism, and the Politics of Friendship.* Durham, NC: Duke University Press, 2006.

Garin, Sheldon, *Beyond Our Means: Why America Spends while the World Saves.* Princeton, NJ: Princeton University Press, 2012.

Geyer, Martin H., and Johannes Paulmann, eds. *The Mechanics of Internationalism: Culture, Society, and Politics from the 1840s to the First World War.* Oxford: Oxford University Press, 2001.

Geyer, Michael, and Charles Bright. "World History in a Global Age." *American Historical Review* 100 (1995): 1034–1060.

Gilroy, Paul. *The Black Atlantic: Modernity and Double Consciousness.* Cambridge, MA: Harvard University Press, 1993.

Grant, Colin. *Negro with a Hat: The Rise and Fall of Marcus Garvey.* New York: Oxford University Press, 2008.

Greene, Julie. *The Canal Builders: Making America's Empire at the Panama Canal.* New York: Penguin, 2009.

Greenhalgh, Paul. *Ephemeral Vistas: The Expositions Universelles, Great Exhibitions, and World's Fairs, 1851–1939.* Manchester: Manchester University Press, 1988.

Grewe, Wilhelm G. *The Epochs of International Law.* Translated by Michael Byers. Berlin: Walter de Gruyter, 2000.

Guttmann, Allen. *The Olympics: A History of the Modern Games.* 2nd ed. Urbana: University of Illinois Press, 2002.

Habib, S. Irfan, and Dhruv Raina, eds. *Social History of Science in Colonial India.* New Delhi: Oxford University Press, 2007.

Hanson, Elizabeth. *Animal Attractions: Nature on Display in American Zoos.* Princeton, NJ: Princeton University Press, 2002.

Harrison, Mark. *Disease and the Modern World, 1500 to the Present Day.* Cambridge: Polity, 2004.

Headrick, Daniel R. *The Invisible Weapon: Telecommunications and International Politics, 1851–1945.* New York: Oxford University Press, 1991.

———. *Power over Peoples: Technology, Environments, and Western Imperialism, 1400 to the Present.* Princeton, NJ: Princeton University Press, 2010.

———. *The Tentacles of Progress: Technology Transfer in the Age of Imperialism, 1850–1940.* New York: Oxford University Press, 1988.

————. *The Tools of Empire: Technology and European Imperialism in the Nineteenth Century.* New York: Oxford University Press, 1981.

Heptulla, Najma. *Indo-West Asian Relations: The Nehru Era.* Bombay: Allied, 1991.

Hight, Eleanor M., and Gary D. Sampson, eds. *Colonialist Photography: Imag(in)ing Race and Place.* London: Routledge, 2002.

Hill, Christopher L. *National History and the World of Nations: Capital, State, and the Rhetoric of History in Japan, France, and the United States.* Durham, NC: Duke University Press, 2008.

Hills, Jill. *The Struggle for Control of Global Communication: The Formative Century.* Urbana: University of Illinois Press, 2002.

Hoage, R. J., and William A. Deiss, eds. *New Worlds, New Animals: From Menagerie to Zoological Park in the Nineteenth Century.* Baltimore: Johns Hopkins University Press, 1996.

Hoffenberg, Peter H. *An Empire on Display: English, Indian, and Australian Exhibitions from the Crystal Palace to the Great War.* Berkeley: University of California Press, 2001.

Hopkins, A. G., ed. *Global History: Interactions between the Universal and the Local.* New York: Palgrave Macmillan, 2006.

————, ed. *Globalization in World History.* New York: W. W. Norton, 2002.

Iriye, Akira. *Cultural Internationalism and World Order.* Baltimore: Johns Hopkins University Press, 1997.

————. *Global Community: The Role of International Organizations in the Making of the Contemporary World.* Berkeley: University of California Press, 2002.

————. *The Globalizing of America, 1913–1945.* Vol. 3 of *The Cambridge History of American Foreign Relations.* Edited by Warren I. Cohen. New York: Cambridge University Press, 1993.

Isserman, Maurice, and Stewart Weaver. *Fallen Giants: A History of Himalayan Mountaineering from the Age of Empire to the Age of Extremes.* New Haven, CT: Yale University Press, 2008.

Jackson, Jeffrey H. *Making Jazz French: Music and Modern Life in Interwar Paris.* Durham, NC: Duke University Press, 2003.

James, Winston. *Holding Aloft the Banner of Ethiopia: Caribbean Radicalism in Early Twentieth-Century America.* New York: Verso, 1998.

Janton, Pierre. *Esperanto: Language, Literature, and Community.* Edited by Humphrey Tonkin. Translated by Humphrey Tonkin, Jane Edwards, and Karen Johnson-Weiner. Albany: State University of New York Press, 1993.

Jensen, Kimberly, and Erika Kuhlman, eds. *Women and Transnational Activism in Historical Perspective.* Dordrecht: Republic of Letters, 2010.

Kern, Stephen. *The Culture of Time and Space, 1880–1918.* Cambridge, MA: Harvard University Press, 1983.

Kevles, Daniel J. *In the Name of Eugenics: Genetics and the Uses of Human Heredity.* New York: Knopf, 1985.

Keys, Barbara J. *Globalizing Sport: National Rivalry and International Community in the 1930s.* Cambridge, MA: Harvard University Press, 2006.

Knock, Thomas J. *To End All Wars: Woodrow Wilson and the Quest for a New World Order.* New York: Oxford University Press, 1992.

Kohler, Robert E. *All Creatures: Naturalists, Collectors, and Biodiversity, 1850–1950.* Princeton, NJ: Princeton University Press, 2006.

Koskenniemi, Martti. *The Gentle Civilizer of Nations: The Rise and Fall of International Law, 1870–1960.* Cambridge: Cambridge University Press, 2002.

Lake, Marilyn, and Henry Reynolds. *Drawing the Global Colour Line: White Men's Countries and the International Challenge of Racial Equality.* Cambridge: Cambridge University Press, 2008.

Lapidus, Ira M. *A History of Islamic Societies.* Rev. ed. New York: Cambridge University Press, 2002.

Large, David Clay. *Nazi Games: The Olympics of 1936.* New York: W. W. Norton, 2007.

Lewis, David Levering. *W. E. B. DuBois: Biography of a Race, 1868–1919.* New York: Henry Holt, 1993.

Linden, Marcel van der. *Transnational Labour History: Explorations.* Aldershot, UK: Ashgate, 2003.

Lydon, Ghislaine. *On Trans-Saharan Trails: Islamic Law, Trade Networks, and Cross-Cultural Exchange in Nineteenth-Century Western Africa.* Cambridge: Cambridge University Press, 2009.

MacCulloch, Diarmaid. *Christianity: The First Three Thousand Years.* New York: Viking, 2010.

MacKenzie, John M. *The Empire of Nature: Hunting, Conservation, and British Imperialism.* Manchester: Manchester University Press, 1988.

MacLeod, Roy, ed. *Nature and Empire: Science and the Colonial Enterprise.* Chicago: University of Chicago Press, 2000.

Manela, Erez. *The Wilsonian Moment: Self-Determination and the International Origins of Anticolonial Nationalism.* New York: Oxford University Press, 2007.

Manning, Patrick. *The African Diaspora: A History through Culture.* New York: Columbia University Press, 2009.

———. *Migration in World History.* New York: Routledge, 2005.

Marchand, Suzanne L. *Down from Olympus: Archaeology and Philhellenism in Germany, 1750–1970.* Princeton, NJ: Princeton University Press, 1996.

Matsuda, Matt K. *Pacific Worlds: A History of Seas, Peoples, and Cultures.* Cambridge: Cambridge University Press, 2012.

Mazower, Mark. *No Enchanted Palace: The End of Empire and the Ideological Origins of the United Nations.* Princeton, NJ: Princeton University Press, 2009.

McNeill, J. R. *Mosquito Empires: Ecology and War in the Greater Caribbean, 1620–1914.* New York: Cambridge University Press, 2010.

———. *Something New under the Sun: An Environmental History of the Twentieth-Century World.* New York: W. W. Norton, 2000.

Morris, Rosalind C. *Photographies East: The Camera and Its Histories in East and Southeast Asia.* Durham, NC: Duke University Press, 2009.

Murray, Bill. *The World's Game: A History of Soccer.* Urbana: University of Illinois Press, 1996.

Nandy, Ashis. *Alternative Sciences: Creativity and Authenticity in Two Indian Scientists.* New Delhi: Allied, 1980.

Nixon, James W. *A History of the International Statistical Institute, 1885–1960.* The Hague: International Statistical Institute, 1960.

Nowell-Smith, Geoffrey, ed. *The Oxford History of World Cinema.* New York: Oxford University Press, 1996.

Okuefuna, David. *The Dawn of the Color Photograph: Albert Kahn's Archives of the Planet.* Princeton, NJ: Princeton University Press, 2008.

Olupona, Jacob K., and Terry Rey, eds. *Òrìṣà Devotion as World Religion: The Globalization of Yorùbá Religious Culture.* Madison: University of Wisconsin Press, 2008.

Osterhammel, Jürgen. *Die Verwandlung der Welt: Eine Geschichte des 19. Jahrhunderts.* Munich: C. H. Beck, 2009.

Palmer, Steven P. *Launching Global Health: The Caribbean Odyssey of the Rockefeller Foundation.* Ann Arbor: University of Michigan Press, 2010.

Patel, Kiran Klaus. "Überlegungen zu einer Transnationalen Geschichte." In *Weltgeschichte,* edited by Jürgen Osterhammel. Stuttgart: Franz Steiner, 2008.

Pedersen, Susan. "The Meaning of the Mandates System: An Argument." *Geschichte und Gesellschaft* 32 (2006): 560–582.

Penny, H. Glenn. *Objects of Culture: Ethnology and Ethnographic Museums in Imperial Germany.* Chapel Hill: University of North Carolina Press, 2002.

Penny, H. Glenn, and Matti Bunzl, eds. *World Provincialism: German Anthropology in the Age of Empire.* Ann Arbor: University of Michigan Press, 2003.

Pinney, Christopher. *Camera Indica: The Social Life of Indian Photographs.* Chicago: University of Chicago Press, 1997.

Pomeranz, Kenneth. *The Great Divergence: China, Europe, and the Making of the Modern World Economy.* Princeton, NJ: Princeton University Press, 2000.

Porter, Andrew. *Religion versus Empire? British Protestant Missionaries and Overseas Expansion, 1700–1914.* Manchester: Manchester University Press, 2004.

Prakash, Gyan. *Another Reason: Science and the Imagination of Modern India.* Princeton, NJ: Princeton University Press, 1999.

Pratt, Mary Louise. *Imperial Eyes: Travel Writing and Transculturation.* 2nd ed. New York: Routledge, 2008.

Raj, Kapil. *Relocating Modern Science: Circulation and the Construction of Knowledge in South Asia and Europe, 1650–1900.* New York: Palgrave, 2007.

Rajan, S. Ravi. *Modernizing Nature: Forestry and Imperial Eco-Development, 1800–1950.* Oxford: Clarendon Press, 2006.

Richards, Thomas. *The Imperial Archive: Knowledge and the Fantasy of Empire.* London: Verso, 1993.

Riddell, John, ed. *To See the Dawn: Baku, 1920—First Congress of the Peoples of the East.* New York: Pathfinder, 1993.

Riffenburgh, Beau. *The Myth of the Explorer: The Press, Sensationalism, and Geographical Discovery.* New York: Oxford University Press, 1994.

Robert, Dana L. *Christian Mission: How Christianity Became a World Religion.* Malden, MA: Wiley-Blackwell, 2009.

Rodgers, Daniel T. *Atlantic Crossings: Social Politics in a Progressive Age.* Cambridge, MA: Belknap Press of Harvard University Press, 1998.

Rogaski, Ruth. *Hygienic Modernity: Meanings of Health and Disease in Treaty-Port China.* Berkeley: University of California Press, 2004.

Rosenberg, Emily S., ed. *A World Connecting, 1870–1945.* Cambridge, MA: Belknap Press of Harvard University Press, 2012.

Rothfels, Nigel. *Savages and Beasts: The Birth of the Modern Zoo.* Baltimore: Johns Hopkins University Press, 2002.

Rupp, Leila J. *Worlds of Women: The Making of an International Women's Movement.* Princeton, NJ: Princeton University Press, 1997.

Ryan, James R. *Picturing Empire: Photography and the Visualization of the British Empire.* Chicago: University of Chicago Press, 1997.

Rydell, Robert W. *All the World's a Fair: Visions of Empire at American International Expositions, 1876–1916.* Chicago: University of Chicago Press, 1984.

Rydell, Robert W., and Rob Kroes. *Buffalo Bill in Bologna: The Americanization of the World, 1869–1922.* Chicago: University of Chicago Press, 2005.

Salvatore, Ricardo D., ed. *Culturas imperiales: Experiencia y representación en América, Asia y África.* Rosario: Beatriz Viterbo, 2005.

———. *Imágenes de un imperio: Estados Unidos y las formas de representación de América Latina.* Buenos Aires: Sudamericana, 2006.

Saunier, Pierre-Yves. "Transnational." In *The Palgrave Dictionary of Transnational History, from the Mid-19th Century to the Present Day,* edited by Akira Iriye and Pierre-Yves Saunier. New York: Palgrave Macmillan, 2009.

Saunier, Pierre-Yves, and Shane Ewen, eds. *Another Global City: Historical Explorations into the Transnational Municipal Moment, 1850–2000.* New York: Palgrave Macmillan, 2008.

Schrad, Mark Lawrence. *The Political Power of Bad Ideas: Networks, Institutions, and the Global Prohibition Wave.* New York: Oxford University Press, 2010.

Scott, James C. *Seeing like a State: How Certain Schemes to Improve the Human Condition Have Failed.* New Haven, CT: Yale University Press, 1998.

Service, Robert. *Comrades! A History of World Communism.* Cambridge, MA: Harvard University Press, 2007.

Silverberg, Miriam. *Erotic Grotesque Nonsense: The Mass Culture of Japanese Modern Times.* Berkeley: University of California Press, 2006.

Stearns, Peter N. *Consumerism in World History: The Global Transformation of Desire.* London: Routledge, 2001.

Stocking, George W. *Victorian Anthropology.* New York: Free Press, 1987.

Strasser, Ulrike, and Heidi Tinsman. "It's a Man's World? World History Meets the History of Masculinity, in Latin American Studies, for Instance." *Journal of World History* (2010): 75–96.

Sufian, Sandra M. *Healing the Land and the Nation: Malaria and the Zionist Project in Palestine, 1920–1947.* Chicago: University of Chicago Press, 2007.

Thompson, Kristin. *Exporting Entertainment: America in the World Film Market, 1907–34.* London: BFI, 1985.

Tomlinson, John. *Globalization and Culture.* Chicago: University of Chicago Press, 1999.

Tooze, J. Adam. *Statistics and the German State, 1900–1945: The Making of Modern Economic Knowledge.* Cambridge: Cambridge University Press, 2001.

Tsing, Anna Lowenhaupt. *Friction: An Ethnography of Global Connection.* Princeton, NJ: Princeton University Press, 2005.

Tucker, Richard P. *Insatiable Appetite: The United States and the Ecological Degradation of the Tropical World.* Berkeley: University of California Press, 2000.

Tucker, Richard P., and J. F. Richards, eds. *Global Deforestation and the Nineteenth-Century World Economy.* Durham, NC: Duke University Press, 1983.

Tyrrell, Ian R. *Reforming the World: The Creation of America's Moral Empire.* Princeton, NJ: Princeton University Press, 2010.

———. *Transnational Nation: United States History in Global Perspective since 1789.* New York: Palgrave, 2007.

———. *Woman's World/Woman's Empire: The Woman's Christian Temperance Union in International Perspective, 1880–1930.* Chapel Hill: University of North Carolina Press, 1991.

Vec, Miloš. *Recht und Normierung in der industriellen Revolution: Neue Strukturen der Normsetzung in Völkerrecht, staatlicher Gesetzgebung und gesellschaftlicher Selbstnormierung.* Frankfurt am Main: V. Klostermann, 2006.

Walters, F. P. *A History of the League of Nations.* 2 vols. London: Oxford University Press, 1952.

Watts, Sheldon J. *Epidemics and History: Disease, Power, and Imperialism.* New Haven, CT: Yale University Press, 1999.

Weinbaum, Alys Eve, et al., eds. *The Modern Girl Around the World: Consumption, Modernity, and Globalization.* Durham, NC: Duke University Press, 2008.

Weindling, Paul. *Epidemics and Genocide in Eastern Europe, 1890–1945.* New York: Oxford University Press, 2000.

———, ed. *International Health Organisations and Movements, 1918–1939.* Cambridge: Cambridge University Press, 1995.

Weston, Timothy B. *The Power of Position: Beijing University, Intellectuals, and Chinese Political Culture, 1898–1929.* Berkeley: University of California Press, 2004.

Wexler, Laura. *Tender Violence: Domestic Visions in an Age of U.S. Imperialism.* Chapel Hill: University of North Carolina Press, 2000.

Wilder, Gary. *The French Imperial Nation-State: Negritude and Colonial Humanism between the Two World Wars.* Chicago: University of Chicago Press, 2005.

Williams, Michael. *Deforesting the Earth: From Prehistory to Global Crisis.* Chicago: University of Chicago Press, 2003.

Winseck, Dwayne R., and Robert M. Pike. *Communication and Empire: Media, Markets, and Globalization, 1860–1930.* Durham, NC: Duke University Press, 2007.

Winter, Jay M. *Dreams of Peace and Freedom: Utopian Moments in the Twentieth Century.* New Haven, CT: Yale University Press, 2006.

Wong, Young-tsu. *A Paradise Lost: The Imperial Garden Yuanming Yuan.* Honolulu: University of Hawai'i Press, 2001.

Worboys, Michael. *Spreading Germs: Disease Theories and Medical Practice in Britain, 1865–1900.* New York: Cambridge University Press, 2000.

Wright, Donald R. *The World and a Very Small Place in Africa.* Armonk, NY: M. E. Sharpe, 1997.

Yanni, Carla. *Nature's Museums: Victorian Science and the Architecture of Display.* London: Athlone Press, 1999.

Yeh, Wen-hsin. *Shanghai Splendor: Economic Sentiments and the Making of Modern China, 1843–1949.* Berkeley: University of California Press, 2007.

Acknowledgments

This book emerged from a larger project on world history under the general editorship of Akira Iriye and Jürgen Osterhammel. I wish to extend special thanks to them for their careful readings, comments, and encouragement. The large volume of which this contribution was a part, edited by me and entitled *A World Connecting: 1870–1945* (2012), also contained contributions by Charles S. Maier, Tony Ballantyne and Antoinette Burton, Dirk Hoerder, and Steven C. Topik and Allen Wells. I am grateful to have worked with all of these fine collaborators.

The ideas and structure of this book were greatly enriched by graduate students both at the University of California, Irvine, and the University of California, Berkeley, where it formed the basis of a special seminar meeting under the sponsorship of Daniel Sargent and Brian DeLay. I especially wish also to thank Shanon Fitzpatrick, Robert Moeller, and Steven Topik for commenting on all or parts of the manuscript. My greatest debt, as always, is to my husband, Norman Rosenberg, for his humor, broad knowledge, and editorial skill.

Kathleen McDermott at Harvard University Press has been a patient and skillful editor without whom the large book and this small volume could not have come to pass. Andrew Kinney, also working with Harvard University Press, continually went above and beyond in shepherding the art program, and Barbara Goodhouse of Westchester Publishing Services was a superb production editor. My heartfelt thanks go out to all.

Index